Praise for

STILL LIFE

An Amazon Best Book of the ˙ ˙

"Hilarious but respectful." — *Wa*

"Engrossing." — *New Yo*

D0777964

"[A] delightful debut . . . Milgrom has in Still Life opened up a whole world to readers." — *Chicago Tribune*

"[A] literate, fascinating history." — *People*

"*Still Life* finds beauty in an unlikely place."
— *Entertainment Weekly*

"Milgrom's eye for detail and sense of humor makes *Still Life* an entertaining and educating look at this intriguing subculture."
— *Florida Times-Union*

"Even in the age of Lolcats and Sugar Bush Squirrel, taxidermy, the subject of Melissa Milgrom's riveting new book, *Still Life: Adventures in Taxidermy,* remains an esoteric and divisive field. But Milgrom proves there's little reason for the latter." — *Salon*

"An absorbing tour." — *Boston Globe*

"If you're an outdoorsman, museum-goer, or a pragmatic animal lover, find this book, grab a shopping bag, and stuff it."
— *Yankton Press & Dakotan*

"Under Milgrom's direction, readers may find themselves more ˙ ˙ rested in — and entertained by — the world of taxidermy than ˙ thought imaginable." — *Christian Science Monitor*

delightful, illuminating journey through a passionate subcul- e that prizes the natural world (even if nature's inhabitants are d when taxidermists work their magic on them)."
— *Shelf Awareness*

STILL LIFE

STILL LIFE

ADVENTURES IN

TAXIDERMY

Melissa Milgrom

MARINER BOOKS
HOUGHTON MIFFLIN HARCOURT
BOSTON NEW YORK

First Mariner Books edition 2011

Copyright © 2010 by Melissa Milgrom

For information about permission to reproduce
selections from this book, write to Permissions,
Houghton Mifflin Harcourt Publishing Company,
215 Park Avenue South, New York, New York 10003.

www.hmhbooks.com

Library of Congress Cataloging-in-Publication Data
Milgrom, Melissa.
Still life : adventures in taxidermy / Melissa Milgrom.
p. cm.
ISBN 978-0-618-40547-3
ISBN 978-0-547-39570-8 (pbk.)
1. Taxidermy—Anecdotes. 2. Taxidermists—Anecdotes. I. Title.
QL63.M55 2010   590.75′2—dc22
2009013511

Book design by Melissa Lotfy

Printed in the United States of America

DOC 10 9 8 7 6 5 4 3 2 1

Frontispiece photograph: The American Museum of Natural History taxidermist James L. Clark grooming an Asiatic lion, 1930. Image #313279, American
Museum of Natural History.

For my cubs,
Sabine and Greta

CONTENTS

My hobby is stuffing things—you know, taxidermy.

—NORMAN BATES, *Psycho*

They are the proof that something was there and no longer is. Like a stain. And the stillness of them is boggling. You can turn away but when you look back they'll still be there looking at you.

—DIANE ARBUS, 1971

STILL LIFE

1

SCHWENDEMAN'S TAXIDERMY STUDIO

"THE SIGHT OF a particularly fine animal, either alive or dead, excites within me feelings of admiration that often amount to genuine affection; and the study and preservation of such forms has for years been my chief delight." I'm quoting William Hornaday, the famous Smithsonian taxidermist and animal-rights activist, who wrote this in his 1891 manual, *Taxidermy and Zoological Collecting*. But the words could just as easily belong to David Schwendeman. Schwendeman was the last chief taxidermist ever employed by the American Museum of Natural History, where he worked for twenty-eight years. Schwendeman is eighty-five, long retired, and likely to show up at the taxidermy workshop his father opened in 1921 in Milltown, New Jersey, now run by his son Bruce. Lately, he says, he's lost his dexterity for taxidermy. Indeed, he says, he's skinned his very last squirrel. Then I show up at Schwendeman's Taxidermy Studio, and he's degreasing a Cooper's hawk, or sculpting a puma tail, or varnishing a boar's nose (to give it the "wet look"), or macerating a bison skull to remove the meat. "Macerating bison's one of the worst smells there is in taxidermy," he says with a devilish grin.

Although Schwendeman's simulations of nature are unsparingly sober, his own nature is curious and wry. Much to Bruce's chagrin, women find David charming, though he is rail thin and pink-complected and he complains that his "computer" has a tendency to backfire. He has fleecy white hair and eyes that work like automatic sensors, picking up every chipmunk and ground-hog that scuttles past his yard—although he's as likely to raise them as he is to trap them in a Havahart.

With his khaki shirts and trousers, zebra-striped toolbox, and pocketknife, Schwendeman resembles the archetypal taxi-dermist, and that's exactly what he is. Schwendeman grew up in a taxidermy studio, passionately devoted to the art and sci-ence of creating the illusion of life. In his prime, he strove for absolute realism, becoming the perfectionist his father never was and his son now strives to be. "I am *skilled;* my father is *tal-ented,*" says Bruce, deferring to the old man who had no use for school after his ninth-grade biology teacher mistook a starling for a flicker. That was that; Schwendeman has sided with the an-imals ever since—a prerequisite, it turns out, for all great taxi-dermists, then and now.

Although the outside world may dismiss taxidermy as the creepy sideline of the *Deliverance* set or an anachronistic throw-back to the dusty diorama, inside Schwendeman's taxidermy is known as a unique talent that is generally misunderstood. "You have to have respect and intuition for the animals to bring out their best characteristics," says David. "You have to have the del-icate finesse of a watchmaker and the brute strength of a black-smith," says Bruce. "You have to be able to mount a humming-bird *and* an elephant." Mostly you have to imitate nature with a fidelity that verges on pathological.

Schwendeman's Taxidermy Studio is the oldest business in Milltown and, not surprisingly, the only place on Main Street that dispenses business cards from the jaws of a leathery old alligator. The workshop was established by Arthur Schwendeman, David's father (Pup-Pup), a habitual truant who learned taxidermy from a female teacher who bribed him with taxidermy lessons so that he'd stay in school instead of running off to fish or hunt. He barely finished the eighth grade. David's mother, Lillian (Mum-Mum), was a patriotic earth mother whose energy for preserving God's creatures was infinite. She was the skinner and made all the artificial ears until she died at age ninety-four. "What you need for this kind of work is a strong stomach and lots of patience, and I have both," she once said. A resourceful cook known to lie about her ingredients, Lillian marched in every Fourth of July parade beside the float carrying one of Arthur's deer heads. Today Bruce Schwendeman wields the calipers and the brain spoons in the studio.

From outside, the sleepy little storefront resembles every other building on Main Street: a 1930s clapboard with two large display windows. Inside, however, the place brims with natural wonders. It's a motionless zoo. Roughly one thousand dusty-eyed birds and exotic stuffed beasts roost on the countertops and hang from the ceiling and walls. It's so cluttered with mounted animals (and skeletons and strange tools) that no one's ever bothered to take an inventory. Some are faded relics from the 1920s; others are so vibrant you want to poke them to see if they will move. A great blue heron with outstretched wings held in place with long dressmaker pins sits on a table near a puma that looks ready to pounce. Intricate snake skeletons lie in long glass-fronted wooden display cabinets. A fluffy Dall sheep seems to have walked through the wall, its hind end hidden from view on the other side.

Once when I visited, 180 birds Bruce had salvaged from an old wildlife museum filled the front room. Another time I encountered a pack of deciduous-forest dwellers (beaver, raccoon, black bear, skunk, turkey vulture, chipmunk, rabbit) preserved at the request of Yale's Peabody Museum of Natural History, which planned to transport Connecticut to Greece for the 2004 Olympics.

I first found myself drawn to Schwendeman's Taxidermy Studio in 1994, when I returned from a trip to Africa to visit my in-laws, who lead safaris for Ker & Downey. The company was founded in 1946 by big-game hunters. Now it's conservation minded and has taken Meryl Streep, Prince Charles, and other famous people on safari in discreet comfort. But not, as it turned out, me.

When I landed in Nairobi, I was informed that I was going to join a group of seasoned guides on a fourteen-day reconnaissance trek through the most barren stretch of Tanzania—an area so remote, the animals had never seen people before. The purpose of the trip was to scout out potential concession areas for future safaris. The guides called it "the real thing." No jeeps or radio—we'd be out of range. It was all very nineteenth-century—the kind of foot expedition the early specimen hunters and museum taxidermists went on when natural scientists were building their amazing collections—only we weren't going to shoot anything.

Coming from New Jersey, I thought it was impossible, even undesirable, to escape civilization, but we did (for a while, anyhow), and the isolation and wildlife were extraordinary, the birds too beautiful for words. On the last night, the leader, dressed in a loincloth, grabbed his shotgun and suggested we take an evening game walk. Somehow, we met up with a group of Belgian hunters who were camping nearby. They invited us back to camp for a drink. While the guides and hunters talked shop, I mistakenly wandered into the carcass room, where the hunters stored their kills. The salted pelts, hung high on pegs,

were eyeless, mangled, and limp. They smelled bloody and me-
tallic: the unmistakable stench of decay. I wasn't sure what was
more shocking: the human violence after all the tranquility or
the idea that someone was going to transform these vestiges into
something else. Trophies, I assumed. I wanted to know more.
Was taxidermy just the creation of an ornamental souvenir? Or
was there more to it?

Taxidermy is the art of taking an animal's treated skin and
stretching it over an artificial form such as a manikin, then carefully modeling its features in a lifelike attitude. The word is derived from the Greek roots *taxis,* "arrangement," and *derma,*
"skin," although its usage became prominent only in the early
1800s when taxidermy began its evolution from a crude way of
preserving skins to advance science into a highly evolved art
form whose chief objective is to freeze motion.

The first person to use the word was the French naturalist
Louis Dufresne, taxidermist at the Muséum national d'Histoire
naturelle in Paris, who wrote about it in the scientific reference
book *Nouveau dictionnaire d'histoire naturelle* (1803). Taxidermy,
he suggested, differed sharply from embalming and other forms
of preservation because its primary goal was aesthetic: to capture
a species' magnificence by faithfully replicating its every quirk
and feature in a realistic mount. In this, taxidermy was a magical mix of science, art, and theater, an incomparable tool for displaying the wonder and beauty of animals, particularly rare bird
species for natural history cabinets—the private collections of
natural wonders and oddities that gave rise to modern museums. (Birds were far easier to preserve than mammals, whose
musculature and facial expressions took decades to hone.)

Two hundred years have passed since Dufresne first used the
term. Nature documentaries and DNA sequencing have long replaced the cabinets of curiosities and study skins (bird skins used

to compare species by type). The grand era of the natural history museum diorama has come and gone. So if the Belgians' animal skins weren't museum bound, what would become of them? What compels people to want to transform animals into mantelpiece trophies, tacky roadside totems, or even diorama specimens? On the one hand, nothing seems as ludicrous as taking an animal and transforming it into a replica of itself. Why kill it in the first place? On the other hand, few objects are as strangely alluring as Flaubert's parrot, Goethe's kingfisher, Truman Capote's rattlesnake, or Charles Dickens's pet raven, Grip. Or, for that matter, as out of context as, say, Fenway Partners' upright grizzly bear on the fifty-ninth floor of its midtown Manhattan office.

There's something arresting and haunting about taxidermy when expertly done by museum masters such as the Schwendemans, and something morbid and kitschy about taxidermy when it's used to make effigies of famous animals such as "Misty of Chincoteague" (the equine heroine of Marguerite Henry's novel; now a moth-cut tourist attraction near Virginia Beach) or Roy Rogers's horse Trigger. It's hard to look at taxidermy and be indifferent, and I can't think of too many art forms—most taxidermists *do* want you to call it art—that stir up such pathos and bathos, as museums and artists such as Damien Hirst are keenly aware. Taxidermy makes you laugh and feel uneasy and inspired all at the same time, a powerful clash.

During the years I spent researching this book, I discovered that the most gifted taxidermists are an almost comically disparate group who argue about everything except this: nothing is either as loved or as hated as taxidermy. When taxidermy slides into one of its inevitable recessions, as it did in post–World War I England or in the ecologically minded 1970s, it isn't merely forgotten; it is reviled. Dioramas are undone; mounts are burned in bonfires, hacked up in HAZMAT tents, stealthily donated to nature centers, or relegated to museum storerooms where no one will ever see them. By contrast, people who love taxidermy will risk imprisonment to import a polar bear or a rare spotted cat for their trophy room or will travel to some far-flung museum just to gaze at an extinct bird of paradise that now exists only in dry storage.

In the Victorian era—the age of scientific exploration and discovery—taxidermy was a faddish craze. As naturalists brought exotic new species home from other continents, armchair enthusiasts filled their parlors and drawing rooms with glass-domed birds, butterfly cases, even their stuffed pets. Back then, every claw and hoof was transformed into some exciting new object: everything from "zoological lamps" (kerosene lamps made of preserved monkeys, swans, and other creatures) to "His" and "Her" elephant heads. Soon every town in England could support a part-time taxidermist. In fact, taxidermy was a prerequisite skill for any serious naturalist—including Charles Darwin, who hired a freed Guyanese slave to give him lessons; otherwise, he never would have qualified for the position of naturalist aboard the HMS *Beagle*. And as I write this, animal lovers in Paris have joined forces to rebuild Deyrolle, the cherished taxidermy establishment that burned down in 2008 after 177 years in business.

Celebrities host weddings under the American Museum of Natural History's ninety-four-foot blue whale (which, by the way, isn't taxidermy—no "derm"—but molded fiberglass; they realigned its blowhole in 2002, so now it's anatomically accurate fiberglass). Even Dolly the sheep, the first cloned mammal, is a stuffed display at Edinburgh's National Museum of Scotland. However, when I first met the Schwendemans, taxidermy was in one of its reviled phases, the height of the antifur campaigns of People for the Ethical Treatment of Animals and the Lynx Educational Trust for Animal Welfare. Advertisements showed beautiful women with flayed dogs draped around their shoulders. People paint-bombed fur coats. It felt creepy (and potentially unsafe) to walk through Schwendeman's door.

Back in New Jersey, when I was telling a hippie-era uncle of mine (who has an unusual tolerance for eccentric behavior) about my trip to Africa, he told me about the Schwendemans. My mother, whose family has lived in the area for as long as the Schwendemans, said, "That dark, dreary place on Main Street that's there year after year? *What goes on in there?*" Everyone knew the queer little shop, but only the most extreme animal enthusiasts seemed to venture inside. Now I had a reason to visit. More than a reason—a compulsion: the beauty of nature and the harsh reality of death were all mixed up in my mind in a way that I didn't understand then and I'm not sure I fully understand now. More to the point, I had seen skinned animals in Africa. That taboo having been broken made it much easier for me to visit the studio.

Bruce Schwendeman and a cross-eyed snowy owl, circa 1930, met me when I arrived. Bruce is a big, brawny guy with graying auburn hair and beard, blue eyes, and high cheekbones. He blushes easily; otherwise he looks nothing like his father. He was wearing the customary denim apron, spattered with blood and hide paste, and had a pencil behind his ear.

Bruce took over the shop in 1977 when he was twenty-six and has run it ever since, working mostly alone, although David shuffles in every day after his nap. Bruce knows the place like a sick child: the mailman's ring at eleven A.M.; the hum of the ten-by-ten industrial freezer in the basement; the slam of the screen door that leads from the workshop to David's house behind it, where both were raised. As a boy, Bruce was paid twenty-five cents for every deer skull plate he scraped clean, a 500 percent raise from what David himself had earned as a child for the same job.

Bruce has a sign in front that basically sums up his attitude toward greeting people: "If you are a salesman, I'll give you two minutes; if you are a liquor salesman with samples you can stay a little while but then you have to get out." Bruce can be gruff at first. If he's just spent a week mounting hooded mergansers in a heat wave without air conditioning (he had), he can also be short-wicked and curt. However, if he senses that you have a genuine interest in taxidermy, he'll let down his guard and talk reverently about every mount. That day he was gruff. I didn't blame him. I wasn't his usual customer—that is to say, a museum curator, an ornithologist, a park ranger, a zoology professor, a hunter, or a roadkill picker-upper. He calls himself a "taxidermologist," a name he uses to distinguish himself, a museum taxidermist, from the "beer-drinking fraternity" that mounts white-tailed deer assembly-line style. "Only five or ten out of one hundred thousand full- and part-time taxidermists are taxidermologists," he said. "We operate same as a museum. Scientific accuracy must be right on. Nothing's typical."

He coined the term in 1980 after years of having to define what he does for people who consider his shop an animal mortuary, or worse. Lately he's been fielding calls from people who think taxidermists drive taxicabs. "I've got a spider in my sink. What kind is it? Do we give fly-fishing lessons?" he says with a groan, shaking his head, rattling off more such inquiries. "How do I get rid of the squirrels in my attic? There's a turtle crossing our yard; is it dangerous? Do you repair fur coats?" At one point, the calls got so ridiculous, he began logging them. He's been keeping that log for about as many years as he's been documenting his encounters with roadkill (1977), though not nearly as long as he's been collecting the shed skins of his pet snakes.

Bruce has a striking command of animal anatomy. Even so, people are often surprised to meet a taxidermist with a master's degree. Bruce studied zoology at North Carolina State University, with concentrations in population dynamics and parasitology. After graduation, Carolina Power & Light advertised a job researching the effects of its power lines on migrating bobwhite quail. His mother (who banned taxidermy from the family home soon after she married David) encouraged Bruce to apply for the job so that he'd have some financial stability. Instead, he put on a denim apron and took over the shop.

Since then, father and son have preserved everything from three-toed sloths to fireflies. Seventy-five percent of the Schwendemans' work is for museums, nature centers, and zoos, including the Smithsonian Institution and the Philadelphia Zoo. Not long ago, they gave the Explorers Club's polar bear a pedicure (artificial claws), and they restored the Harvard Club's elephant head by sealing its cracked trunk with Yale paper napkins saturated in Elmer's glue. Mostly they are known for their work at the American Museum of Natural History (AMNH), to which they have an unshakable loyalty. That loyalty does not lie primarily with the curators and exhibition staff, which have sent laughing gulls, sea otters, galagos (bush babies), lemurs, and hornbills to them for mounting since the late 1940s, but with what they call the "stars of the show": the animals. And, naturally, with the taxidermists in whose footsteps they proudly walk.

Because of this, they tend to know every mount that's ever been taken off exhibition or altered and every exhibition hall that has been dismantled to make room for something new — something undoubtedly louder and with more special effects and animatronics — the direction museums have been going since the 1960s, when taxidermy displays gave way to IMAX theaters and robotic dinosaurs. "When I was a boy, you went to the museum to see the *animals,*" says David, groaning as if in pain. "You went to see the elephants. Nowadays everything's getting gimmicky." They fondly remember, for instance, the old bird halls filled with unadorned glass-fronted wooden cabinets. They blanch when they recall how the museum dismantled Dogs of the World, a gallery of stuffed canines. And they smirk with delight when they describe gory displays sanitized by the museum, such as a vulture picking at a zebra's exposed entrails. "It seems to me that they didn't want the public to see blood and guts," David says, laughing. Often they will try to convince a museum that its old mounts are treasures worth conserving, even if the mounts were preserved by naturalists who knew little about the species (compared to what biologists know today) and are anatomically outmoded: the AMNH's primate hall's aggressive lemurs and monkeys, for example, or the Vanderbilt Museum's thirty-two-foot-long whale shark. (Bruce spent four years restoring William K. Vanderbilt II's megaspecimen, which he believes is the world's largest mounted fish.) At Schwendeman's Taxidermy Studio, the AMNH's very first mammal mount—the ferocious African lion it purchased from the famous Parisian firm Maison Verreaux in 1865—is referred to as it is in the mammalogy department: "Specimen Number 1."

Bruce jokes that one day he'll write a book about the AMNH called *Skeletons in the Closet.* Until then, he is happy to point out all the fabulous artifacts that David has retrieved from the museum's dumpsters or was given on indefinite loan. "Their garbage forms the nucleus of the treasures of our museum," Bruce said, leading me back to the workshop through a corridor of wooden display cases, which contained, among the bronzes and death masks, two huge condors (Andean *and* California!) and a passenger pigeon.

Most of the animals are uncanny replicas. Others have

been transformed into tiny people, inkwells, or whatever, and he called these items "novelty mounts." A frog strumming a banjo and boxing squirrels were displayed on a glass shelf; Arthur mounted them years ago. Above the cash register, a yellow-eyed jackrabbit looked crossbred with a pronghorn (antelope). "Every taxidermist worth his weight has a *jackalope!*" Bruce said, beaming. Jackalopes are the weird invention of Wyoming taxidermist Douglas Herrick, who one day in 1932 tossed a dead jackrabbit onto the floor of his workshop. It landed under some deer antlers, spawning the gaudiest icon of the American West. "We have two types," Bruce boasted. "That one came with a certificate of authenticity!"

From a taxidermological perspective, you might think Bruce finds novelty mounts unseemly. But he views them as part of taxidermy history. Victorian homes contained an omnium-gatherum of such artifacts, including anthropomorphic mounts, as viewed through the eyes of Beatrix Potter fans. That said, the most novelty Bruce is willing to offer his clients is bear rugs, which he believes demean bears. "It's disrespectful to, you know, vacuum [a bear rug]," he says. "It's like man's dominance over nature."

Beyond the museum, swinging double doors flanked with the sail of a sailfish and the saw of a sawfish had stenciled on them NO ADMITTANCE. I followed Bruce past the sign and into the workshop: a large cement room, poorly ventilated, with three small windows that let in barely any light. Hanging from a chain above the sink was a woodchuck pelt, and lying upside down on a chair was Arthur's old stuffed terrier, a rental prop for TV commercials. Mostly the shop was full of strange tools with frightfully descriptive names: toe probes, lip tuckers, tail splitters. In the center of the room what looked like a dissection was taking place on a large worktable, which was lit by a single bulb that dangled from a ceiling strung with antlers. That day Bruce's friend Kurt Torok, who helps out in a pinch, was preserving a bald eagle for a nature center.

Kurt's fingers were bloodstained from the pile of fat, brains, and leg muscles he'd been extracting from the bird like a hellbent surgeon. Now he was scraping meat off the skin — "fleshing" to a taxidermist—so the skin would absorb borax, a preservative used to soak up fat and repel insects. In taxidermy, an animal starts out looking like the animal, gets mangled beyond recognition, and then ends up looking like the animal again. This eagle was mangled beyond recognition. Kurt pointed to a bald patch on its belly where its feathers had been ripped out by a truck, then he extended its long yellow talons. Its purple carcass dangled from a skinning hook near Bruce. A fan sent the stench of rotten meat circling around the humid workshop.

Kurt went over to the skinning hook and took down the carcass. He set it on the worktable, then began cutting into it with poultry shears. It still had the skeleton inside, which seemed odd; I had always thought taxidermists used skeletons as armatures to support the skin, but I was wrong by about three hundred years. In the 1700s, when taxidermy manuals were useful only to specimen collectors who wanted to know how to preserve birds for transport, people did use skeletons as armatures. In fact, they had all kinds of convoluted ways for preserving animals. One of the first people to describe his methods was the French naturalist R.A.F. Réaumur. In 1748, Réaumur offered four ways to preserve birds for travel: he stuffed their skinned bodies with straw, hay, and wood; he soaked them in spirits, then packed them in barrels of oat or barley chaff; he essentially mummified them with preserving powders; and, of course, he baked them. E. Bancroft's method for preserving Guyanese birds for natural history cabinets (1769) resembles a recipe for coq au vin: after he stuffed the skinned birds with salt and alum, he marinated them in rum for two days, then baked them. When death came knocking for George Washington's golden pheasants (a gift from Louis XVI), Charles Willson Peale (portraitist, naturalist, and fossil hunter) desperately wanted the skins for his Repository for Natural Curiosities in Philadelphia. In 1787, he sent Washington these instructions: "If the weather should be warm, be pleased to order the Bowels to be taken out and some Pepper put into the Body, but no Salt which would spoil the feathers." Washington agreed: "He made his Exit yesterday, which enables me to comply with your request much sooner than I wished to do."

Some taxidermists steamed wings, talons, and webbed feet to make them supple. Others coated bodies in liquid varnish or preserved skins with sal ammoniac (ammonium chloride), corrosive sublimate (mercuric chloride), or mixtures of wine, turpentine, and camphor. In 1771, Captain T. Davies described how he extracted bird tongues, brains, and eyes through the mouths of his eviscerated creatures. Then he stuffed their heads with camphor-soaked cotton and inserted black eyes that he had made from candle wax.

If these methods sound nothing remotely like taxidermy, that's because the first taxidermists were not taxidermists. One of the earliest documented taxidermy collections was preserved in the early 1500s by chemists. A Dutch nobleman's prized cassowaries, which he had brought home from India, suffocated in an overheated aviary (his furnace door had been left open and baked the birds). Distraught, the owner had the leading local chemists devise a method for preserving them. They treated the skins with spices, crudely mounted them using wires, and affixed them to a perch, frozen in time.

For the next three hundred years, the practice of taxidermy was, in a nutshell, a series of attempts to animate nature while preventing it from taking its course. Before arsenical soap was used as an insecticide and preservative, most mounts lasted no more than thirty years before they became moth-eaten or began to decompose. Except for the duchess of Richmond's African grey parrot in Westminster Abbey and George Washington's pheasants at the Harvard Museum of Comparative Zoology, few specimens predate the 1830s. This would all change when taxidermists—notoriously secretive—began to divulge their private formulas.

Kurt glanced up. A sly smile spread across his face. He considered the purple carcass. "Wanna sex it?" David, who was sitting in his rocker, snickered. I reached for my car keys.

"Quit showing off!" Bruce shouted. Although he knows that scientific specimens are always identified by their sex, age, and location where they were collected, he wanted me to view taxidermy as dignified and had no patience for taxidermy jokes. "Look at what their [people's] exposure is: *Psycho,* Jeffrey Dahmer. And all of the horror movies, like *Dracula,* always have taxidermy on the walls. Disney has a problem with taxidermy. In *101 Dalmatians,* taxidermy was evil—they wanted to make a coat out of puppies. Even *The Simpsons* had a runaway parade float, and someone almost got speared by a mounted swordfish! So it's perpetrated as a weird thing, not necessarily a bad thing, just unusual and creepy."

Taxidermy does have a creepy reputation, but taxidermists can blame only so much of it on Hollywood. Taxidermy was considered shady even in its heyday. In fact, except for five years in the 1880s, when taxidermists banded together to form the Society of American Taxidermists (SAT), the first professional taxidermy association (whose members would eventually revolutionize museum displays), again in 1972, when the National Taxidermists Association was formed (followed by Britain's Guild of

Taxidermists and others), taxidermists, who tend to be solitary workers, purposely cut themselves off from the outside world. No other profession has so steadfastly barred visitors from its dreary workshops, a decision that makes sense if you've ever seen someone flesh a bald eagle with tweezers.

Before refrigeration, it was even worse. Back then, taxidermy workshops were vile. Gruesome dissections took place in dark, smelly rooms that were stifling hot in the summer. Arsenic, formalin, carbon tetrachloride, and other dangerous chemicals that taxidermists used as preservatives were stored in open containers and filled the workshops' stagnant air with carcinogenic dust.

That said, the ghastly workshop is only one reason for taxidermy's insularity. The other reason is that taxidermy is an incredibly time-consuming handicraft. Few have ever prospered by stuffing other people's animals. "You don't become rich as a taxidermist," says Bruce. For this reason alone, it seems, taxidermists have always been incredibly suspicious of one another—citing the first law of nature, self-preservation, as the cause. Before 1972, taxidermists hoarded information, passing it down strictly from father to son, master to apprentice. Countless recipes for saline pickle (a tanning solution) and arsenical soap have died with some stingy taxidermist. When the French apothecary Jean-Baptiste Bécoeur, for instance, invented arsenical soap in 1743, he refused to share the recipe with other naturalists because he wanted a job with the Cabinet du Roi, the royal collection that became the Muséum national d'Histoire naturelle after the French Revolution. He didn't want to help his rivals because their birds might outshine his own. (He didn't get the job.) Exceptions existed, of course. William Hornaday found his colleagues' behavior exceptionally puerile and said so in an 1880 issue of *Science:* "If painters and sculptors had always been as narrow-minded, jealous, and absurdly exclusive of their knowledge as we have ever been (with but few exceptions) their art would stand no higher to-day than ours."

Now Bruce wanted to dispel some misconceptions. He started with the popular notion that taxidermists derive pleasure from killing animals. The Schwendemans never kill animals for taxidermy, acquiring their specimens from natural death or roadkill—except for a Norway rat that Bruce's sister drowned for the AMNH's exhibition on epidemics. ("They didn't send us a decent specimen," he explained. "Central Park has the smelliest old rats.") Other fallacies are that taxidermists start the day off with a beer (David drinks only after five); that nothing repulses a taxidermist (Bruce faints at the sight of human blood, especially his own; he also thinks it's gross to preserve dogs and cats); and, most important, that taxidermists "stuff" animals.

Before taxidermists made careful studies of animal anatomy, they did stuff skins with sawdust and rags, making for lopsided and disfigured specimens. Even John James Audubon, who shot and preserved thousands of birds to use as models for his illustrations, failed to mimic life until he invented a way to wire wings in naturalistic poses. Today highly skilled taxidermists mount animals with unerring perfection using an astonishing range of prefabricated manikins and fake animal parts—rippled tongues, plastic claws, colorful glass eyes—that used to take pioneering taxidermists years of careful field observations to sculpt by hand (which is why the Schwendemans sarcastically call it "modelmaking"). However, much like store-bought Halloween costumes, store-bought anatomy means limited choices of species and poses. "You can't buy a manikin for a dwarf galago from a supply catalog!" Bruce says. The best taxidermists still insist on sculpting their own forms, trusting their own articulations even over those at museums, whose models vary from era to era.

Bruce practices what he calls "good taxidermy": respect for the laws of nature and conservation. For David, whose work had to meet the imposing standards of renowned mammalogists, herpetologists, and ornithologists, that's a given, and therefore he loves to provoke Bruce. Whenever Bruce says an animal was "liquidated," "collected," "culled," or "dispatched," David thunders, "Killed!" When Bruce says "sportsman," David groans "hunter." David also prefers "workshop" to "studio." "Oh, we could get *fancy* and call it a studio," he says, rolling his eyes.

David is extraordinarily unpretentious. People from the AMNH remember him as a humble, hardworking naturalist with an uncanny intuition for animal forms. For example, when Rose Wadsworth, the museum's former exhibition coordinator for living invertebrates, brought him a flying lizard from Asia that he had never seen, he positioned it with the sensitivity of a local who had grown up with it in his own backyard. Indeed, to understand David you have to understand his deep devotion to wildlife, especially birds.

David is a purist: a birder's birder. He loathes the term "bird watcher," for instance, because it implies lists and rarity. David would rather observe a common species a million times, just to see the sunlight hit its covet feathers as it banks into a salt marsh, than to glimpse an exotic species for a nanosecond and then race off to see the next one. For David, the walk counts more than the birds. In this, he's the definition of the old-school taxidermist — a field naturalist who believes the only way to replicate an animal faithfully is to study it in its native haunts.

The first day I met him, however, David wanted to talk about eating bald eagle. (Taxidermists love to joke about eating specimens, especially if a specimen is rare, endangered, or politically charged.) So what does it taste like? I asked.

"Like bald eagle!" he said with a chuckle.

Then he went over to the eagle carcass, glanced at it, and said, "Looks like ovaries. An adult female."

He sat back down and rocked in the afternoon heat. The rocker is the center of David's universe, the focus from which all the significant places in his life radiate, like the points on a compass: "up there" (the AMNH), "back there" (his house), "in here" (the workshop), and "the cabin" (the log house his parents built by hand and lived in until they died). Dressed in khaki from head to toe, worn leather work boots, and a leather belt with a brass buckle, he looked like a safari guide who got lost and ended up in New Jersey. He had folded paper for jotting field notes in his breast pocket and a small jackknife in his pants pocket, and he was smoking a pipe. He handed me a business card that said DAVID J. SCHWENDEMAN, CHIEF PREPARATORY TAXIDERMIST, AMNH, RETIRED.

"I was in my teens when I did my first mount. I mounted a starling," he said.

"Mine was a grackle," said Bruce. "Pup-Pup's was a pigeon. Mum-Mum's was a blue jay."

"My mother was really a skinner; she could skin anything," enthused David. He puffed on his pipe and continued. "She used to bake those pies. Is that what you'd call a blackbird pie?"

"Four-and-twenty blackbirds," said Bruce as he fastened antlers to a deer head manikin he was filing into shape.

"When the blackbirds migrated, we'd get a bunch. We used to eat grackles by the hundreds. During the Depression, we'd eat anything," said David.

"Heck, we do now," said Bruce. "But we're *not* a butcher shop! It's a fringe benefit, not the norm."

David got up and shuffled out of the workshop and into the yard. He checked his cage of promethea moths, then went over to see if his bamboo garden was producing. When he lifted a capful of O'Doul's out of the soil to see if it had attracted any slugs, it was impossible to picture him in any city, much less New York. As far as David is concerned, the AMNH is a city itself. He simply bypassed Manhattan by riding the C train directly into the museum, commuting the thirty-five miles with a briefcase concealing dead beavers and shrews and the occasional poison dart frog. In twenty-eight years, the only city sidewalk he ever touched was the one he had to cross to go birding in Central Park.

Sometimes when David is feeling wistful, he grabs an old binder labeled "Taxidermy Notes and Formulae" and flicks through its yellowing pages. Whenever he does this, his eyes sparkle and it's as if he's back on the fifth floor of the AMNH in the exhibition department's rich art studios. One day he grabbed the binder and with trembling fingers showed me his secrets for making lifelike plants and animals. It was astonishing to see his range of skills. The book was filled with hand-written recipes and experiments, things that evoked chemistry equations or a wizard's book of potions. One entry had his "star-fish solution" (equal parts formalin, water, and glycerin); another, "how to clean an oropendola nest" (make a spray from ten ounces of water, Elmer's glue, and one and a half ounces of glycerin). There was his "formula for bleaching bones" (a paste of hydrogen peroxide and magnesium carbonate), his method for hatching snapping turtle eggs (Mortimer lived for fifteen years), and an entry called "how to make artificial frog eggs."

He pointed to a section called "scorpion experiments," then to "how to anesthetize a lizard" and "relaxing bat study skins." There was a section called "how to make a Plexiglas water line for wading wood storks," his "snake-tanning formula," and instructions for how to fasten a diving cormorant to the wall so that it looks as if it's flying. And there was more: How to "clean live coral. How to make "slushy snow": combine clear resin, a touch of white pigment, and cabosil (a thickening agent); add enough small glass beads to create the consistency of cream (gives it luster); add ten drops of catalyst; let it set up for fifteen minutes). How to "set up earthworms for casting": inject the worms with vinyl acetate before molding. How to "make artificial algae": boil Angora goat hair with yellow-green fabric dye. And on and on.

David was born in 1924, three years after his father sold his first deer head and Lillian skinned her first pheasant. The original workshop was in the family home, in what is now David's kitchen. It sold bait and tackle and was open 24-7. People would ring the buzzer at three A.M. looking for shiners, and David would trudge down in his pajamas to fill orders, sarcastically mumbling, "I've been waiting up all night for you." In the early years, their customers were local hunters who wanted their pheasants and small mammals mounted, and the place took on the seasonal rhythm of a farm: rails, grouse, quail, and pheasants in early fall; deer and ducks in mid-fall; turkeys and bears in spring; fish and woodchucks in summer. Before they had a freezer, Lillian would skin the birds while the hunters waited, and she'd hand back the meat wrapped in paper. (Now Bruce tells his customers to get two: one for mounting, the other for dinner.)

As a boy, David hung around the shop, cleaning deer skulls and getting in his father's way. He loved to wander outdoors to listen to spring peepers (little frogs), green frogs, and katydids. Mostly he trapped foxes and went frogging, birding, and hunting for tree stumps. Sometimes he'd grab a camera and wade into the swamps behind the house, looking for red-winged blackbird or least bittern nests and grebes. He'd come home sopping wet, and Arthur would scold him by saying it was okay to watch birds now, but as a man it would be a problem. He never stopped. Once, when he was fourteen, he sat by the old dirt road that ran by their house sketching a little green heron. A man rode by on horseback and took him for a Boy Scout. David was infuriated. "You had to be a *Booooy* Scout to look at birds!" he says with a mock whine. "Now it's strange here," he says reflectively. "I think they spray. I haven't seen a bat all summer. Used to see them flying around. Now it's all houses; it's all gone now."

Birds are the workshop's specialty. However, the first animal the Schwendemans mounted for the AMNH was a venomous lizard: a Gila monster. Gila monsters are classified as *Heloderma suspectum*. They have forked tongues and scaly bodies that are typically two feet long. Arthur's brother boxed up the live lizard and mailed it to Milltown from Arizona. Arthur put it in a cage and kept his distance, in case it spit poison. "Boy, did I want to touch that thing, but we weren't allowed, because we didn't know if it was alive or dead," David recalls with boyish enthusiasm. It was dead, so Arthur mounted it, and the uncle called up the museum and asked if they wanted it. They did—and then they offered Arthur a job. Arthur hated cities and said he would work from home. But when David turned eleven, he begged his mother to sign him up as a museum member. It was 1936—the heyday of the diorama—and that year "members day" fell on the museum's most momentous occasion: the ribbon cutting for the Akeley Hall of African Mammals.

For taxidermists and curators alike, African Hall represents taxidermy's highest merger of science, art, technology, and institutional support. Carl Akeley, the taxidermist whose dream it was to build the hall, was also a hunter-naturalist, whose adventures in Africa had made him an American legend. For young David, whose parents hadn't begun to use manikins yet, African Hall—with its startling dioramas and eight trumpeting elephants—was the taxidermic equivalent of shooting a rocket to the moon. The taxidermists who had worked on the exhibits had actually gone to Africa to collect the flora and fauna, which they painstakingly preserved over twenty-five years. David rode home from the opening dazed. "What we did wasn't like that," he says. He began dreaming about becoming a big-game taxidermist, just as other boys dreamt about becoming Babe Ruth. A while later, a local butcher gave him a calf head so that he could pretend to be Carl Akeley. But when he pulled the head out of the burlap sack, it had been bisected and was rotting. David dug a hole and buried it. He also buried the museum taxidermy idea.

During World War II, David joined the Marines, and from 1943 to 1946 he was stationed in Guam. "Should I tell her what I did?" he asks Bruce. "Big, bad Marine!" Bruce chides. While other soldiers admired pinups, David watched butterflies. He wanted to preserve a few spectacular species, so his parents sent him his collapsible butterfly net and cyanide killing jar. But when they arrived, David was too embarrassed to run around the military base waving the butterfly net.

After the war, when he got married, his wife said she hoped he didn't expect her to do what his mother did. He didn't. "Most *men* wouldn't do what my mother did," he says: skin a bear with a single-edge razor blade; shoot blue jays from the kitchen window; wade into ponds in a long dress and chest waders to collect geese that she was raising and selling; chip ice off the roof of her log cabin at age ninety-one; use her skinning knife to stab an apple slice after the knife had been in arsenic and minimally wiped off on her apron. The Schwendemans credit her longevity to arsenic exposure: they say she stored it in her fatty tissues and reabsorbed it as she aged. When they told me this, I shot

Bruce a sidelong glance, and he said defensively, "Arsenic is an overrated poison!" by which he meant that people who are not taxidermists tend to view arsenic myopically: nothing more than a deadly carcinogen.

Taxidermists typically overcompensate when defending their maligned profession, but arsenic as elixir was exceptionally suspect—at least to me. To Pat Morris, a retired University College London zoologist and taxidermy historian, it had some merit. In 1982, he compared the life spans of thirty-two nineteenth- and early-twentieth-century taxidermists with their civilian counterparts. The taxidermists outlived the civilians by forty-two years. According to Morris, the average taxidermist in 1901 lived to 76.4, whereas the average male lived to be 34. The alleged reason: metabolized arsenic. Also, as Morris surmises, job fulfillment. The Schwendemans, who resist change, used arsenic until the mid-1980s.

One day in the late 1940s, a local taxidermist showed up at the workshop with a bag of pheasants and grouse. Arthur mounted the birds in Milltown, and the taxidermist brought them to the AMNH, which hired Arthur to preserve study skins for its ornithological collections. Soon Arthur and David were delivering batches of birds to Seventy-ninth Street and Central Park West every month. "Just like we do now," Bruce says.

On one delivery trip, the head of exhibitions offered David a summer job. Work was generally slow in the workshop during the summer, and his parents said they could manage, so he took the job. He went "up there" for two months, and he stayed for twenty-eight years.

It was 1959, "the beginning of the end" of the old-style natural history museum. Back then, displays were permanent, mostly dark galleries of dioramas, not the blockbuster traveling exhibits popularized during David's lifetime. Dioramas are perhaps the most laborious form of exhibition design, and therefore they cost millions of dollars to make. In the 1950s, museums had to compete with new sensations such as television and air travel for the public's attention. When David showed up at the AMNH, the major halls were undergoing renovation, and only two taxidermists remained on staff. They were making artificial plants. One of them greeted David by saying, "Quit while you're ahead! Taxidermy's lousy." David changed out of his commuting clothes (a suit and tie), put on his khaki uniform, and got busy preserving study skins.

"It was the heyday of 'quality comes first,'" Bruce recalls. *Up there,* David quickly learned the difference between a commercial taxidermist's trophy and a museum taxidermist's scientific specimen. A trophy is a generalized depiction (it could be *any* zebra), whereas a museum specimen is a specific individual (*that* zebra). A commercial taxidermist must work quickly to turn a profit; a museum taxidermist must bring the latest phylogenetic information to life and receives all the time and scientific data he needs to achieve his goal. A museum taxidermist must know how to mount the rarest and most exotic species—even extinct prehistoric creatures. He has to "relax" (soften and rehydrate) one-hundred-year-old study skins and articulate intricate skeletons. A museum taxidermist's mounts must last indefinitely and will be seen by millions of people.

David relished every moment of every job. Mostly he loved the stimulating atmosphere. *Up there,* he met famous scientists and artists whose fidelity to nature was even more extreme than his own. One of those people was the landscape artist James Perry Wilson, who worked at the museum from 1934 to 1957 but never stopped visiting it after he retired. Wilson was a Columbia University–trained architect, an amateur meteorologist, and a self-taught artist who painted thirty-eight diorama backgrounds at the AMNH. He was so talented that people at the museum said that he could paint atmosphere. "He could paint the feeling of the temperature of a hot climate," says David. One day David experienced Wilson's exactitude. David was installing bobolinks (small, sparrowlike birds) in a diorama when Wilson showed up to have a look. The diorama depicted the birds migrating south through a night sky illuminated by a crescent moon. Wilson asked about three things: the locality, the time of year, and the direction of migration. The diorama artists told him the birds migrated east of the Great Plains and wintered in South America. Wilson thundered, "Well, the crescent is facing the wrong way! It should be reversed!" They reversed the crescent.

At the museum, David got to open all the doors of the most amazing cabinet of curiosities in the world. He got to visit the museum's gargantuan freezer ("As big as this whole building!") to select, for instance, penguin skins from the quarry collected on one of Robert E. Peary's polar expeditions. While inside, he'd steal a glance at the huge stacks of folded elephant skins and the full-mounted tigers and pandas. Soon he befriended the collections manager of ornithology, who let him select his own skins from the vast storerooms filled with more than a million preserved birds.

His primary pleasure, however, was learning how a diorama is made. Dioramas are three-dimensional time capsules of vanishing landscapes. Like meticulous stage sets, they simulate reality with dreamlike precision. Dioramas depict places in the world that are no longer as beautiful or as "natural" as they used to be. From 1890 to 1940, dioramas were the primary way American museums educated the public about the ecological interdependence of species and their habitats. The AMNH's dioramas were (and still are) considered the most magnificent in the world, and David has repaired and restored them all.

His favorite diorama is the Yosemite Valley Group in the Hall of North American Mammals. It's not the coyotes or the Anna's hummingbird that draws him to it, but the background painting of the meandering Merced River as it flows through Bridal Veil Meadow on a bright June morning. The river winds down from glacial mountains and forms a clear pool in a landscape of azaleas, rhododendrons, and mariposa lilies. Wilson painted it in 1946 after he spent two days in Yosemite searching for the perfect spot. "By God, it looks like if you walked in there, you'd get wet!" David exclaims. "I mean, you can see through it! You can see the bottom! The effect is so fantastic!"

The first diorama David worked on was the Japan Bird Group in the Hall of Birds of the World. One day he described the process for me. As taxidermist, David was an integral part of the exhibition team, which included a background painter, a foreground artist, and an ornithologist who oversaw the scientific accuracy of the display, selected the species, and approved the final mounts. Most of the work took place directly inside the diorama shell, as they installed the exhibit from the curved back wall to the front window.

While the background artist painted the scenic backdrop (using a grid system devised by Wilson for translating two-dimensional studies and photographs onto rounded contours), David was up in the fifth-floor studios animating pheasants and sparrows in a way that brought the ornithologist's vision to life. After the background was painted, the foreground artist added layers of wire, burlap, and plaster to mimic the surface of the land. As the artist carefully put his mosses, grasses, and shrubs on top of his topographical stage set, David installed his birds in batches, as specified by the ornithologist. Finally, after everything, including the intricate lighting, was adjusted to suggest sun and shadow, the case was tightly sealed with a thick plate-glass window, tempered to reduce glare. "It was a beautiful exhibit, a beautiful diorama," he says.

Museums often credit their patrons, scientists, curators, and artists by posting their names in their grand galleries. For the Japan Bird Group, the museum listed, among others, the background painter, the foreground artist, the person who collected the birds—everyone, it seemed, except David. "They didn't have my name! You know, the taxidermist!" he says. "And you look at the *damn* thing—I'm sorry—and you look at the diorama, and you see the birds. Who cares about what kind of moss they have? . . . I complained to the birdman—the ornithologist, who I worked with more closely than anyone else, . . . and after a while, they did change it and put my name on the group."

While David was telling me this, Bruce flushed, then said, "Can I interject? This points to a couple of things. One is that the taxidermist was overlooked. They did admire his expertise, but he wasn't the scientist, and he wasn't asked to go on the collecting expedition, and his name was often left off of the diorama. And yet the birds were the stars of the show!"

Other bird groups followed, including the Chilkat River Bald Eagle Group in the Hall of North American Birds. David had to create the illusion that the eagles were soaring down into the river to catch salmon. To capture the drama of eagles in flight, he devised a method for inserting threadlike steel wires into their pinion feathers, so the birds would appear to be resisting the wind.

In the late 1960s, he worked on the first renovation of what is now called the Millstein Hall of Ocean Life. When the hall first opened in 1933, its dioramas depicted the fragile marine habitats of walruses, elephant seals, and other large mammals hunted to near extinction for their fur, their environments decimated by the petroleum industry. In 1969, the museum gutted the hall, replacing its original seventy-six-foot great blue whale model (designed in 1908 by the legendary paleontologist Roy Chapman Andrews) with the ninety-four-foot fiberglass model that dominates the hall today. David made the replacement whale's huge fake eye. Mostly, however, he recast plaster fish in lightweight fiberglass so they'd be able to hang from a boom. (Taxidermists don't use actual skin for fish mounts anymore, because the skins curl, ooze grease, and ruin the paintings.) By the early 1980s, David's taxidermy jobs at the museum had dwindled, and he was mostly restoring faded old mounts. For the Hall of Biology of Birds, he had to revive five hundred birds preserved in the 1930s. The heron's wings had snapped, the Andean condor had shriveled, and ultraviolet light had discolored the crimson breast of the trogon and turned the pink flamingo white. "Capturing the iridescence of the colors with paint is the most difficult part of the work," he said at the time in the employee newsletter. Other jobs followed: tail extensions for Carl Akeley's elephants; feather cloaks for the Hall of Pacific Peoples; and gardens and gardens of artificial plants. When he retired in 1987, his colleagues threw him a big party and baked him a cake in the shape of a muskox. "And they did a nice job on it, too!" says Bruce.

After he retired, David put on a denim apron and joined Bruce in the family workshop, mounting specimens for the AMNH, which no longer had a taxidermist on staff. In 2002, they preserved cormorants and a sea otter for the second renovation of the Hall of Ocean Life. Bruce had to implant 120 monofilament whiskers into the sea otter by hand, something he calls "a cold-sweat job." They also preserved the laughing gulls in the Hall of Saurischian Dinosaurs. The gulls sway above the maniraptor case like a fantastic mobile. If you walked into the hall and gazed up at them, as I have done many times, you'd realize that taxidermy is indeed magical. When the birds arrived in Milltown, they were frozen and bloody; missing feathers, feet, and eyes; and marred with bullet holes (airports shoot down nuisance birds before they fly into airborne planes and cause crashes).

In 1995, Bruce mounted forty West African mammals and birds for the Hall of Biodiversity, a new-style diorama that takes you through an African rain forest. Some of the primate skins were one hundred years old and arrived at the shop without reference. "Reference" is the scientific data taxidermists use to make their replicas. It can be photographs, skeletons, diagrams, even DNA sequencing, anything that helps them sculpt forms that support the biological narrative. Every detail of the animal's anatomy must be convincing in order to pull off the trick: a jaguar's whiskers can purr or roar; a hunting dog's perked ears can sense danger or sniff prey. Taxidermists call this "translating reference." They translate reference all the time. Without a skeleton, however, they have to improvise. When taxidermists improvise, they often turn to the natural world. David walked over to his garden, clicked open his jackknife, and chopped down bamboo stalks of varying lengths and widths to mimic primate femurs and tibias. Then father and son sat side by side and made skeletons out of homegrown bamboo.

At first I just liked to hang around Schwendeman's Taxidermy Studio and listen to David and Bruce banter back and forth. Then I started to notice that each time I visited, they were working on a different species that required an entirely new set of skills and anatomical knowledge. During these visits, I began to realize that these two taxidermists, often stereotyped as "animal killers," were teaching me to see the infinite variation in all living things. I figured that if I hung around the Schwendemans long enough, maybe they'd open up to me, and eventually they did.

Soon it was evident that taxidermy was a thriving subculture that extended far beyond Main Street. Some 100,000 taxidermists, mostly commercial practitioners, exist, and they come alive in *Taxidermy Today, Breakthrough,* and other trade magazines. I wanted to meet them. I wanted to find out if they shared the Schwendemans' extraordinary skills and fascinations. So in April 2003, I left Milltown and the cloistered world of these taxidermologists, with their eagle dissections and stories of Mum-Mum the skinner, and booked a room at the Crowne Plaza in Springfield, Illinois, where taxidermists from across the globe were gathering to strut their stuff as celebrated animal artists.

2

THE CHAMPIONS

HAVING DRIVEN FOURTEEN HUNDRED snow-slick miles from Cody, Wyoming, Ray Hatfield was now in the lobby of the Crowne Plaza in Springfield, Illinois, pushing a brass luggage cart with a snow leopard perched on it. He pushed it onto the elevator, rode up to the ninth floor, and then rolled it down the hall to room 918, where he placed the leopard on one of the double beds, its spots curiously blending in with the oak-leaf pattern of the bedspread. Hatfield walked slow circles around the leopard, inspecting it for imperfections. In his hand was a gunmetal silver blow dryer.

Hatfield runs Nature's Design Taxidermy, a big commercial studio, which serves mostly hunters. He is tall and soft-spoken, with tawny hair and aviator eyeglasses that adapt to the sunlight. On the drive to Springfield, he'd delivered several trophies to customers along the way: elk and deer, a buffalo, an ibex, and a Marco Polo sheep. A few mounts, including the snow leopard, got wet when melting snow leaked into his cargo trailer. Under normal circumstances, damp capes ("cape" is the term used for the animal's pelt, or skin), if quickly caught, are an easy problem to fix. On this day, however, Hatfield couldn't risk even a minor flaw. "I'm trying to get all of its hairs separated down to the skin and make all of the hair patterns lie in place," he said, clutching a wire brush that rapidly filled with soft golden fur. "Everything has to be just right for the competition."

Hatfield was hopeful of winning a ribbon with the leopard, but his expectations were not high. In this he was realistic. Three hundred fifty taxidermists from twenty-two countries were competing for twelve Best in World titles and $25,600 in cash prizes. For the next five days, Springfield would be what Atlantic City was to beauty queens and Indianapolis is to racecar drivers: the most extraordinary gathering of competitors in the field.

But Hatfield wasn't there only to win medals. No one was, actually. That was just the pretext. Taxidermy competitions have long been the single most important place — outside of natural history museums — where taxidermists can highlight their artistry. Indeed, the American taxidermy competitions of the early 1880s gave rise to a new movement in artistic taxidermy. The winners went off to work at the leading museums, transforming their halls from dreary morgues of systematic classification into galleries of simulated nature. Elevating taxidermy's status was a goal in Springfield as well. Hatfield, for one, was slated to lead a two-day seminar in which he'd demonstrate how one expertly preserves a leopard. Equally important, the World Taxidermy Championships (WTC) offered him a rare opportunity to talk shop with world-class taxidermists from places such as the Milwaukee Public Museum, the Natural History Museum of Los Angeles County, the Smithsonian Institution, and museums throughout Europe. Birdmen from the United Kingdom were flying in, as were fish carvers from Switzerland; midwestern cat ladies with a motherly devotion to lynx, bobcats, and tigers; and "Team Sweden." Arriving from Russia was Vladimir Sukchare, who in 1977 helped excavate and preserve one of the Zoological Museum of St. Petersburg's Siberian baby mammoths. And, accompanied by her father in a matching red polo shirt that said AMY'S ANIMAL ART, was doe-eyed Amy Ritchie, a home-schooled teenager from Midland, North Carolina, whose business cards said PRESERVING THE BEAUTY OF GOD'S CREATIONS. Among the elite were skilled amateurs from many rural outposts and small towns in America, people who prepared deer heads in their garages or plaster-cast fish in family-run shops. All were converging for a long weekend of friendship, competition, and, as the World Show's glossy brochure put it, "inspirational fellowship."

The lobby of the Crowne Plaza was a veritable Noah's ark on luggage carts. A taxidermist from Nebraska carted a prairie chicken and a mink; a competitor from Pittsburgh had a black squirrel and a freeze-dried snowshoe hare. Green sandpipers, cougars, geckos, a Bengal tiger, brant geese, chum salmon, marmots, rattlesnakes, and snapping turtles were all being wheeled this way and that in the eccentric migration. The bellhops stood by and watched. They had nothing to do, really, because only a slacker would hand over a mount that he had been preserving for a year or more to the untrained hotel staff.

Cradling a red-tailed hawk in his arms was a taxidermist from Indiana, who paused to say that his raptor wasn't a raptor at all. It was a fake. "It's a re-creation made out of turkey, chicken, and goose feathers," he explained, as if it were perfectly normal to turn chickens into hawks. He was entering it into the show's most fascinating category: Re-Creations. According to the rule book, "Re-Creations are defined as renderings which include no natural parts of the animal portrayed . . . For instance, a re-creation eagle could be constructed using turkey feathers, or a cow hide could be used to simulate African game." Imitation or not, this hawk looked ready to stalk prey in Lake Springfield's wetlands. Here, in this convention hotel set amid chain restaurants and highways, a dead circus was coming to life.

I got in line to register, feeling like a vagrant species blown in by an errant trade wind. In here, a person could not easily hide his or her exotic plumage. Nearly everyone in line was male, and nearly all of them wore camo, stars and stripes, or denim. Several guys had deer tracks tattooed across their forearms. Others wore animal T-shirts or shirts emblazoned with Smith & Wesson logos. A man in a PETA shirt caused a stir until people realized the acronym stood for People Eating Tasty Animals.

The participants, many of whom were from blue-collar families or had grown up on farms, considered themselves outdoorsmen and hunters, and they reflected a distinctly American approach to taxidermy, one linked to hunting in the spirit of Daniel Boone and Davy Crockett. Lured by the infinite bounty of the unexplored wilderness, early white hunters such as Boone and Crockett considered the American West a sportsman's paradise (a sportsman being someone who hunts for pleasure, not profit; someone who does not, for instance, shoot wolves with machine guns from airplanes, but rather gives his prey a "fair" fight in the wild). The most emblematic American sportsman of later generations was Theodore Roosevelt, whose Boone and Crockett Club (1887) promoted what Karen Wonders describes in her Ph.D. dissertation "Habitat Dioramas" as "sportsmanship through travel and the exploration of wild country, through the preservation of big game and through the scientific study of animals in the wild." In the early days of the Republic, big trophies, such as those displayed by Thomas Jefferson at Monticello, were thought to disprove the European claim put forth by the French naturalist Comte Georges de Buffon and others that animals shrank and became muted in the New World and men lost their virility. Once that theory was debunked, a sizable moose head (or a record marlin) became more personalized. Rich sportsmen from Europe and the United States wanted their kills and catches preserved to commemorate their prowess as marksmen and adventurers. Soon the American West was dotted with taxidermy firms such as Jonas Brothers in Denver, whose trophies glamorized the thrill of the hunt and who also did amazing museum mounts. Today the big commercial firm Animal Artistry in Reno, Nevada, which has prepared mounts for the likes of General Norman Schwarzkopf and country music singer Hank Williams Jr., maintains that tradition.

In the gleaming lobby of the Crowne Plaza, however, one could not easily discern mere hunter from true sportsman. Nevertheless, the guys in line did seem to know everything about each species they had prepared for competition.

As Hatfield and I made our way through the parking lot to his cargo trailer, we passed two truckloads of driftwood being sold for bases. All around us, drivers were carrying odd-shaped bundles. Talons, claws, and webbed feet poked out of blankets and garbage bags that had been cut and taped to accommodate the peculiar forms.

Hatfield swung open the trailer doors and stepped inside. Leaning against the walls like furniture in a U-Haul was a herd of western origin: a buffalo, two six-point elk, and a large mule deer—deliveries for the way home. "Those are elk legs that go to another guy," he said, pointing to a pair of detached limbs. "It'll be a lamp." In the middle of the truck was an enormous mass covered by a blanket. Ray heaved off the blanket, and there sat his monstrous Barbary lion: a mature male with yellow eyes, a grandiose mane that extended down over its belly, and an upright tail exposing a painstakingly crafted hairy scrotum. The species no longer exists in the wild. An Ohio zookeeper had sold the lion to Hatfield for $8,000 after it had died of natural causes. "I've done about eighty lions, and this is by far the largest," he said with the same nonchalance he had displayed while blow-drying the snow leopard. After the show, the lion was going to the collector who had bought it for $20,700. He paused, considering how to haul this king of beasts to the hotel ballroom where the competition was being held. Even without its artificial sandstone outcrop, the lion was far too big to wheel in on a luggage rack.

Outside the ballroom was the grooming area. Here, in a wide corridor, competitors frenetically combed, fluffed, and beautified their mounts before taking them inside for judging. For the most part the human:animal ratio was 1:1. But there was also Cally Morris's flock of turkeys. According to the World Show brochure, Morris is a renowned "turkey man" whose turkey-mounting seminars are standing room only. Hazel Creek, his studio in Green Castle, Missouri, mounts eight hundred turkeys a year for international clients (turkey hunters mostly). A former world champ, Morris won Best in World Bird in 1997 with a turkey and has taken numerous other awards since. Here he was competing with five eastern wild turkeys in their late-winter plumage. The gobblers strutted down a leaf-strewn trail. "This one right here is about to get his rear end kicked," someone pointed out. Everyone agreed that the turkeys—with their white crowns, obscene red wattles, and retractable snood covers—were exceptionally handsome. Equally striking were Morris's grooming crew. The young men in baseball caps and matching denim shirts preened the gobblers with oversize tweezers until each plume lay perfectly atop the one beneath it. As a finishing touch, one worker grabbed a feather duster (of all things!) and brushed the birds off.

While the turkey mounters exemplify the high level of obscure expertise some taxidermists bring here, the deer-head guys represent the most popular category, because theirs is the most hunted animal in the United States. And like the turkey guys, the deer-head guys had their own obsessive preshow rituals. Darrick Bantley, for instance, a twenty-three-year-old taxidermist from Ebensburg, Pennsylvania, was spraying compressed air onto the glass eyes of his one-and-a-half-year-old whitetail mount. "A live animal doesn't have dirt on its eyes," Darrick's father, Dan, explained. Dan Bantley, a round-faced, round-bellied man with lank silver hair and a mustache, was founder and president of the Pennsylvania Institute of Taxidermy and host of a taxidermy show on cable TV. This week he was scheduled to lead the financial seminar "Business: The Lifeblood of a Studio." He was also on hand for some impromptu coaching of his son, which, at the World Show, means ensuring that every anatomical feature — from veining to pupils — is impeccable. Poses, he said, should reflect "the nuance of nature, not the hand of man." Darrick's young buck, for instance, appeared to be "flehmening" — that is, it was eager to mate. Its upper lip was curled, and the glands inside its nose were visibly aroused by the scent of estrogen. The deer resembled a snorting, rearing horse on a merry-go-round. Someone at the show said that "antler-fixated" taxidermists sculpt mounts in their own image, and one had to wonder what inspired this particular one.

Darrick bent down and with ophthalmological precision shined his penlight onto the buck's glass eyes. Dust-free. Nearly every participant had such a light with which to inspect his mounts for flaws. While Darrick was examining the deer's nictitating membrane, or third eyelid (a transparent inner eyelid), Dan recited what I came to consider the World Show's unofficial motto: "First comes anatomical accuracy, then art."

Nearby, a sixty-two-year-old cattle-brand inspector from Texas considered his mount: a longhorn calf eyeball-to-eyeball with a writhing rattlesnake, barbed wire, and a sign that said I'M WARNING YOU. "I was just going to have his mouth open saying 'I'm gonna get you,' but I didn't think it was appropriate with a little calf like this." A woman from Ontario, Canada, gave her two mating bighorn sheep the once-over. "He's romancing her, to say it politely," she said, smiling with satisfaction.

When Ken Walker and John Matthews, two taxidermists from the Smithsonian's National Museum of Natural History, walked in, everyone set down the feather dusters and penlights and looked up, dumbstruck. The Smithsonian taxidermists brought integrity to the show. They brought respect to taxidermy. But that's not why everyone paused mid-groom. The two men were carrying a life-size giant panda!

"I've shot bigger pandas than this!" someone joked from the crowd. It was Dan Bantley walking over for a closer look. Only about sixteen hundred giant pandas still exist. Killing one for any reason is almost treasonous (the punishment for poaching a panda in China is ten years in prison), but that doesn't deter everyone. Black-market panda skins can fetch $100,000 to $300,000 apiece. For all these reasons, everyone gazed at the animal until they realized that this panda wasn't a panda. It was another entry in the Re-Creations category.

That was obvious because the person who had created the panda was the two-time world champion, Ken Roy Walker. If you had to choose a taxidermist who epitomizes the spirit of the WTC, it would be Walker. Although he's a fierce competitor, his unapologetic love of taxidermy, his good-natured spirit, and his ability to inspire others make him a celebrity in the field. Not to mention his uncanny gift for sculpture. Whenever anyone in taxidermy speculates about who will be the next Carl Akeley—which is to say all taxidermists, all the time—Walker's name usually comes up.

Walker is forty-eight and lives with his family in Alberta Beach, Canada, a small vacation town situated on Lac Ste. Anne, about an hour northwest of Edmonton, the city where he grew up. He is handsome in a rugged, Burt Reynolds kind of way. He's about six feet tall and has bright blue eyes, thick bristly brown hair, and a matching Vandyke beard. There's something of the bearcat in him — the directness of someone who trusts his own instincts. Walker has a big, friendly smile and tends to disarm people with his impromptu impersonations of Bugs Bunny and Kermit the Frog. He also enjoys bragging, in a gently provoking way, that he is among the politically *incorrect*. Because of this, he never seems pretentious, even when he's promoting himself — something he admits he does quite flagrantly. How else do you become famous as a taxidermist?

If you said Walker's passion for taxidermy borders on the fanatical, you'd be right. He's been this way ever since he was a kid. Even if you find taxidermy bizarre, you have to admire his willingness to sacrifice everything — except his independence — for the profession. Before one World Show ends, he's already gearing up for the next one. At the last WTC, for instance, Walker took third place in Re-Creations with a saber-toothed tiger. The winner was a Labrador duck. "I stood in front of that duck and said, 'What could beat that duck?'" he told me. "I was strategizing. A panda could beat the duck. I didn't want to make *American Beauty*. I wanted to make *Jurassic Park*!" Sometimes other taxidermists are jealous of him. They think it's unfair that he's able to spend weeks and weeks on a single mount, when they have to take on commercial jobs for the money. He tells them, "I'm not here to beat *you*. I'm here to beat the *winner*."

Like most exceptionally curious people, Walker can talk endlessly about topics he finds captivating. He's been exasperating people with his passions ever since he was a boy. "When he was dedicated to something, that was his life," his mother, Patsy Walker, told me at the next World Show. "He'd just keep adding on." When he was four, for instance, he held the dry-cleaning man captive in the doorway, reciting an entire dinosaur encyclopedia verbatim. "You better take that kid somewhere — there's something wrong with him!" the man told Patsy. Another time, Patsy had to rescue Aunt Pauline when Walker, who had just learned how to fish, showed up at Pauline's house insatiably curious about bullheads. "Is he pestering you?" Patsy gingerly asked Pauline. "No," she demurred, "but all his wheels are turning." Of course, those incidents were nothing compared to the time five-year-old Ken visited Aunt Mary's house with his pet frog. Mary was sunbathing in a bikini. The frog leaped out of Ken's hands and landed in Mary's bikini top. The top fell down, she went nuts (her boobs were flopping all around), and Ken burst into tears, hysterically crying, "Don't kill my frog, Aunt Mary!"

Because he either loves something or finds it terribly boring, Walker pretty much hated school, even preschool. His parents still call him "a play-school dropout." His teachers had little patience for him. When he was in third grade, he'd show up for school with his pockets full of dead muskrats that he had trapped that morning and would skin at home after lunch. If he found a topic interesting, he'd interrupt the class with innumerable questions. If he found it boring, however, he'd wait for the teacher to mess up some fact so that he could correct her. One teacher got so fed up with him she asked if he'd like to teach class. He ran to the front of the room and started to talk and talk.

Luckily, Ken's parents, who are terrifically good-humored, found his idiosyncrasies a sign of intelligence, and they supported him by letting him "tear apart animals in the garage" as long as he cleaned up the "scrunge." "Sometimes I didn't like it when my garage bench was covered with guts," said his father, K. D. Walker. "But I let him do what he wanted." They did this because he was unwavering. When he was drawn to something, he doggedly stuck with it, even turning down a family trip to Disneyland so that he could work at a taxidermy shop. That was in junior high. Now the thing that fuels his curiosity is formulating scientific theories about how prehistoric animals lived (or died out) and then using that information to resurrect them.

He also loves hunting. "It cleanses my soul," he told me later that year at the Smithsonian Institution, where he was working on a contract basis. Indeed, Walker dresses like a hunter even when he's indoors. At the World Show, for instance, he wore a khaki hunting shirt with a built-in shoulder patch to cushion the recoil of a shotgun, even though he never left the hotel. In his view, worshiping nature and shooting animals are perfectly compatible endeavors. "A cougar lives outdoors, and he loves to hunt. Our DNA is ninety percent the same as the cougar's," he reasoned.

In the 1980s, Walker owned a bear-hunting outfit called Svartbjørn (Black Bear), guiding mostly Norwegian hunters through Alberta's vast subalpine forests. He moonlighted as a Roy Orbison impersonator. "I can *really* sound like him," Walker said, staring into my eyes and nodding.

Relating to animals so viscerally is one reason—indeed, the most important reason—Walker excels at taxidermy. "You can almost hear a heart beat. You can almost see the spark of life, and it's a gift to bring the spark of life back," he said. "As a taxidermist who can do his job, I'm indispensable. But as an individual, I'm going to do it *my* way." He paused and then said, "Some people fit into history nicely. Others have to bully their way in."

At the time, Walker was three months into a nine-month contract at the Smithsonian, which was erecting a new mammal hall and had to hire independent taxidermists because it had closed its taxidermy workshop in the late 1960s. Before he'd left for the museum, however, Walker, who had never seen a real giant panda, had begun to make a fake one. Not a run-of-the-mill forgery, but a panda so convincingly real that you could almost hear its heart beat.

The first step had been finding suitable skins. "I was a bear-hunting guide, an outfitter, for ten years, so I have plenty of hides in the freezer, but I didn't have the right brown ones," he said, explaining that he needed two black bear skins for the job. Black bears can range in color from blond to brown to black. Ken needed two brown-colored bears in their blond phase. That means that the fur appears brown but is actually blond at the roots. "I needed the bear to be shot on September tenth, so its hair wouldn't be too long," he explained. "If you tell people that, you can usually get one in a week," he added in the same dispassionate tone you'd use to order a mobile phone. I stared at him, perplexed, and he softened and said, "When I'm driving, I'll swerve in the street to miss a frog, but I'm by *no means* a bunny hunter." (A "bunny hunter" is the hunting equivalent of a "Sunday painter.")

When Walker arrived at the Smithsonian, he had access to unbelievable reference: the frozen carcass of Hsing-Hsing, one of the two pandas Mao Zedong gave President Richard Nixon on his historic visit to China in 1972. (Nixon gave China a pair of muskoxen in return.) Hsing-Hsing had died at the National Zoo in 1999, and the museum had acquired his carcass, storing it in three parts: the carcass, the cape, and the head. "They're afraid to mount it," Walker said, shaking his head with frustration. The museum saw it as a potential political fiasco. Nixon's panda had become a powerful symbol of East-West détente, and no one wanted to offend the Chinese. Somehow, in spite of this,

Walker got permission to make a template of it. "You think of the odds," he mused. "There I was with the only panda specimen available, the only *fresh reference*—meaning carcass—right there in the freezer!"

Much like a forensic scientist outlining a murder victim on a sidewalk, Walker traced Hsing-Hsing's carcass onto paper and used the template to make his own panda's inert body. He bleached the blond bear's cape white using Clairol hair dye, then he cut and sewed it and another cape together. Using a brown bear face as a model, he cast its lips, teeth, ears, and tongue. He reshaped bear claws to use as panda claws, inserting an extra one into each paw to serve as the panda's sixth "false" digit. "Being a visionary taxidermist, I knew what it was going to look like," Walker said with the élan of a champ. "But I had never seen a panda before, and there I was holding one!"

Now, at the competition, Smithsonian lead taxidermist John Matthews (Walker's boss) described "Thing-Thing" to the crowd: "That's a reproduction. Ken made that out of two different black bears, and he put them together. Now he's going to put a whole mess of bamboo trees on the base." Like reporters covering the spectacle this would have been had Thing-Thing been Hsing-Hsing, the taxidermists fired questions at Walker.

"Is it a male or a female?"

"You cannot tell the sex of a panda unless you perform surgery. It's more or less generic," Walker said, boring holes into the platform and planting bamboo.

"I got knocked once for not having nipples on a black-squirrel mount that was peeping into a hollow log," noted Randall Waites as Walker cemented bamboo stalks onto the base, bending one near the panda's mouth so it appeared to be playfully munching. "Which way's the sun shining?" Waites asked as a follow-up, eyeing the bamboo to see if it was bent in the proper direction — that is, oriented properly given the sun's supposed alignment.

Under his grandiose handlebar mustache, Matthews broke into a huge smile. "This is the Super Bowl of taxidermy right here!" he said.

That night Jody Green, a commercial taxidermist who was manning a booth at the taxidermy trade fair, and Dan Bantley sat in the hotel lobby talking shop over a beer. They discussed the ordeal of molding stellar lip lines. They described the limitations of prefabricated deer forms (not enough slack around the neck). Then they analyzed a snapshot of a deer eye, passing it back and forth like a shared cigarette. *Exactly where should the eyeball sit in this particular socket?* Perhaps it was the beer or the long day of travel, but soon I was bleary-eyed. *How much of the eyebrow do you see if the eye is positioned at thirty-three degrees?* The questions revealed an aesthetic that favored literal representation, to say the least. I got the impression that if they could outfit a deer with a working heart and lungs, they would. Why not simply go to a forest or drive to Springfield's Henson Robinson Zoo and see the real thing? I wondered. Why kill it just to obsessively bring it back to life?

The moon rose, and a guy walked by with a mute coyote tucked under his arm. Green and Bantley were too engaged to notice. "We're all trying to duplicate nature," said Green.

"You always go back to nature," Bantley agreed.

"We're judging another man's interpretation of nature. My job is to use my interpretation of nature to judge another guy's interpretation of nature," said Green.

"What's different between this deer and a real one?" Bantley mused, explaining not only what taxidermists think about when they lie awake at night but, more important, what will be on the minds of the judges the next day at five P.M., the start of the competition.

"When you go into that room, you're looking for that top-end deer. I'm looking for something that pleases me *and* that's your top-shelf deer," said Green. "That's the drawback to this whole thing. There's some interpretation in it."

Taxidermy is so outsider, it's not even included in Outsider Art fairs. Competitions are where taxidermists have always demonstrated the potential of their art. The first American taxidermy competition was held in 1880. It was organized by the Society of American Taxidermists, a brotherhood of scientists, professors, museum men, and taxidermists who wanted to elevate taxidermy from amateurish craft to professional-grade fine art by proving that it could be both scientifically sound and artistically evocative. No longer would the isolated taxidermist, too "jealous" to share his knowledge and too steeped in "conceit" to seek it out, languish in anonymity. Instead, taxidermists would "throw open their studio doors to the public until the only secret left was to imitate nature." Or, as G. E. Manigault, an honorary SAT member from the Natural History Museum at the College of Charleston in South Carolina, put it in 1880, "There's no reason why the taxidermist should not hold his head as high as any man. He is eminently a student of nature, and when, as a result of his observations and skill, he is able to produce a counterpart to life itself, he is entitled to rank on the same level as painter or sculptor."

Getting from point A to point B, however, took years of determined struggle by these talented artisans, who would eventually transform Chicago's Field Museum, the Carnegie Museum of Natural History in Pittsburgh, the Smithsonian Institution, the AMNH, and other museums into grand galleries of artificial realism. But of course, this being taxidermy, the momentum gained in the 1880s had all but evaporated by the mid-1970s. By then, taxidermists had forgotten the whole "good PR" thing, and their mounts were crude and sensational (with some exceptions). Predators baring sharp teeth and suffering from gaping arrow or bullet wounds glamorized man's dominance. Some taxidermists also had apparently stopped studying anatomy and turned out bobcats with stumpy forearms, deer with misaligned joints, and other monstrosities. Scientists, curators, and other potential employers stayed away. Soon taxidermists faced a pre-1880 dilemma: where to demonstrate their expertise to a public that equated their craft, through years of negligence and unscrupulous taxidermists (who preferred shotguns to binoculars), with shooting Bambi's mother.

In 1974, a taxidermy maverick name Joe Kish, disappointed by the mounts he saw at a National Taxidermists Association convention, believed that taxidermists needed to improve their craft. So he decided to host the first American taxidermy competition since 1880. Kish is an industry insider who ran a taxidermy magazine for nine years. When I met him in Springfield, he was living on a three-hundred-acre exotic-game ranch in Mountain Home, Texas ("Texadermy" to Kish). One night Kish and I met for a beer in the hotel bar. Smiling under the brim of a stars-and-stripes baseball cap, he explained how taxidermy had been slumping in the 1970s. By then, most museum workshops had shut down, and the 1973 Endangered Species Act was, taxidermically speaking, limiting available subject matter. People were trading in shotguns for cameras. Kish has an impressive résumé—Carnegie Museum, Denver Museum of Nature & Science, Jonas Brothers, and Cabela's hunting stores—but in the 1970s, even as he was doing top-notch work, he feared that his profession was becoming obsolete. Remembering how the SAT competitions had revolutionized taxidermy in the 1880s, he organized his own competition, hoping for similar results.

The first SAT exhibit, a six-day event, took place in 1880 in Rochester, New York, then the taxidermy capital of the United States. Rochester was where the famous specimen emporium and museum supplier Ward's Natural Science Establishment was located. Founded by Professor Henry Augustus Ward in 1862, Ward's hired the best taxidermists, including the seven SAT founders. Ward's resembled a college campus—except the entrance gate was adorned with massive whale jawbones and every building overflowed with treasures that would eventually form the core collections of the Field Museum, the Harvard Museum of Comparative Zoology, Princeton University, and many others. In the late 1800s, famous taxidermist-explorers from Europe passed through Ward's, talking of grand expos in France, England, and Germany where taxidermists displayed futuristic mounts to a public hungry for sensational renditions of nature. In spite of this, Professor Ward was profit driven and reluctant to change (to become too artistic) at a time when museums had no dioramas. Taxidermy was then primarily a tool used for comparative morphology (the study of the form and structure of an organism). Birds, for instance, were stuffed, tagged, and lined up in uniform rows for comparison by type.

Forty-four members from seven states—the largest gathering of taxidermists ever—and hundreds of eager spectators attended the first SAT show. What they saw inside that gaslit hall dazzled them: staggering creatures from the farthest reaches of the earth, everything from bison to iridescent hummingbirds. Most of the mounts were crudely executed, typical of the era, but then there was William T. Hornaday's *A Fight in the Tree-Tops*.

Tree-Tops wasn't a single menagerie specimen stuffed with straw and hemp until it bulged, but a rain forest melodrama in which two male Bornean orangutans viciously fought over a female, while swinging from artificial vines! The larger of the two males had bitten off the middle finger of the other, and the victim's face writhed in agony as blood oozed from his mutilated hand. Hornaday himself called the apes "hideously ugly" and the display a "trifle sensational." That was intentional; he wanted to create a stir similar to the one Parisian taxidermist Jules Verreaux's shocking *Arab Courier Attacked by Lions* had caused at the 1867 World Exposition in Paris. He succeeded.

The greatest American taxidermist of his era, Hornaday was also an ardent evolutionist and passionate naturalist. He knew that scientifically sound fighting apes would incite both the lurid public and the sober scientist, and that's exactly what happened. The judges—leading museum men from Cambridge, Princeton, and Manhattan—awarded *Tree-Tops* the top prize. As much as Hornaday loved the limelight, however, he loved animals even more, and scholars do consider *Tree-Tops* to be the first large mammal group appropriate for scientific display. As a result, it revolutionized taxidermy by inspiring others to aim for accuracy in their art.

Hornaday, a towering figure and eloquent speaker who dined with Andrew Carnegie (a lifelong friend and SAT patron) and other elites, wielded tremendous influence in the scientific community. He served as the first director of the National Zoo and was the director of the New York Zoological Park (Bronx Zoo) for thirty years. His ardent conservation campaigns brought national attention to the plight of the American bison, the northern fur seal, and the white rhino. His efforts to save the passenger pigeon, a species that vanished in 1914, were, sadly, less successful.

Hornaday went to work for Ward's in 1874, during its glory days. Previously, while at Iowa State College, he had read books by world-renowned naturalist-explorers, including John James Audubon's *Birds of America* and Paul Belloni Du Chaillu's *Explorations and Adventures in Equatorial Africa*. At Ward's, he also hunted specimens for science.

He got the idea for *Tree-Tops* on a two-year collecting expedition through the East Indies and Borneo. Ward's sent Hornaday there to collect crocodiles, Bengal tigers, water buffalo, primates, and other exotic species for his museum clients. While he was in Borneo, the twenty-four-year-old Hornaday spent hours on the banks of the Sadong River sketching orangutans and gibbons, more convinced than ever that Charles Darwin's theory of evolution was right. This did not deter him from his primary responsibility: to shoot them. In all, he killed forty-three primates (twenty-seven orangutans), surpassing Darwin's colleague (and friendly rival), the British naturalist Alfred Russel Wallace, who in 1855 collected twenty-four for scientific study and display.

In 1879, Hornaday returned to Ward's with a diagram of a *Tree-Tops*–like primate group, vines and all. Henry Ward was skeptical. At the time, no museum had a display case combining large mammals and artificial foliage—a "habitat group" to museums. Ward doubted that any museum would pay for something so expensive to make, so cutting-edge, and so violent. It was one thing to admire an orangutan in a painting or to read about one in an explorer's tall tale. But to see "real" primates engaged in bloody combat without having to trek to Borneo was something else altogether. How better to depict how species fight for survival?. Ward gave in, and Hornaday went to work.

That August, Hornaday presented *Tree-Tops* at the annual meeting of the American Association for the Advancement of Science, an organization of scientists and museum men devoted to advancing science and serving society. As he described his field studies (explaining, exuberantly I imagine, how orangutans are not ferocious—indeed, they can be quite docile and playful), the attending scientists were riveted. Then he unveiled his case, and the orangutans appeared in the room as if by magic. Here was the jungle complete with creeper vines, moss, and bellicose apes. Even Hornaday could not convey in words this type of theater, which was electrifying, if a bit overwrought. The scientists were tantalized. After the lecture, George Brown Goode, curator and assistant secretary of the Smithsonian, offered Hornaday the position of chief taxidermist at the National Museum of Natural History. Albert S. Bickmore, founder of the American Museum of Natural History, commissioned a tame *Tree-Tops* for his museum.

In 1883, the Smithsonian bought *Tree-Tops* and displayed it in its Hall of Mammals for a curious public eager for science. Sometimes Hornaday would visit the museum to see if his masterpiece held up in light of the latest phylogenetic discoveries. He was never anything less than sanguine. "Yes; even forty years after we are not ashamed of it; for it is sufficiently near to the standards of to-day to be entitled to a place in the sun," he boasted in his 1925 memoir, *A Wild-Animal Round-up: Stories and Pictures from the Passing Show.*

Tree-Tops was dismantled in the 1950s, its individual orangutans displayed in the World of Mammals Hall until 1999, when they were taken down and put into storage. If you saw the apes now, you'd think the taxidermy was crude, and you'd be right. The top taxidermists at the WTC today could sculpt a far more realistic and technically accurate primate—that is to say, one that was fleshier and less grotesquely savage. At the time, however, Hornaday's experiment was radical, equivalent to adding Technicolor to *The Wizard of Oz.*

Even so, it was the *live* animals that truly captured Hornaday's heart. "I love nature and all her works but one day in an

East Indian jungle among strange men and beasts, is worth more to me than a year among dry specimens," he wrote in 1885.

In spite of Hornaday's breakthrough display, that year the SAT dissolved, mired in debt. Its third and last exhibit received mixed reviews: apparently some mounts showed a bit too much imagination—as if the mirrors held up to nature were from a fun house. By then, its remaining officers found the organization too unwieldy to manage; although everyone wanted to win ribbons, only a few would share their secret formulas and methods.

The SAT was far from a failure, though. Hornaday, for one, claimed that it had grandly served its purpose and was therefore no longer necessary. In fact, its most gifted members, such as Carl Akeley and Frederic Lucas, had already taken positions with the leading natural history museums, erecting astonishing dioramas unrivaled to this day. The era of "stuffing" animals, Hornaday later remarked, was finally over.

Nearly ninety years later, in 1976, an optimistic Kish sent out a thousand invitations to his first Taxidermy Review Show; 125 taxidermists responded. The show was a success, and Kish organized his second competition the following year. This show featured an awards banquet held at the Denver Playboy Club. Difficult as it was to surpass sexy women in bunny ears displaying ample décolletage and mounted animals, the newly formed National Taxidermists Association, which had initially rejected the very idea of competitive taxidermy, decided to hold its own competition, also in Denver. Kish competed in this show, too, taking Best of Show with a mounted bobcat. Undaunted, he also ran his Taxidermy Review Show for another four years.

Meanwhile, a paint company executive named Bob Williamson had decided that competitive taxidermy was more fun than selling taxidermy paint, so he set out to host his own competition, which he boldly called the World Taxidermy Champion-ships. Soon he had copyrighted the name and the competition categories. (Try passing yourself off as a World Taxidermy Cham-pion, and you just might get sued!) The first WTC took place in 1983, drawing nearly three hundred taxidermists, including a few competitors from Canada and Europe.

In 1994, however, Williamson sold the WTC to a former schoolteacher named Larry Blomquist, who—together with his wife, Kathy (whom he poached from *Taxidermy Today* maga-zine)—has run it (and *Breakthrough* magazine) ever since.

Many participants asked me why I was at the WTC. They found it incomprehensible that someone who was not a taxidermist, a hunter, or a zoologist would find taxidermy so intriguing. The subtle shame lived on, even here among the elite. Usually this was manifested by self-deprecating humor—humming "Duel-ing Banjos" from *Deliverance,* for instance, or claiming that one's genetic makeup contained the "Taxidermy gene" ("T gene" for short)—a propensity to procrastinate. Some taxidermists went so far as to compare themselves to serial killers—an industry cliché based on the belief that as kids, serial killers abused their pets. (Jeffrey Dahmer did consider taxidermy as a profession, and he did skin dogs.) Several of the taxidermists who had at-tended college or graduate school wanted it known. Others spoke of children and grandchildren who were now enrolled. A woman whose husband was a bird judge told a story that epit-omized the unease felt by the entire field. When her daughter was in third grade, her teacher asked what her father did for a living. The eight-year-old mumbled, "He's a taxidermist."

"A tax attorney?" asked the teacher.

"Oh, yes!" said the daughter with relief.

• • •

"The fine arts never respected taxidermy and never will," Kish told me. "If you take five of the best sculptors who ever lived and ask them to sculpt something, you'll get five different results. If you ask the five best taxidermists in the world to mount a white-tailed deer, aside from some stylistic differences, they'll all pretty much look like white-tailed deer. We're trying to duplicate something that nature already created. It's kind of like medical illustration."

Jack Fishwick, a tall, thin, bespectacled taxidermist from England who works for natural history museums throughout Europe and whose specialty is birds ("*small* birds"), was far more blunt: "Even though I do it, I think it is *totally* weird. *Bizarre!* It's a pointless exercise, because it will never be perfect. No matter how good you are, you'll only get a semblance of life. It'll never be alive again. A sculptor can make things soft and flowing to give the impression of speed or agility, but a taxidermist is restricted to re-creat[ing] nature *exactly.*"

By day two, the Crowne Plaza was a fourteen-story *Wunderkammer.* The grand ballroom contained 701 competition mounts. The seminar rooms hosted live taxidermy demonstrations — the zoological equivalent of Thomas Eakins's painting *The Gross Clinic.* And many of its 288 hotel rooms were inhabited by beasts and birds that looked freshly plucked from the forest or the tundra or the veldt. This presented something of a challenge to the hotel staff, who suffered random encounters with snarling effigies, a series of unintentional practical jokes.

One day after lunch, I stopped by my room to make a call. The door was open and the housekeeper was making my bed, so I stood outside with the floor supervisor, a twenty-five-year-old from Lima, Peru. When I asked him what he made of all this, his eyes brightened and he said, "The housekeepers called me a few time: 'Someone has to come and open the door for me because there's a tiger!' They get scared of small snakes." He pointed down the hall. "The housekeeper over there—we told her to be careful of room number 615. There's a big anaconda in there from Peru."

Ken Walker stood in a packed conference room preparing to give his talk, "Competition Techniques and Strategies." As people searched for seats, he arranged a bear skull and two sets of plastic jaws (cougar and bobcat) on a long table. The "jaw sets" resembled wind-up toys—pink-gummed dentures that chatter across your desk. He was using them to animate his talk —not that he needs props to enliven his speaking. Like Hornaday, Walker can hold a crowd captive. He's a world-class talent and a Smithsonian taxidermist; everyone here wanted to know how to sculpt forms the Ken Walker way, which is to say with grace, speed, and accuracy.

"Why even compete? It's a waste of money," he began in his Canadian accent. "Really, isn't it the person who has the most *green* ribbons who wins? I realized early on in my career that I wouldn't be rich. So why not be famous? I've never taken the safe road. You learn nothing from winning. But those third-place ribbons taught me a lot." As he talked, his hands were shaping a tiny marten out of warm gray clay. He's been working with clay since he was a kid fascinated with Claymation movies. "Okey-dokey. This is my therapy since they let me out. I couldn't get that needlepoint down." He's only half joking, because later in his talk he would compare taxidermy to flower arranging. It's the same thing—an obsessive fabrication of microhabitats.

Like a coach, he spoke in platitudes:

"Procrastination is justification for failure."
"You have no control over your competition."
"A piece is never finished—you can groom it until all the
    hair's gone."

"I strive for the artistic over the technical, but you're looking for the perfect marriage of both."

"A judge spends on average [of] ten minutes for each bird,
and you spent an entire year."

"I've never mounted a piece for a judge in my life. I mount
everything for *myself*."

The crowd was writing furiously. "To win at the highest level,
you want to make your own jaw sets," he said, holding polyurethane cougar fangs in his right hand and fake bobcat teeth in
his left. With snarling jaws in each of his hands and, of course,
his own straight white teeth, he resembled a three-headed de-
mon casting an evil spell. His next topic was how to soak, freeze,
cast, and pickle tongues. "There's nothing worse than paint on
a tongue," he said. "I feel like I can taste it."

As he finished, the elevator across the hall opened to let
someone off. Inside, Ray Hatfield was riding down to the ballroom. He raised a friendly hand. Next to him, on a brass baggage cart, was his radiant snow leopard.

The World Show is not a survival-of-the-fittest event, but something of a twisted 4-H fair, where teams of scrutinizing judges
holding dental mirrors and penlights examine mounts from
nearly every phylum and order for anatomical accuracy and artistic merit. Using an official score sheet—a checklist, really—
of competition criteria, they determine a total score. The life-
size mammal score sheet, for instance, has 139 items, including correct use of paint for nose interior; appearance of seams;
cleanliness (bloodstains); odor (strong animal smell or "raw"
rancid smell); fullness of lips; tail area (sex organ); and inner
ear anatomy. Twelve Best in World titles and numerous first-, sec-
ond-, and third-place ribbons are awarded during the show. Anyone from its four divisions (Master, Professional, Novice, and

Freeze-Dry) can win the Carl E. Akeley Award. Though named for the most famous taxidermist ever, the prize has the less lofty purpose of proving that "taxidermy is indeed a valid form of wildlife art."

It was six P.M. Wednesday, the start of the competition. When I entered the ballroom, an official manning the door eyed me suspiciously, until he noticed my shiny black STAFF badge (given to me by the show's promoters) and motioned me in. To the right, an entire wall was covered with deer heads—facing up, down, and all around (each one subtly different, but they all looked the same to me). To the left, nothing but porcelaneous fishes. Throughout the ballroom, hundreds of mounts jockeyed for position under glimmering chandeliers. A quick scan revealed Hatfield's monstrous lion; Cally Morris's gobblers; an Alaskan lynx; a muskrat and a green sandpiper pondside; a Gaboon viper with a tarantula and scorpion; a snow-covered snarling coyote; a porcupine climbing up a frost-covered tree; and, over in Re-Creations, Walker's fake panda. Although the black-footed ferret and the ring-tailed lemur are officially considered endangered, nothing, I was told over and over, was poached or smuggled. "You get caught, you're dead meat," said one official.

Farther inside, a lime green chameleon snared beetles with its long translucent tongue, and three crows happily roosted in a pumpkin patch. A garish pink tongue the size of a tube of toothpaste emerged from the woolly face of a bison. The bison was attempting to lick its own nose, a naturalistic moment that caught the judges' attention. "I love the tongue! It's awesome," enthused mammal judge Wendy Christensen-Senk, a taxidermist with the Milwaukee Public Museum. "Look at that tongue!" crowed another judge. The chameleons inspired similar remarks. Although the judging had just begun, I could tell the bison was a top contender.

Each mount was like a song by an enthusiastic, if sometimes off-key, singer. Walker compared taxidermy to karaoke, and when you think about it he's right: each animal was some taxidermist's passionate attempt at mimicry. The hooded crow perched on a gargoyle of Charles Darwin was a British taxidermist's ode to evolutionary science. An Osceola turkey in the snapping jaws of an alligator depicted a rare scene from Florida's swamps. Some mounts were weird stabs at humor: for example, two mandarin ducks with a plaque (engraved!) that said YOU THE MAN. More bizarre still were the truncated beasts. The howling coyote with a mini–World Trade Center wreckage built into its eviscerated furry torso was especially confounding. Bearing the title *Predator Who Survives,* the coyote had been sawed in half and turned into a shrine.

Several mounts entered by foreign participants were like national anthems. The Russian competing with a Siberian sturgeon was one case in point. But no mount evoked its country of origin as distinctly as a Swiss participant's minnow-size fish. With chronographic precision, the display—an aquarium lit with high-tech fiber optics disguised as aquatic plants—was accompanied by a thick binder documenting the laborious process of how one transforms a real fish into an exact replica. I couldn't help but wonder just how long it would take this exhibitor to tackle, say, a whale shark.

Although every judge knew certain basics (bobcats attack from the ground, leopards from high up in trees), some mounts required more specialized knowledge. And for these, Christensen-Senk had her own reference files. At one point, she grabbed a photo of a groundhog and was able to bust a participant who was attempting to pass off a porcupine made from a groundhog manikin. (Porcupines have super-long quills, which can hide imperfections. Christensen-Senk noticed the flawed profile in a nanosecond.) Sniffing the ibex while running her hands up and down its furry frame, she said, "It smells like an ibex. I like the pose, but it's a *commercially available* pose." She held the participants to rigid standards, knowing which parts were purchased and which hand-cast. Nearby, John Matthews, from the Smithsonian, shined his flashlight down a white-tailed deer's throat and said, "Look how bumpy it is at the base." Anything with an open mouth was simply howling for scrutiny, and variations of Matthews's comment echoed throughout the ballroom.

While the mammal judges examined tongues for taste buds, inner nostrils for septums, and backsides for anuses, I tagged along with the bird judges, whose visual dissections were somehow less invasive. (As Kish told me, bird taxidermists are usually expert naturalists because they go outdoors and closely study bird behavior.) Bird taxidermists are, for the most part, birders. However, whereas birders tend to seek out rarity, bird taxidermists are interested primarily in common species: nuanced archetypes. Tagging along with the bird judges felt a lot like walking through a nature preserve, although it's much easier to spot a clapper rail in a ballroom than in an overgrown salt marsh. The five judges moved in a flock from bird to bird, troubled by unsightly covet feathers, crude eye rings, and other misdemeanors. Although I hadn't seen many of the species before, a bird book was unnecessary. The judges—one of whom had memorized every single Latin species name—were five walking field guides, and I jotted down their comments.

ROCK PTARMIGAN: "The left eye is off."
NORTHERN SHOVELER: "No detail in the mandible. He's not aerodynamic. Secondary wings are distorted."

AMERICAN WIDGEON: "I like the drop of the crop and the
flatness of the wings. Each wing is a unit working. I like
the rump."

EASTERN WILD TURKEY: "It's the plastic foliage I find so
disturbing. But it's a damn good turkey."

ANOTHER TURKEY: "This turkey here, he's after that grass-
hopper. He's got attitude!"

CAPERCAILLIE: "Exposed wires in the Master Division is a
no-no."

MALLARD: "Silly duck!"

WATERFOWL: "Looks like they've walked here from Chicago! Waterfowl have sleek, feminine feet."

The bird judges argued and squawked until their eyes landed
on a mount that left everyone speechless. It wasn't something
regal and symbolic like a bald eagle or exotic like a brilliantly
plumed macaw, but two English tree sparrows, one protecting
its nest from the other: a subtle narrative with a delightful mise
en scène. Bird droppings indicated that the sparrows inhabited
the area. A feather in one sparrow's beak animated the process
of building a nest. Crouching down to see it from all sides, the
judges detected not a single flaw. "The sideshow is three hundred sixty degrees," they agreed, gazing into the little world before them as if it were alive. The sparrows, lovingly preserved by
Uwe Bauch of Ammelshain, Germany, exemplified the category.
In fact, they exemplified the show.

It was nearly midnight when I opened my notebook and
read the list of birds I had seen. As I wondered aloud whether I
could add a few species to my life list, the British bird judge Jack
Fishwick snapped, "This is a *death* list! You can add them to your
death list!"

In the morning, my eyes ached, my mind was reeling, and I
understood why taxidermists use the word "anatomical" to de-

scribe each other—as in "He's getting too anatomical." I had had enough anatomical minutiae for now—maybe forever. But I still hadn't been down to the taxidermy trade fair—the subterranean world where you can buy products and services that may, on the surface, seem illegal, immoral, or haltingly bizarre: lion pelts with intact claws, whiskers, tails, and manes; chicken feet injection fluid; frozen raccoons ($50 each); artificial coyote throats; mink teeth; fish eye sockets; fox urine; and tanned sable scrotums ($7.50 apiece).

The first thing that caught my attention was a live demonstration that had attracted a crowd of spectators. A taxidermist in blue surgical gloves was sewing the cape of a big-horned aoudad sheep, a species normally found in northern Africa. (This one had died at an exotic-game ranch in Texas or Missouri.) Answering questions as he drew a threaded needle through its skin, he could have been demonstrating how to operate a new car or refrigerator. I watched for a bit, amazed and bewildered. Then wandered down an aisle, passing rows and rows of polyurethane deer, boar, and bear manikins resembling yellow fetuses, until I came upon a freeze-dried monkey holding a tiny, hand-lettered sign that said FREEZE DRY YOUR PETS! I quickly moved on. At the end of the row, shoppers at a booth of tanned pelts peeled back skins one by one as if they were broadloom carpet samples.

The range of anatomical wares was dizzying, and they were all unfathomably legal. At Skulls Unlimited, the world's largest osteological specimen supplier, a Goth-looking salesman manned a table of skeletal remains (mandibles, skulls, exotic horns). He was describing how taxidermists, skeleton assemblers, and museums use dermestid beetle colonies to eat the flesh off skeletons so that their intricate structures stay articulated. At the Tohickon booth, thousands of glass eyes, each painstakingly crafted, stared up at browsers. The fox, bobcat, and lynx eyes were hand-veined and hand-colored, and they had the accurate slit pupil (offered in two widths, depending on whether the taxidermist wants to portray his mount in daylight or at dusk).

Only Fred Fehrmann, the bearded owner of a fake-fur factory in Lawrence, Massachusetts, seemed vaguely out of place — that is to say, urbane, East Coast, and decidedly not anatomical. This despite the pronunciation of his name: "fur-man." Fehrmann manufactures polyester fur of the theatrical variety, the kind of synthetic tresses big Hollywood productions use to create monsters, yetis, and talking lemurs. Fehrmann's typical clients are LA prop men, Manhattan costume designers, and stylists who don't, for instance, shoot lions in order to make lion costumes. Banking on his success in show business, Fehrmann thought he'd have crossover appeal with taxidermists. He was mostly wrong. "That stuff is made to fool a camera, not a taxidermist," said Walker indignantly. Although taxidermists freely use fake septums, fake eyelashes, and fake claws, they'd rather die than use fake fur. More modelmaking. This may explain why Fehrmann's booth was quiet, drawing few taxidermists but lots of children, who came by to pet swatches of the Grinch, the Teletubbies, the Hamburglar, and Rum Tum Tugger from the Broadway musical *Cats*.

For me, Fehrmann's booth was a respite, a chance to rest my eyes and enjoy a bit of mainstream culture. However, tongues were my destiny, because soon I was at the "Jaw Juice: Stronger Than Critter Breath" booth inspecting rippled bobcat tongues with Jan van Hoesen, one of taxidermy's pioneering cat ladies. I had interviewed van Hoesen earlier that day in her hotel room, and I knew that her presence at a booth was something like having Venus Williams browse in a pro shop — a celebrity endorsement.

Van Hoesen is a former junior high school science teacher with a passion for felines, especially lynx and bobcats. After attending her first taxidermy competition in the 1980s, she was appalled by the ferocity of the mounts. Determined to depict animals humanely, she decided to eschew prefab anatomy (aggressive and mean) and cast her own custom bobcat (playfully stretching). She entered the bobcat into the 1992 World Show, took Best in World Mammal, and inspired many followers. "I really love the fluidity and gracefulness of the animals and the wonder of their movement," she said. "I don't like to see them snarling. That's more of a he-man thing. After all, how many women and families with kids want to have a vicious, snarling cat in their living room?"

This may explain why the shoppers at the fair were predominantly men. Even so, van Hoesen was inspecting howling, snarling, and panting tongues and talking shop with the Jaw Juice owner. She agreed to try his new bobcat jaw set, then examined his fake coyote throats and beaver teeth, explaining in a teacherly voice how beaver teeth are self-sharpening and grow throughout a beaver's lifetime. I had not seen any self-sharpening, ever-growing beaver teeth so far, but where artificial tongues are sold, there's bound to be fake saliva. *Jaw Juice!* "It's kind of niche," said the owner's son. I nodded. Then he squeezed a dribble of it (a clear adhesive) onto an artificial coyote tongue ("panting") and dried it with his own breath.

Before the World Show, I half jokingly told the Schwendemans that I'd come back to New Jersey so transformed and excited about taxidermy that I'd want to mount something myself. But now as I riffled through "how to stuff a squirrel" videos, my mind swirling with detached limbs and a sea of flat fur, glass eyes, and a freeze-dried monkey before me, I felt a dull nausea rise up, and I doubted that I could skin and stuff a chicken.

Just then, Ken Walker, who was strolling from booth to booth, stopped by. Walker has the alert eyes of a hunter, and those eyes landed on the manuals in my hands before I could hide them. I didn't want to get him going. There's nothing Walker likes more than to convince someone to pick up a scalpel for the first time. His face lit up. He launched into a mini-version of his lecture upstairs customized for a wary outsider. Within seconds, he handed me a manual and a video for the aspiring squirrel stuffer. I hesitated. I wasn't sure I wanted to buy these things just now, but then I remembered how he had told his seminar audience that he never takes the safe road, and I paid up. After that, Walker led me to another booth so that I could see his red fox display. Its silky fur was so smooth that I petted it impulsively, forgetting how important coat sheen is to a taxidermist. Before I could muster an apology, Walker had grabbed a comb from his back pocket and fluffed it back up.

Meanwhile, upstairs, the judges, having already selected the winner in each category, were wrangling over which one would win Best of Show. In a way, the job was ludicrous, because the judges had to compare a bison with a Gene Simmons (of Kiss) tongue to a bogus giant panda to a pair of delicate tree sparrows. I could sense the rivalries among the various factions, especially between the bird and deer judges. ("The deer guys are neurotic, and the bird guys are nuts," explained Paul Rhymer, a Smithsonian taxidermist whose father and grandfather also had worked for the museum.) Eventually, the judges handed their ballots to head judge Wesley "Skip" Skidmore, curator of animals at Brigham Young University's Monte L. Bean Life Science Museum. The winner would be announced that night at a banquet in the Grand Hyatt ballroom.

I retreated to my room to dress for the ceremony. With its mundane décor, creature comforts, and view of Hooter's, the room had no regional feel. It was certainly devoid of taxidermy's roiling subculture. It was, in a nutshell, predictable, and I embraced its blandness. I tossed my purchases into my suitcase so that I didn't have to look at them, then opened the mirrored closet doors and selected an outfit. As I slipped into black dress pants and a trim brown turtleneck, then tied a giraffe-print scarf around my neck in a fashionable knot, I suspected that my outfit was all wrong; it was far too casual.

And it was. The World Show banquet wasn't a church picnic in the boondocks, but the Grand Ole Opry, the Academy Awards, and the Super Bowl halftime show combined. The women arrived in long shimmering gowns, festooned with bright jewelry. The men, shaved and showered and camo-less, were dressed in dark suits and ties or dress shirts and slacks. Larry Blomquist, the master of ceremonies, wore a black tuxedo; his cohost and wife, Kathy, wore a sleek black gown and cherry red lipstick. Everyone was dressed to kill.

The mood was buoyant, convivial, familial, as everyone exchanged greetings, bought rounds of drinks, and found seats among their friends. Ray Hatfield tried to tame his lively daughters. Skip Skidmore, Jack Fishwick, and Ken Walker resembled corporate lawyers. As they made their way to their tables, stopping to chat and shake hands along the way, it was hard to picture young Skidmore preserving his pet hamster Little Nipper, Walker tracking bears, or Fishwick dissecting "confusing fall warblers." There were a few exceptions, of course, notably a ponytailed fish carver in a Hawaiian shirt, who reflected the individualism most taxidermists embrace.

The lights dimmed for a moment of silent reflection, followed by the Lord's Prayer, recited in unbroken unison. Then two teenage girls in prom gowns sang "The Star-Spangled Banner." During the national anthem, I glanced at my paper place

mat with its photo of geese flying over a taxidermy trout and logos for the National Rifle Association, the National Wild Turkey
Federation, and the Safari Club International, the largest hunting lobby in the world. Our caesar salads arrived, and the ceremony began in earnest.

Seated on my left, a trade-show salesman from Louisiana described his fear of Chicago; he expressed his reluctance to soak
in the hotel's hot tub because of its potential to double as a toilet. A fresh-faced blond taxidermist from Michigan sat across
from us. Stories of his African bow-hunting adventures kept me
riveted during what turned out to be a very long evening.

In the end, the ceremony resembled a large family reunion,
an American jamboree. But the family wasn't too insular to keep
the Best of Show prize from going to a European — Uwe Bauch,
for his tree sparrows. As we left the ballroom, I asked everyone
why the tree sparrows had taken the top prize and not, say, the
bison. Over and over, they repeated — as if it were obvious — essentially the same answer: the sparrows looked truly alive.

Aside from an excursion or two, I hadn't left the hotel in five
days. While I was packing the next morning, I began to feel
like I was trapped in a tightly sealed diorama. I needed some
fresh air.

Through the window, high above the parking lot, I watched
Ray Hatfield roll his African lion back to his cargo trailer. His
wife pushed the sandstone base. They trudged in single file,
their daughters straggling a few paces behind. Hatfield hadn't
won any of the top prizes. His lion and snow leopard had taken
second place in their respective categories. "The judging was really difficult this year," he later said matter-of-factly, and he was
right. The low scores arguably reflected the most intense scrutiny ever witnessed at an American taxidermy competition. In

fact, after the show several people complained to the promoters that the judging had been too harsh and nitpicky. Hatfield, however, wasn't among them. Yes, the judging had been painstaking and exacting. "But that's good," he said, squinting in the bright sunlight. Good for taxidermy.

As three grimacing men hoisted the lion into the trailer, I pictured father, mother, and daughters driving along Dirksen Parkway en route to Cody, Wyoming, delivering the moose, the elk, and the mule deer mounts on the way. But the World Show wasn't entirely over. That night was the BYOB wind-down party: a few more hours of solidarity before everyone headed back to their individual workshops.

The distinct shadow of a bird of prey appeared at the edge of the parking lot, and I unlatched the window and leaned out to see whether it was the same counterfeit hawk I'd seen when I'd arrived. The air was cool and invigorating, and as I craned my neck to find the source of the shadow, a real bird cried out, eerily piercing the silence. It was probably some common bird—a grebe, perhaps, or a killdeer—but its call was strong and clear and full of life.

THE MAN WHO HUNTED FOR SCIENCE

VETERINARIAN-RADIOLOGIST William J. Hornof is x-raying dead elephants to see if they can be saved. "It's too late. They're dead," he jokes as he walks under the biggest bull, a regal specimen shot in 1910 by taxidermist-explorer Carl Akeley after two years of hunting. (Only two-hundred-pound tusks would do!) The bull measures roughly ten feet six inches at the shoulders and twelve feet at the top of its head and appears to extend its trunk as if disturbed by an intruder. It's one of eight freestanding elephants that form the monumental centerpiece of the American Museum of Natural History's Akeley Hall of African Mammals. And Hornof, a silver-haired Californian with radiant blue eyes, is in New York City on this sunny June day in 2004 to see whether the museum can prevent them from suffering a second death—that caused by too much petting. Lately the elephants have also been fraying around the ears from something completely foreign to their central African habitat: air conditioning.

Usually the hall swarms with excited schoolchildren. "Hello, little gorilla!" they shriek, pressing their noses to the diorama glass as they have for more than seventy years to see if the gorillas will tumble and bark and beat their chests. Sometimes the kids draw the scene as if it is actually the Congo, not viewing an exact replica—they haven't lost the ability to imagine that it is real. Naturalists and artists come here to escape the city. The hall is a shrine for everyone at the World Taxidermy Championships who considers Carl Akeley the greatest taxidermist who ever lived.

Of all the early taxidermists, Akeley is the one I found most intriguing. He lived during taxidermy's golden age, when taxidermists of his stature traveled in sophisticated circles, were handsomely paid, and made astonishing exhibitions. The French have a word for work of his magnitude: *naturalisation*. *Naturalisation* is the *gourmandise* (gluttony) of taxidermy. No one consumed nature like Carl Ethan Akeley.

In his era, Akeley was famous. His adventures still draw comparisons to Indiana Jones and other swashbucklers. But Indiana Jones never killed a leopard by shoving a bare fist down its throat, sewed the scalp back onto a mauled Nandi spearman, or raised a vervet monkey on Central Park West. (J.T. Jr. had her own bedroom.) Mostly Akeley is known for blazing a trail that took taxidermy from the single menagerie specimen to the majestic diorama, which is why it made sense for me to start my search for him here, at his masterpiece, African Hall.

But on the day I show up, a sign saying DO NOT ENTER blocks the entrance, and Hornof and a squad of conservators are x-raying the elephants. They want to see whether the superficial cracks have caused internal structural damage and if so, how to make the elephants sturdy enough to be preserved for future generations.

"Okay, I'm going to have to shoot this one," Hornof says, pressing the shutter of the x-ray camera, which resembles a yellow scuba flashlight and is typically used to diagnose injured racehorses.

"Okay, we're ready to shoot! Ready to shoot!" shouts Stephen Quinn, AMNH senior project manager (aka "Mr. Diorama"). Everyone races out of the radiation zone, then returns to analyze the elephant's scaffolding on a computer monitor.

The two-story hall is dark green serpentinite (a volcanic stone from Vermont) and has twenty-eight dioramas that form an oval around the elephants. Each bay contains an intimate scene of Africa at dusk or at twilight or in the bright midday sun. The hall's subtle light and dramatic shadows have been compared to watching Africa through the windows of a magical train that does not disturb the animals. I'm upstairs near the colobus monkeys, resting my elbows on the marble balcony as if it were a rocky escarpment. Without the usual crowds, the Cape buffalo and mountain nyalas look ready to gallop out of their glass cages and into Central Park. It's a compliment, and something of a taxidermic cliché, to say that a mount is so lifelike you could swear it moved, but the animals here look suspended in motion. Every muscle, whisker, and wrinkle work together to convey, say, the direction of the wind or the scorching heat of the desert.

The next time Hornof yells "Shoot!" a vision of Akeley's famous elephant hunt with Theodore Roosevelt comes to mind. In 1909, the Smithsonian sent Roosevelt (and 260 porters) to Africa to collect specimens, and the AMNH sent Akeley on a similar expedition. The two safaris merged in Kenya, as planned, for a drink and an elephant hunt. Akeley spotted the perfect cow for his museum group, Roosevelt bagged it, and Roosevelt's son Kermit shot its calf. At least that's what Akeley used to say. One biographer suggests that Akeley secretly substituted a larger cow for the president's. Although he craved the publicity of a Roosevelt mount (Roosevelt was his hero), he craved perfection even more. Such was his vision of nature.

It took Akeley and three assistants six years to mount three of these elephants. He and forty native porters skinned and skeletonized them using jackknives in the steamy veldt. Each elephant was painstakingly reduced to four rolled-up skins, preserved with brine and local beeswax. Each skeleton was scraped clean and numbered for anatomical reference. Before Akeley, no one had achieved such startling realism. The elephants appear to trumpet through the hall, displaying the attributes Akeley most admired in them: sagacity, versatility, and comradeship. Paleontologist Roy Chapman Andrews, the intrepid explorer, described them like this: "If you want to see a live elephant, you can go to a circus or a zoo. But if you want to see the way an elephant lives, you go to a good museum of natural history. And you owe much of what you see there to the genius of Carl Akeley."

It takes a certain driving passion to want to reproduce a twelve-thousand-pound elephant in all its savage splendor. To duplicate the flora and fauna of an entire continent requires the stamina of a madman. Akeley had the energy of three men and the will of twenty. His quest for realism was insatiable. Every twig, every grain of sand, every star in the sky had to match what he himself had witnessed on one of his expeditions.

I wanted to know more about Akeley. I was especially curious about African Hall, his magnum opus, because I was going to the Smithsonian to watch Ken Walker and the other taxidermists work on its new mammal hall, and I wanted to see what museum taxidermy was like at its peak. In the AMNH archives, I saw Akeley's most intimate handwritten notes, in which he wonders whether a taxidermist can ever be a true artist—especially in the eyes of J. P. Morgan and other rich patrons of the museum. I came across an inventory of every tool and artifact in his studio, which was located in one of the old mammal halls and was called "the elephant studio" by everyone, including, I imagine, the security guards who'd see Akeley working late into the night and hand him a flashlight so that he could get around the place in the dark. I read letters from his divorce lawyer, in which "grounds for desertion" and "tanned topi skins" are discussed with equal importance. Stacks of telegrams fill the archives. They are marked Kabale, Nairobi, Arusha—alluring places where he embarked on his daring wildlife expeditions to collect the skins for these dioramas. One cable reports his tragic death in the Congo in 1926.

If taxidermy were a profitable profession, Akeley's life would be a rags-to-riches story. Clarence Ethan Akeley (later called Carl) was born in 1864 and grew up on a farm in Clarendon, New York, in near poverty. A quiet loner who hated school, he was happiest wading in the fields and swamps around his home, gazing at his friends the birds and other creatures. Not long after Akeley visited the stuffed menagerie of an Englishman who dabbled in taxidermy, he preserved a neighbor's canary that had frozen to death. "Please don't cry," the twelve-year-old said, consoling the grieving owner. "I think I can fix the canary for you. It won't sing, but I think I can make it look as if it could." After that, he borrowed a taxidermy book and spent hours in his room, dissecting and preserving dead animals. Taxidermy was then a popular hobby. Theodore Roosevelt's father nurtured his young son's love of birds and the outdoors with taxidermy lessons. Not so for Akeley. His parents, stern farmers, found taxidermy macabre, impractical, and a waste of time. One relative had this to say about Akeley's "queer" obsession: "Shouldn't he be put away, where in confinement he might recover from his apparent madness?"

A less driven person would have been discouraged; Akeley, not quite sixteen, was not. He quit the farm and had business cards printed: ARTISTIC TAXIDERMY IN ALL ITS BRANCHES. Three years later, in 1883, he began an apprenticeship at Ward's

Natural Science Establishment. When he showed up there, he must have been astonished by what lurked inside: barrels, boxes, and crates brimming with the most exotic beasts and birds — kangaroos, koalas, opossums, fish, polar bears, dugongs, gorillas, narwhales — all of which had been snared in Professor Henry Ward's "universal dragnet." "Neither the elephant nor the whale is too strong to break through," enthused Hornaday, who had left Ward's in 1882 and himself had once sent twenty-six cases of crocodiles, tigers, Indian bison, and "monkeys galore" to the emporium. Although Ward had posted a sign on the gate that said, "This is not a museum but a working establishment," people were no doubt transfixed by the place. Inside, a colorful group of long-bearded Europeans and other free spirits scraped whale bones, polished rocks, assembled buffalo skeletons, and preserved orangutans. One hall contained human skeletons (hung by their necks) and mottled snakeskins; another held all the wonders of the sea — shells, corals, starfish, and sponges. There were fossils and meteorites, the strangest and most marvelous things imaginable.

All these treasures ended up in museums and colleges. Chicago's Field Museum was founded in a single day when dry goods tycoon Marshall Field saw Ward's magnificent quarry at the 1893 World's Columbian Exposition in Chicago, paid $100,000 for the entire hoard, and set up shop. Another big customer, Louis Agassiz of the Harvard Museum of Comparative Zoology, bought hundreds of specimens from Ward's: he wanted to acquire the entire animal kingdom in specimen form to disprove Darwin's theory of evolution.

Unscientific and profit driven, Ward's was basically a taxidermy factory — this in spite of Hornaday and the other SAT founders who worked there. At Ward's, men literally stuffed animals. The specimens had no vitality, none of the gloss or vibrancy of wild creatures. Akeley was appalled. He saw men filling raw skins with greasy bones, straw, and rags until they bulged, creating disfigured zebras with exposed seams and lopsided deer. They weren't anatomically sculpted; they were, as he put it, "upholstered."

But that's exactly what most museums wanted pre–*Tree-Tops:* specimens as raw data. The first natural history museums attempted to create a complete inventory of nature by accumulating everything that roamed, swam, and crawled the earth. They were primarily formed around magnificent private collections, the stately cabinets of kings, princes, and rich adventurers who explored the unknown reaches of the earth or hired others to hunt for them in search of new species to bring back to England, Europe, and America. The British Museum, for example, was founded in 1753 when England bought Dr. Hans Sloane's amazing personal collection: 19,290 animal specimens and fossils. In 1869, the year it was founded, the AMNH purchased Prince Maximilian of Wied's preserved menagerie of 4,000 birds and 600 mammals, reptiles, and amphibians. The AMNH later bought paleontologist James Hall's fossil collection (1875); P. T. Barnum's iguana and "one Human Hand"; and Jules Verreaux's unrivaled collection of 2,800 stuffed birds, 220 animals, and 400 skeletons. Most early preserved specimens were crude approximations, but since science had never seen anything as strange as, say, a kangaroo—Captain James Cook brought the first kangaroo skin to London in 1771—they were still marvels to behold.

Taxidermy fared better at the small private museums such as Charles Willson Peale's Repository for Natural Curiosities in Philadelphia (1784–1845) and William Bullock's London Museum of Stuffed Animals (1809–1819), but these immensely popular establishments had been closed long before the big museums were ready to embrace artistic taxidermy for public education ("rational amusement" in Peale's day; "edutainment" in ours). Still, Peale's repository bears mentioning. Peale was a famous portraitist who used his artistic skill to animate taxidermy. He had no formal scientific training, but he believed in portraying nature accurately, to the extent that he manufactured glass eyes and carved limbs out of wood, even displaying his birds in front of painted skies. (In Europe, birds were displayed scientifically, singly on white paper.) Although his birds were arranged systematically (unlike the kaleidoscopic curiosity cabinets of the sixteenth and seventeenth centuries), his repository also contained a five-legged cow, stuffed monkeys posed as humans, an exhibit debunking the popular notion that elk breathe through their tear ducts, a lock of human hair from an albino, four-inch shoes worn by a Chinese woman, a snake den, and, in the yard behind Independence Hall, a live menagerie. What cemented his fame as a naturalist, however, wasn't his artificial ponds, his superior use of arsenic, or even his prairie wolf clobbering a mule deer, but rather his "mastodon" skeleton, which was really a mammoth he called "the Carnivorous Elephant of the North." When Peale wasn't singing "Yankee Doodle" inside the mammoth's reticulated skeleton with a cohort of chums or conversing with his sons—Raphaelle, Rembrandt, Titian, Rubens, Vandyke, Charles Linnaeus, and Benjamin Franklin (some of whom shot the birds that he himself preserved)—he liked to think the massive skeleton proved that animals were indeed as large in America as they were in Europe (and so, incidentally, were American men). You get the picture.

By the mid-1800s, especially after Darwin introduced his theory of evolution, museums, obsessed with taxonomy, prepared specimens in a way to facilitate comparative morphology—the study of an organism's form and structure. Comparative morphology did not happen on the banks of the Sadong River, but inside the dark museum, aptly called the "closet." Although this practice allowed science to progress, it basically killed taxidermy. The big public museums, you see, generally employed the worst taxidermists—or, rather, the fastest ones: taxidermists whose unintentional anatomical blunders would prejudice the way people would view dodos, goblin sharks, and other species for generations. Pioneering field naturalists were horrified. "That which once was a bird has probably been stretched, stuffed, stiffened and wired by the hand of a common clown," ranted the eccentric British taxidermist-explorer Charles Waterton in 1825. It was entirely unlike the bird itself, which was "touched by nothing rougher than the dew of Heaven."

Only a handful of pioneers in Germany, France, England, and Sweden preserved animals and birds with any liveliness, and those who did tended to favor combative tigers and camel-riding Arabs mauled by lions. Although these sensational displays riveted crowds at world's fairs and expos, they failed to show how an animal truly behaves in the wild. This would eventually change when American and Swedish museums embraced public education in the form of grand public displays (birds followed by mammals). But when Akeley arrived at Ward's, taxidermy was still amateurish, either too dead or too alive.

Fueled by a restless ambition, Akeley left Ward's in 1887 to prove that taxidermy could be scientifically sound, technically ingenious, and evocatively beautiful, and that he—"nothing but a taxidermist"—could be a true artist. His goal was to revolutionize taxidermy by approaching it as a sculptor, and after thirty years of tireless experimentation, he did just that. Instead of stuffing a skin full of rags and bones, he studied anatomy, replicating every muscle in clay. Eventually, he devised a method for stretching the animal's skin over a plaster replica of its body that was so finely contoured no one could deny that taxidermy was art. His manikins were so strong, lightweight, and accurate that museums such as the Smithsonian use a variation of his method today. In 1889, Akeley created the first habitat diorama in America: muskrats for the Milwaukee Public Museum, which still has it on display.

It was the grand era of the scientific field expedition. Museums no longer relied only on private collectors and places like Ward's for their specimens. They sent their own teams of explorers, naturalists, and taxidermists to exotic lands, where they collected an astounding number of specimens. From the 1880s to the 1930s, Americans led the pack. These hair-raising journeys involved not only the thrill of the hunt but also the less celebrated task of skinning the animals and curing thousands of exotic pelts in primitive conditions, then shipping them back to the museum across oceans and deserts in hermetically sealed "chop boxes" (boxes used to transport food on safaris). When the precious skins arrived at the museum, taxidermists spent years preserving them using rudimentary tools, limited scientific knowledge, and no refrigeration.

In 1887, the AMNH sent an expedition to Montana's badlands in search of bison. It was the first of more than one thousand such collecting trips sponsored by this museum alone. In 1931, the Harvard Museum of Comparative Zoology sent a six-man team to Australia. "We shall hope for the specimens of the kangaroo, the wombat, the Tasmanian devil, and the Tasmanian wolf," wrote museum director Thomas Barbour. They returned to Cambridge with more than one hundred mammals and thousands of insects.

Some expeditions were much less fortunate. Around 1900, Carl von Hagen, a German butterfly collector, went to Papua

New Guinea to collect butterflies. After he netted an exceptionally beautiful *Ornithoptera paradisea,* he himself was captured and eaten by cannibals. Ironically, his 110-year-old winged trophy survived and now resides at the Harvard Museum of Comparative Zoology, its magnificent day-glo green and black wings as vibrant as ever.

In 1916, an expedition headed by Roy Chapman Andrews crossed southern China on horseback in search of dinosaur fossils and, according to one account, the elusive "blue tiger" and other new species. They never found the mysterious tiger but managed to send home more than three thousand zoological specimens (about two thousand mammals and mammal skeletons, eight hundred birds, and two hundred reptiles), two-thirds of which had never been seen before in the United States.

Taxidermists who collected animals for museums considered themselves conservationists, not trophy hunters, even though their expeditions were funded primarily by wealthy patrons who wanted to hunt for big game—especially with Akeley. Today you can see their quarry (and their names) in the AMNH's Hall of North American Mammals and other grand galleries. Although Akeley did discard the occasional elephant (uneven tusks; facial tumors), Cape buffalo (scorched pelt), and diseased hyena, he claimed that he never shot for sport or for profit. That's why he could look you in the eye from under his pith helmet, a smoking .475 Springfield rifle in his hands, and say, "As a naturalist interested in preserving African wildlife, I was glad to do anything that might make killing animals less attractive."

Animals were, after all, his dearest friends, and, like most taxidermists, he viewed them anthropomorphically. He considered elephants chivalrous, lions regal and fearless, kudu stylish and graceful, hippos and rhinos stupid and blundering, ostriches wary and clever, and buffalo vigilant and vindictive. The only animal he ever truly disliked was that "sneaky carrion eater" the leopard. In the shy, gentle gorilla, he found his "kin"—a species that "desired to be loved."

The place that enchanted him most was Africa, where he led five scientific field expeditions. He was seized with the idea of re-creating Africa in America on his first expedition for the Field Museum in 1896, but the notion didn't fully take hold until 1909, when the AMNH sent him back to collect elephants for it. (He would spend the next seventeen years at the museum, but he refused to take a position on staff, instead preferring to be paid in stipends.) By then, Africa had changed. It was no longer pristine and wild but marred by civilization. Hunting safaris had become big business, led in vehicles, not on foot. Forests that had once teemed with exotic birds and beasts were now, taxidermically speaking, picked over, and it took Akeley two years to find four elephants splendid enough to represent the largest land mammal on earth.

One day Akeley was on Mount Kenya, taking photographic reference of the elephants' habitat, when he startled an old bull in a bamboo forest. When the bull charged, his gun jammed. He escaped with (relatively) minor injuries: a broken nose, swollen eyes, cracked ribs, punctured lungs, and a torn cheek that hung off his face, exposing his teeth. Only an elephant charge could pry Akeley off the trail. He spent weeks on a camp cot recuperating, his bandaged head making him look like a mummy with eye slots. While he healed, however, the driving forces that gave meaning to his life crystallized into a plan that would consume him for the rest of his days.

He would re-create Africa in Central Park, of all places, to prove that the Dark Continent was actually flooded with sunlight. He would do this not by satisfying the public's urge for sensation, but by crafting forty flawless dioramas, each a sincere

and scientifically faithful record of the beautiful creatures as
Akeley himself had come to know them: in the jungle, at peace.
After all, as he put it, "Why in hell should a good sculptor waste
his talents on reproducing a lie?"

The work was backbreaking. So was the pressure to record
the scene before the animals became extinct and their virgin
habitats were trampled. Already the last quagga (an extinct ze-
bralike quadruped) had been wiped out. Akeley figured he had
twenty-five years to collect the specimens; it was, as he used to
say, "now or never."

So there was the matter of time. More so, there was the matter of Akeley, an uncompromising nature freak. He was restless, impatient, eager to move from one challenge to the next,
a man with a furious temper who laid into anyone not as exacting as he, but whose stern expression melted away at night
in his studio with friends. In the archives, I found a memo in
which someone suggests that Akeley—who was short an antelope bull for the hall—take the skins of two females and transform them into a single male. Akeley flew into a rage, tearing
into the person who dared him to cheat nature. Painstaking per-
fectionism, of course, can drive those in charge of budgets and
deadlines—namely, museum administrators—nuts, and in the
end Akeley's crowning achievement may have been that the museum shared his indomitable vision and left him alone.

In 1912, the president of the AMNH was Professor Henry
Fairfield Osborn, a paleontologist who founded the museum's
Department of Vertebrate Paleontology. When Akeley presented
Osborn and the trustees with his sketch of African Hall, they immediately accepted it. The museum already had an Africa hall,
essentially a trophy room. This was a bit more ambitious. Yet
countless delays put construction on hold for the next thirteen
years, during which time Akeley preserved his elephants, dreaming of Africa.

In her fascinating memoir *The Wilderness Lives Again,* Akeley's widow, the mountaineer Mary Jobe Akeley, describes his process of collecting, skinning, tanning, and mounting a single elephant (thirteen pages of tight prose, which, incidentally, matches up with what Hornof, Quinn, and the conservators discovered with their x-rays). Basically, this is what he did. After the elephant was shot in the bush, he shaded it under a tarp to slow it from decomposing. After he photographed it for reference, he took detailed measurements with a tape measure and calipers, compensating for variations that make a dead animal different from a living one, such as deflated lungs, a limp trunk, and flaccid muscles. Next he cast the skull and leg bones in plaster and made a death mask of the face to capture its fine musculature. Without this data, the animal would have been a trophy (a generalization); Akeley's elephant would be an exact duplicate.

Properly skinning an animal is incredibly difficult, particularly in primitive conditions. Akeley skinned animals like a Park Avenue plastic surgeon. All his incisions minimized future seams, so they'd disappear when the animal was assembled later. The legs were cut on the inside; the back was cut longitudinally along the spine; the head was cast, cut off. Once skinned, the elephant was fleshed, a far more grueling task. It took Akeley and his team of porters four to five days to remove and prepare the thick, two-thousand-pound hide, using small knives so that they would not mar the skin. When the salted skin arrived in the museum workshop, it was hard and stiff and had to be tanned—a twelve-week process of daily turning to achieve optimum suppleness. (Mary Jobe Akeley said that her husband's tanning formula—undisclosed—was so good that he never lost a wrinkle, a wart, or a tick hole.) Eventually, the two-and-a-half-inch-thick hide was reduced to a quarter inch of leather (soft as a glove) and was ready for mounting.

Akeley always made a miniature clay model of every animal as a guide. Then he outlined the elephant's body on the floor in chalk and built its internal scaffolding on top of that, starting with a steel backbone, neck, and legs and working outward. Eventually, he had an armature made of steel, wood, and the elephant's own bones, which he covered with wire mesh and three inches of clay to mimic its muscles. He placed the tanned skin over the clay muscles, manipulating every fold and wrinkle until it looked like a real elephant. Then he cast the form in plaster to make his manikin. There's actually a whole lot more to it than that, and when you consider that, for instance, a hairless black rhino is nothing at all like an eighteen-foot giraffe or a fleshy-faced gorilla and that each one requires specific anatomical knowledge and reference (which, of course, had to be personally obtained in the field), you can get a sense of who Akeley was: by his own definition, "a fool."

It's a good thing we have fools, however, because a person would have to be incredibly passionate about something to keep it alive for thirteen years of setbacks. From 1912, when the plan was accepted, until 1925, when it was a reality, Akeley got divorced, suffered from depression, mourned the death of Theodore Roosevelt, and served in World War I. He was a major in the Corps of Engineers, where he invented the first cement gun—used to fortify the Panama Canal—but he refused to wear a uniform because if he did, he couldn't call his colonel a "damn fool."

Finally, in 1925, George Eastman of Eastman Kodak and banker Daniel Pomeroy agreed to fund an expedition to Africa to collect six key animal groups for the hall. "Soon I shall be on my way to Africa, this time accompanied by artists and taxidermists, happy in the knowledge that my years of preparation are ended and my big work actually begun!" Akeley exclaimed.

He was now past sixty, a national celebrity, his daring exploits featured in every newspaper and magazine. He was also happily remarried to Mary Jobe Akeley and spending every waking hour planning the yearlong expedition. But even in a moment of repose, smoking a pipe in his studio, Akeley looked tired. Deep crevices in his face showed the strain of keeping alive his dream. His hair was now silver, his strong shoulders were slumped, and the scar from the elephant charge ran across his cheek like a river on a well-worn map. "If I die before it is finished," he said, pointing to his scale model, "the whole concept and plan is there."

Eight grueling months later, the Akeley-Eastman-Pomeroy Expedition had collected all the skins, bones, and habitat accessories for seven museum groups—a staggering accomplishment. Yet even with many porters, the safari was difficult. Eastman bickered with Akeley. Landscape painter Arthur Jansson had had enough of bellowing hyenas and fled. Museum taxidermist Robert Rockwell shot the wrong immature giraffe, infuriating Akeley. "The trouble with you, Rockwell," he seethed, "is that you are putting your judgment above mine." Rockwell shrugged it off: "As I looked levelly at Carl it came to me that here was a tired, aging man beset by difficulties, yet furiously intent on carrying out successfully the vision of a lifetime."

Akeley reluctantly checked into a Nairobi hospital with what he said was a fever (malaria and dysentery). The Associated Press reported a nervous breakdown caused by utter exhaustion. Before entering the hospital, he took a detour to the Rift Valley to outline Rockwell's next assignment—to hunt for buffalo on the Tana River, ninety miles northeast of Nairobi. Rockwell, having just killed and flayed five reedbucks, a Grant's zebra, a steenbok, and a hyena, also must have been wiped-out. But his fatigue was nothing compared to Akeley's. As Rockwell eyed him lying on a cot in a land cruiser, barely able to smoke his cigarette, Rockwell said, "If you drive yourself any more than you've been doing, you're liable to leave your bones in Africa."

"I don't know of any other place I would rather leave them," Akeley said flatly in reply.

Three weeks later, Akeley was ready for the final leg of the expedition. He was bringing the renowned painter of the American West William R. Leigh ("the Sagebrush Rembrandt") to a lush rain forest on Mount Mikeno in what was then the Belgian Congo—to the vista he had specifically chosen for the panoramic backdrop of the gorilla group: the eleven-thousand-foot saddle between Mount Mikeno and Mount Karisimbi. The "Kivu volcanoes," as Akeley called the part of the Virunga mountain range bordering Lake Kivu, span Rwanda, Uganda, and the Democratic Republic of the Congo. Virunga National Park, the oldest national park in Africa, which Akeley helped establish as a gorilla sanctuary in 1925, is located here. It's also the place where Dian Fossey, the American zoologist who wrote *Gorillas in the Mist,* was murdered in 1985 while protecting gorillas from poachers.

The place Akeley had chosen was the mossy wonderland where he had come in 1921 to film and then shoot his prized gorilla specimens: the Old Man of Mikeno, the Lone Male of Karisimbi, and his namesake, Clarence. It's also where he tied himself to a tree on the precipice of a canyon to steady himself while skinning and skeletonizing Clarence.

Akeley had already mounted these gorillas and two others in New York. He also had the footage of the live gorillas (the first ever taken), as well as footage of his beloved volcanoes. (He invented the first portable motion picture camera just for this purpose.) You might be tempted to think that Akeley already had everything he could possibly need to make a convincing diorama, but you'd be wrong. Akeley wanted the expedition to experience the place firsthand. The only way to truthfully exhale the spirit of any place, Akeley thought, was first to inhale it. That the spot was halfway up a steep, active volcano, whose slopes were covered with thick jungle, mud, and thorny nettles, didn't matter. Neither did the torrent of rain or Akeley's condition.

So once Akeley was out of the hospital, he and the remaining expedition members left their motor caravan in Kabale, Uganda, and set off, first by canoe and then on foot, to reach Akeley's old camp on Mount Mikeno. The trail followed stupendous waterfalls, thousand-foot chasms, and thick stands of bamboo that had to be struck down to clear a path. After days of twenty-five-hundred-foot ascents and descents in the pounding tropical rain, Akeley, knee-deep in mud and dressed in a Burberry raincoat, broke down and had to be carried by stretcher. Most men would have pitched camp and called it a day, but Akeley wasn't most men; he was a taxidermist.

Eventually, the group reached a lush wilderness marked by wild celery and lichen-covered vines that dangled from moss-covered canopies. Signs of gorillas were everywhere. Akeley looked up from the stretcher and said to his wife tenderly, "Mary, this is the Kivu at last. Here the fairies play! Isn't this forest the most beautiful, the most ancient in all the world?"

Conditions were dismal in the dark forest. Sheets of cold rain and sleet pounded the troupe. Akeley staggered the last two miles into his old camp. He was suffering miserably from fever-induced chills and was nauseated. He stayed in his tent the next day and rested while Leigh, armed with art supplies, trekked deep into the jungle to find the panoramic vista.

It was forty degrees on the frost-covered mountain, and the air was thin. Akeley, delirious, began to hemorrhage. His pulse weakened, briefly responded to hypodermic shots of caffeine, and then stopped. Hours later, Leigh found the chosen vista and began sketching it, while everyone else worked for the next four days preparing Akeley's burial. They embalmed his body with formalin, which they had brought to preserve plants for the dioramas, so that it would last while they built the casket. Then they dug his grave in the hard lava rock.

In the archives, I found the telegram Mary Jobe Akeley sent to the museum: "My husbands sprit passed November 17th Hemorage. Slope Mikeo. I remain Supervise completion background accessories. Goulla Koodoo according to plan Inform Pomeroy . . . Inform families. Friends."

A week later, she wrote again: "But there is a voice from somewhere which urges me to carry on, and in my imperfect way, complete as far as possible the work he planned, and which he talked to me constantly. So I am going hard and driving hard to get the work accomplished by the end of December."

Leigh had already painted a full panorama of Mount Mikeno and Mount Karisimbi, which he would use to create the backdrop of the diorama. (These heavy-framed, diptychlike field sketches now hang in the Explorers Club in Manhattan.) Dr. Jean-Marie Derscheid, the Belgian zoologist who sat with Akeley on his deathbed, took the first accurate topographical survey of the region. And for the next seven weeks, Mary Jobe Akeley and the remaining expedition members furiously collected flowers, moss, grass, twigs, and stems to replicate back at the museum. They even managed to take home an entire gorilla nest and the actual tree trunk where the Lone Male of Karisimbi was killed. Eventually, they left the Congo but not Africa. They still needed swamp reeds from Mount Elgon (lion diorama) and plants from the Rift Valley (greater kudu diorama). Finally, they carefully packed up all the skins, skeletons, and plants and shipped them to New York. The only thing they left behind was Mary's wedding ring; she had buried it with her husband.

Back at the museum, James L. Clark, taxidermist and sculptor, was now in charge. He made several trips to Africa to ensure that Akeley's vision was not compromised. For the next eleven years, Clark, Rockwell, and the other taxidermists mounted the skins, using Akeley's methods. In 1929, seventeen years after Akeley had first presented his plan to the museum, New York City gave the museum $1.25 million for a new wing to house the dioramas, as specified by Akeley, who would settle for nothing less.

African Hall was supposed to be named for Theodore Roosevelt. When Akeley died, the museum had a change of heart and named it after Akeley instead. The idea that an entire hall would be named for a taxidermist (rather than a president) was unheard of. Did this prove that a taxidermist could be an artist?

At Akeley's memorial service, famous people in the arts and sciences praised Akeley the inventor, Akeley the explorer, Akeley the sculptor, and Akeley the conservationist. Yet when it was his turn to speak, Frederic A. Lucas, the museum's honorary director (and a Ward's graduate), could not find the right word to describe his friend's profession. He only knew what *not* to call him: a taxidermist.

> In spite of the thousands of words . . . recorded in our ponderous dictionaries, there are some that seem still to be needed, among them one to define the modern taxidermist . . . Animator might be suggested for one who puts life into such a hopeless looking object as the skin of a rhinoceros, but for the present we will stick to taxidermist . . . So we have only the word taxidermist to cover all grades of preparators including those who have been aptly styled perpetrators, whose work can only be considered as art because it certainly is not nature.

Even Akeley's biographer Penelope Bodry-Sanders (a person so devoted to his legacy that in 1998 she trekked to his ran-

sacked grave and, weeping, expressed a desire to hold his vandalized bones) drew a blank: "There should be a more elevated
title for work of Akeley's stature, but there is not."

On May 19, 1936 (Akeley's seventy-second birthday had be
been alive), the museum held the ribbon cutting for the Akeley Hall of African Mammals. It contained fifteen animal groups
(not forty as originally planned) and eight mind-numbingly real
elephants — his scale model come to life. "It has a three-way grip
on the brain and the heart," wrote *The New Yorker.*

Akeley didn't live to see his dream realized. But somehow,
twelve-year-old David Schwendeman had convinced Mum-Mum
to take him to the museum on members day, which happened to
be the same day as the ribbon cutting. David doesn't talk much,
but he's told me the story of the ribbon cutting several times,
and each time he does, his eyes fill with tears, his arms get goose
bumps, and he shakes his head a lot and says "gee whiz" as if it
were a dream. Which, indeed, it was: Akeley's, of course, and, as
it happened, his own.

On that day, Schwendeman stood in the dark hall with Mary
Jobe Akeley, Daniel Pomeroy, and Roy Chapman Andrews — cou-
rageous people whom he had read about in magazines — while
African drummers pounded tribal rhythms. He was stunned by
what he saw: three-dimensional portraits of Africa that transported him to the Rift Valley, the Serengeti, and Mount Kenya.
David gazed at the elephant herd slowly crossing the plains, then
circled the hall, pausing to admire the mountain gorillas. In the
center of the diorama, the huge silverback beat his chest while
his family peacefully munched leaves in an artificial habitat that
was implausibly real: ferns embedded with spore cases; ripe Ru-
wenzori berries; lichen-covered moss; and seventeen thousand
wax leaves, each made individually by hand. All of this in front
of a simmering panorama of the Virunga range, whose volcanic

smoke seemed to billow out of the glass and into Central Park. The only thing missing was Akeley's grave.

It was like peering out of a canvas tent onto bright, enchanted Africa—an Africa that existed only briefly in the early 1900s, when nature and a man with a prophetic quest to document a vanishing world intersected at exactly the right time.

4

HOW THE ORANGUTAN GOT ITS SKIN

ERECTING A MAMMAL HALL in a post-expedition world is something like building an indoor skiing facility in Dubai or planting a tropical rain forest in a mall café in New Jersey. And that's mostly because, as one taxidermist put it, "it isn't cool to go out and whack endangered species."

Nevertheless, in 2003, the Smithsonian was in the throes of the most stupendous undertaking at the National Museum of Natural History since it opened on the Mall in 1910: the making of its Kenneth E. Behring Family Hall of Mammals. Smithsonian lead taxidermist John Matthews was in charge of the animal preservation team, and he needed to hire a master sculptor. So he called panda forger Ken Walker to see if he'd take the job.

Walker wanted it—what taxidermist wouldn't?—but obtaining a visa was difficult. The first time he had applied to work in the United States, he was rejected for, as he puts it, being "uneducated." "I wasn't offended," he says. He applied again. This time he wrote "artist" on the form. Again his application was denied. "They classify me as a *hobbyist*," he says, livid. "I've decided to dedicate my life—which is really all I've got—to this, and for someone to diminish what I do because of their personal perspective offends me. It all boils down to prejudice."

Finally, with the help of the Smithsonian, he obtained a visa as a "specialist." But before he packed up his red toolbox and shipped off a few capes to mount in his spare time (well, more than a few: twenty-one orange-footed martens, six black bears, four wolverines, three fishers, and one grizzly bear), he hung 690 pounds of moose meat in the family freezer—enough to feed his wife, son, and daughter while he was away for the nine-month contract. ("There's no steroids," he explains. "It's good stuff.")

I hadn't seen Walker since the WTC in April, and he was still gloating about taking Re-Creations with the panda. "A polar bear would have made a better panda," he said, mulling it over. "I can get a polar bear for a hundred dollars a foot . . . but I can't bring it into the United States." Since everyone loved the panda, he figured he'd become rich by selling fake pandas to museums and wealthy collectors, and this kept him happy while he cast galago tongues and retrofitted old giraffes at the Smithsonian.

He had been at the museum for seven months, living in a rented room in La Plata, Maryland, when I visited the taxidermy lab there. It was a hot, sticky week in July—for an Albertan, insufferable. Yet adapting to the muggy climate had been far easier for Walker than adjusting to life at the largest museum complex in the world.

You see, in Alberta, Walker answers only to himself. ("My independence is more important to me than anything," he says.) At the Smithsonian, he had a boss (John Matthews); his boss had a boss; his boss's boss had a boss. The line of bosses led directly to the chief justice of the Supreme Court and the vice president of the United States. There were bosses to tell him how to handle the scientific specimens, bosses to tell him how to pose each animal in each case, even bosses whom he had to consult before making the most minuscule change, such as trimming an artificial branch that obstructed a colobus monkey (denied!). At the Smithsonian, he could not monkey around. He had to behave. He had to attend an orientation where he learned that inappropriate behavior—sexist behavior—was not tolerated. Walker was afraid that he'd compliment a curator's dress and be fired. Even weekends were a strain. Although his coworkers invited him to go out with them in the city, he preferred to stay in Maryland and fish. I thought he'd love the capital; he hated it. Too conservative? I asked. "No. Too liberal! The first thing Hillary Clinton did when she moved into the White House was take down the mounts. John and I want to write a letter to Bush asking him to reinstate them!"

The taxidermy lab where Walker worked was actually in Newington, Virginia, a Beltway community of industrial warehouses and shopping centers. The lab was set back off the road on a lot that resembled a construction site. A bulldozer was parked in the rubble outside, and the sign in front read POTOMAC VALLEY BRICK.

When I visited, Matthews suggested that I stay at a nearby motel and he'd pick me up in the morning. The place he recommended was a 1954 roadhouse called the Hunter Motel. The Hunter's restaurant just happened to be the taxidermists' favorite place for chicken-fried steak, and while the restaurant did have oodles of rustic charm, the motel itself left something to be desired. It was directly under an I-95 exit ramp, and I could hear pickup trucks revving their engines in the parking lot all night. My room featured fake wood-grain veneer—nine distinct tree species laminated to make the headboard, the TV stand, the lampshade, and so on. The hollow door to the room had no deadbolt, and someone had scrawled THE HUNTER in thick marker on one of the pillows, which had the whiff of a horror movie. Since I couldn't sleep, I thought about scary things. Thankfully, I didn't know what had happened to the Hunter's previous owner (allegedly gunned down), and the scene in *Lolita* where Humbert Humbert takes the nymphet to the seductive Enchanted Hunters hotel had escaped my mind. I was, however, consumed with an Italian movie I had recently seen called *The Embalmer* (2002). This movie centers on an Italian guy named Peppino Profeta. Profeta is a taxidermist and, as it happens, a homosexual dwarf. He has a greasy comb-over, a raspy asthmatic laugh, broken teeth, an amputated finger, and a stockpile of disfigured stuffed animals. When Profeta's not misusing his taxidermy skills by preparing human corpses for the Mob, he likes to molest his handsome apprentice, who doesn't seem to mind.

In the morning, I stood outside the Hunter waiting for Matthews. It was hot in the sun, even at eight A.M., and I paced back and forth in the parking lot as I-95 became choked with commuter traffic. I wondered what the area had looked like pre-highway. Today the Hunter seemed unsuitable for hunting of any kind. You'd be lucky to see a Norway rat cross this migration of honking SUVs.

Matthews soon pulled up in a black pickup, a shiny Ford with a bumper sticker that said SPORTSMEN FOR BUSH. I followed him under a train trestle, then along a winding industrial road that switchbacked past blank warehouses. As I drove, I thought about how lucky I was that the museum had granted me permission to tour the lab. I'd wandered through the most amazing museum halls; now I was going to see how a mammal hall is made from scratch. It was an exceptional opportunity, sort of like visiting Ward's Natural Science Establishment, because the Smithsonian can get any specimen it wants—even a Tasmanian wolf, a marsupial that became extinct in 1936. Its universal drag-net is backed by the U.S. government. More important, it owns the National Zoo.

Plus, I had heard that after the opening of the new hall, the museum might shut down the lab. This might be the end of taxidermy on a grand scale at the Smithsonian. It might be the end for John Matthews. It felt like the right historic moment to be here.

In twenty minutes, we were at the lab. The taxidermists, who were putting in ten- to twelve-hour days to make the deadline, had been at work since six A.M. Their official hours were six A.M. to four P.M., Monday through Thursday, but lately they had been working every day. "We've done ninety percent of the skin-ning and seventy-five percent of the mounts," Matthews said, leading me inside the cool cement-block warehouse.

The lab was monstrous: fifty thousand square feet of taxi-dermy divided into three huge rooms. The front room had the computer, a sofa, a coffee table, and an immature giraffe in a gantry (posed for a water hole group). Boxes and crates lined the walls. Inside any given crate might be the rare skin of a black-footed ferret or the world's largest moose. For the past two years, the most amazing creatures had been arriving from zoos, primate labs, and research centers around the world. The skins came in plastic coolers and FedEx boxes; they came packaged in huge wooden crates and foam-lined containers. Medium-size mammals—frozen raccoons and lemurs—were shipped over-night in coolers with hinged lids. One time, a primate lab forgot to include a colobus monkey's detached head and had to send it express the next day.

Beyond that room was the actual workshop, and past the workshop was a twenty-five-thousand-square-foot storage area containing shelves upon shelves of trophies (private donations) and historical mounts extricated from old dioramas. Imagine Ikea if Ikea sold only stuffed animals.

A museum storeroom is a sad and spectacular place to see. Only when you walk past shelves loaded with Galápagos tortoises, black-maned lions, elephant skulls and rows of stiff domestic dogs, huge vipers from the 1800s, and the first preserved gorillas can you begin to grasp the incomprehensible slaughter committed by museums whose lust for nature in the form of collecting expeditions was boundless. While researching this book, I was exceptionally lucky to tour the British Natural History Museum's Wandsworth facility in south London with fish curator Oliver Crimmen (who periodically visits the animals so that they aren't forgotten). It's a humongous, maximum-security, climate-controlled animal morgue. Each specimen—there are thousands—is a death as well as a reincarnated life lovingly preserved by some taxidermist at a given point in time. They are frozen records, dilapidated facsimiles, time capsules of vanished worlds, testaments to an era when British imperialism dominated the race to acquire the most "type specimens" (the archetype, the standard to which all others are measured) for its national collections. Wandsworth is a heart-rending record of what humans are capable of doing when they love something too much.

Before we entered the workshop, Matthews checked his e-mail. He was visibly on edge, and everyone knew why. The big opening was in mid-November—only four months away—and four months is nothing in taxidermy.

Except for the stars-and-stripes button-down shirt he had worn to judge mounts at the World Show, I had only ever seen him in a Smithsonian shirt. The Smithsonian sun logo appeared on his chest day after day, like a sailor's tattoo of a heart with the word MOM in the center. He owns around two dozen Smithsonian shirts; the one he had on that day was red.

Matthews grew up in Plymouth, Massachusetts, and has a strong Yankee accent and a New Englander's reserve. He is broad-shouldered and muscular, with clear blue eyes, thick graying brown hair, and a prominent handlebar mustache that brings to mind a daguerreotype.

Matthews mounted his first specimen, a rabbit, in an after-school program when he was thirteen. "I just liked to see how things came apart and went back together," he said. "I've always liked animals. I loved nature, loved to watch it . . . It's strange. I just kept picking up animals that were hit on the side of the road, and then people started bringing me things to mount." For a while, he ran his own taxidermy studio on Cape Cod. He's also worked at a nuclear power plant and spent some time building ships. Sometimes rich hunters hired him to accompany them to places such as Spain, Africa, and Argentina, so that he could demonstrate how to properly skin their kills. "In the taxidermy trade, I've never worked for anyone else except the Smithsonian," he said.

In twenty-nine years as a taxidermist, his sole ambition has been to preserve animals—exactly. "I'm not going to change nature," he says. "We don't know anything about life systems, but [we do know] everything that supports the musculature."

Matthews, himself a championship taxidermist, holds competitions in high regard because they provide standards in an otherwise unregulated field. Whereas most European taxidermists must pass a practical exam and serve as an apprentice before they can work commercially, in the United States generally all a taxidermist has to do is pay a nominal fee to the state fish and wildlife department and show someone there a mount or two. That said, no title in the taxidermy world ranked higher than lead taxidermist at the Smithsonian Institution.

Matthews's salary was $58,000, half of what he says the same work would have brought in commercially. Still, the honor far eclipsed the money. "It's a prestigious job and a legacy. A commercial taxidermist doesn't have the time for details, but a museum taxidermist should be as flawless as possible. The anatomy should be perfect; all the nasal and inner ear detail, all the idiosyncrasies should be as close to perfect and anatomically accurate as possible," he said. "I just spent a week and a half on the koala bear. I'd *never* spend that much time on a commercial mount."

The gigantic workshop was sparkling clean, with super-high ceilings lit with long fluorescent tubes. Long worktables spread with specialized equipment and anatomy books were equipped with ventilation hoods for sucking out toxic fumes given off by the Bondo and lacquer the taxidermists used. But most prominent were the animals. Strikingly beautiful, some mounts were more than one hundred years old; others were rare and exotic endangered species, hardly any examples of which still exist in the wild. They leaped and yawned, stretched and drooled, nursed their young and showed off their defining features. The towering Russian brown bear on hind legs looked as if it remembered how it got here and wanted revenge. The arched-backed clouded leopard flaunted its sharp canines and papillae-studded tongue—weapons it used to devour its mates, thereby ensuring its status as the most endangered wild cat. Matthews shined a flashlight into its custom-made eyes; they gleamed like roadside reflectors.

The room radiated the energy of 274 animals representing four continents telling the story of evolution. The smallest, the feathertail glider (an extremely rare marsupial from Australia), had already been skinned (by Matthews, in front of research scientists) and mounted. The largest, the fifteen-foot reticulated giraffe (now a pile of foam parts and a frozen pelt), had to be assembled on-site in Washington, the only way the giraffe would fit through the door.

Matthews led me deeper into the lab, introducing me to the mounts as if they were childhood friends. I envied his ability to feel so deeply for each species. We passed the lowland gorilla (knuckle-walking), the brush-tailed porcupine, the gray fox, and the South American tayra. Three tree kangaroos were frozen in flight, hopping across the cement floor. They made me want to hop, too.

Matthews knew every inch of the lab. In 1997, when the museum had received a $20 million donation from California real estate developer Kenneth E. Behring for the hall, Matthews had been appointed lead taxidermist. It was an immense responsibility to help collect, refurbish, and mount 274 animals in three years, especially when you consider that the Akeley Hall of African Mammals took twenty-five years to create (and killed Akeley).

This year the Smithsonian's secretary, Lawrence M. Small, wasn't a paleontologist or an astrophysicist, but a former Citicorp banker with no museum or academic experience. (Small resigned in 2007 after an audit showed that he had spent museum money on chauffeured cars, private jets, posh hotels, and other luxuries.) When Small took the job, he promised to "modernize everything of consequence," a dubious concept to research scientists and curators (literally, guardians of the collection), who feared that the Mall was becoming a mall. Soon every exhibit bore a logo: the Fujifilm Giant Panda Habitat; the O. Orkin Insect Zoo; the Lockheed Martin IMAX Theater at the National Air and Space Museum; and, most perplexing of all, a museum visitors' guide sponsored by Philips Petroleum with a back-page ad promoting oil drilling in Alaska.

Outside funding is essential at most museums, even this

one, which gets 70 percent of its annual budget from the U.S. government. Museums have always operated this way. Carl Akeley and Roy Chapman Andrews had to entice rich industrialists and other patrons to fund their expeditions, too. At the Smithsonian, however, researchers and curators feared that the private money would affect content, resulting in exhibits that are "dumbed down." In 2001, for instance, thirty-six curators at the National Museum of American History signed a protest memo saying, "Secretary Small has obligated the museum to relationships with private individuals that breach established standards of museum practice and professional ethics."

Kenneth Behring had given more money to the Smithsonian than anyone in the museum's history. When he gave Natural History the $20 million, followed three years later by $80 million for American History, the museum was finally able to renovate its gorgeous Beaux Arts building (1910), which housed two mammal halls, World of Mammals and North American Mammals, with their habitat dioramas, and Life in the Sea, with its great blue whale.

One reason the museum wanted the new hall was because it believed people were no longer aware that they were mammals; indeed, the museum thought, people didn't consider themselves animals at all. As the exhibition team hired outside architects and designers, it began to establish what the new hall would be about (210 years of mammal evolution), who the intended audience would be (families with children under age ten, 60 percent of its demographic), and what story to tell (in a nutshell, "Welcome to the Mammal Family Reunion. Come Meet Your Relatives!"). Mostly the hall would show the diversity of species and how mammals have adapted over time to a range of environments and climates, which, given global warming, is an incredibly important trait to highlight.

Now the museum had to decide how to convey this. The "concept people"—a group of highly accomplished scientists, designers, writers, and curators—investigated whether, for instance, the exhibit should be based on phylogenetics or ecosystems; whether dioramas or freestanding mounts enhanced with fog machines and simulated thunder should be used. Meanwhile, Matthews, a "production person," was dispatched to Newington to outfit the lab with the best tools and equipment.

Deciding to forgo traditional dioramas ("stagnant"; "animals in their dullest moments"), the concept people called for installations with more drama, more high-tech wizardry, and more interactive special effects, such as flip doors, pushbuttons, digitized animal sounds, and kids-only crawlspaces. This is what I believe associate director for public programs Robert Sullivan meant when he told reporters at a press conference that the new hall contained the "ooh factor" and the "gross-out factor."

Smithsonian taxidermist Paul Rhymer explained it like this: "Kids don't give a shit about those dioramas. It's the MTV generation. They want new images, and this exhibit gives it to them. I had to be converted to that point of view. This hall treats taxidermy like sculpture. The starkness shows off the work. Or maybe I'm buying the party line. That's okay. [It's] okay to be a company man on this one."

Once the concept people chose the environments (arctic, rain forest, temperate forest, and prairie) and their corresponding inhabitants—274 of the 5,000 known mammal species and 1 extinct one—it had to acquire the specimens. Historically, as we have seen, museums have obtained specimens by shooting them in the wild. That clearly was not going to happen here. Instead, the museum took specimens off of its own exhibits and excavated others from its dusty attic. It circulated a wish list to far-flung labs and zoos, requesting 450 additional skins and carcasses. And it acquired two amazing private collections of 250 specimens each: one from Roger Martin, a taxidermist from North Carolina, the other from Kenneth Behring.

At seventy-four, Behring was a real estate magnate and the former owner of the Seattle Seahawks football team. He also was an internationally famous big-game hunter with more than 300 kills recorded in the official record book of the Safari Club International (the world's largest hunting lobby, which, incidentally, has its own taxidermy museum in Tucson, Arizona). Behring was not someone Walker would ever call a bunny hunter. Neither would the Humane Society or scores of other environmental organizations. When the Humane Society, for instance, got wind of Behring's donation, it posted a statement on its Web site describing the time Behring shot one of the last remaining argali sheep in existence (Kazakhstan, 1997). Instead of censuring Behring for killing an endangered species on the brink of extinction (only about one hundred existed in the wild), the Smithsonian, having just accepted the $20 million, attempted to import its trophy remains as a scientific specimen. Eventually, after much bad press and public outcry, the museum dropped the permit application.

Because of all this, some museum people and a host of environmental groups suggested that it was unethical to accept money and trophies from someone—even a great philanthropist such as Behring—who had been seemingly indiscriminate in his choice of kills (Behring says he shot the sheep in the company of Russian scientists who wanted to study it) and that the museum was allowing him to buy his way into the exhibit. Collections manager Linda K. Gordon, the person at the Smithsonian who personally accessioned each of Behring's trophies, denied this. "Of course he was interested in seeing those specimens used [in the exhibit], but there was no stipulation of that or content," she explained to me one day by phone.

She went on, "We were all concerned that the big-game aspect of this would make a big flap in the press, and that never happened. We were always waiting for the other shoe to fall, and [the] public programs [department] was careful to emphasize that no specimens were killed for the exhibit—and that is true—*more or less*—*almost* true."

At that moment, it occurred to me that when all was said and done, the most controversial aspect of the new mammal hall was, ironically, its most traditional feature: it had been funded by a big-game hunter.

The morning I visited the lab, Matthews sat at a worktable, preserving an exceptionally rare and wonderful creature: the okapi (*Okapia johnstoni*). Okapis are shy ruminants that live in the eastern Congo. They are equally strange and beautiful. They have a zebra's striped hind legs, an antelope's body, and a giraffe's face and long tongue. So unusual are they, in fact, that when Sir Harry Johnston brought the first okapi skin to England at the turn of the twentieth century, the Zoological Society of London thought it was a horse and classified it as *Equus johnstoni*. The society later articulated an actual okapi skeleton, realized it was not a horse, and reclassified it. Here in the lab, the okapi may look like a taxidermist's fanciful creation (like the jackalope), but in the forests of the eastern Congo, its shadowy brown coat camouflages it in the trees, which is how the species has survived (so far). Although scientists discovered okapis only a hundred years ago, they are already headed for extinction. Matthews treated his okapi skin like a precious jewel.

This okapi didn't come from the Congo; it died at a California zoo. That was evident by its overgrown hooves, which would have been filed down in the wild. Captivity alters the way animals look; captive animals are rarely as beautiful as those in the wild, which is why taxidermists find them aesthetically subpar.

"It's like masturbation versus sex," Walker explained (after he was back in Alberta and could say whatever he wanted).

"We never got the perfect specimen [for the hall]," explained Matthews, filing. "At least half [had] had a necropsy [an animal autopsy] done on them when they showed up. All of the internal organs were removed—the eyeballs, brain, thyroid were all removed. They cut off the top of the head to take out the brain. They were cut everywhere—the head, the bottom, the sides—so research scientists could get a life history." Take the gorilla, for example. When it arrived via FedEx, it had no eyelids and was missing a nipple.

It was fascinating to watch the taxidermists transform zoo captives into wild savages. For instance, zoo rodents' overgrown teeth had to be cosmetically trimmed with wire cutters to make them look as if the animals had foraged for food (when in reality they had been served take-out). Clearly, this went beyond creating the illusion of life. Instead, the taxidermists were creating the fantasy of a life never lived.

Taxidermists as a rule dislike fiction, because they believe it's impossible to improve on what nature has already perfected. But sometimes, apparently, you can, and the taxidermists in this lab were doing just that. If William Hornaday, chief taxidermist at the Smithsonian in the 1880s, were here now, he probably would be disgusted by the condition of the skins.

I wonder, though, if he ever encountered the following situations. To transform Behring's galloping oryx into a nursing mother, the taxidermists had to rehydrate and remount the skin, reshape its muscles, and raise its head. The threadbare sable antelope had bald patches on its rib cage, requiring skin grafts, and the immature giraffe needed replacement leg rods. Whereas Theodore Roosevelt's white rhino needed only a simple cleaning, the antique Bengal tiger's stripes had faded and needed to be painted back on with Garnier Nutrisse "Luscious Mango" hair dye. Finally, the fifteen-foot giraffe required a penile implant: twenty-five pounds of clay.

Matthews had to make every blemish disappear before November. The job required thousands of hours of painstaking work and had to be done fast. But how? Akeley had demanded that his taxidermists join his expeditions so they could take scientific measurements in the field. Hornaday had pleaded with museums to reject pelts from donors who did not know how to properly collect them. Matthews hired an Alberta bear hunter who did a mean Roy Orbison imitation.

"They needed me to come down to make forms for skins that were in bad condition," Walker explained. "I can come uncannily close, down to the bump on a Roman nose." He sat hunched over a worktable, darning a bush baby skin. Among taxidermists, Walker is famous for big predators, so I was surprised to see him preserving such a delicate primate. While he drew a threaded needle through the skin, he hummed along with a CD of his brother's bluegrass band, named String 'Em Up, of all things. When he looked up, a big smile spread across his face, and he said, "A song has to *sound* inspired—whether it is or isn't!"

As it happens, Walker had found his calling after reading *My Way of Becoming a Hunter*. Robert Rockwell had published the memoir in 1955, when he was seventy, after a tremendous career mounting all kinds of fabulous creatures for all the big museums, including this one. In 1910, after passing the required civil service exam ("highest score"), Rockwell was offered ninety dollars a month ("excellent") by the Smithsonian and took the job—for nine months (just like Walker). His high expectations, however, were dashed when his "pompous" boss, George Turner (another Ward's graduate), had him transform five decomposing fur scraps into a South American spectacled bear. It was "far from a work of art," but it satisfied Turner. Nothing irked Rockwell more than having to perform taxidermic somersaults for a boss who knew nothing about, say, ungulates. "Those who understand animal anatomy know that the rump of a Grevy's zebra is totally different from the horse and even from the Grant, Chapman, and Mountain species of zebra, but Turner was quite unaware of this," Rockwell observed. "I took care that the hindquarters of my full-size clay model were correctly proportioned, but my boss immediately objected. He often did this, and frequently was in the wrong, as a look at the live animal would have shown him."

Rockwell went on to become an exceptionally accomplished museum taxidermist, working on the American Museum of Natural History's Hall of North American Mammals. But he felt stifled at the Smithsonian and said so in his memoir. I read several passages to Walker, who nodded his head in recognition. Then he bagged the bush baby and led me around the workshop. "I put the other taxidermists at ease because I have no political aspirations for this place," he said, and for that reason he made an exceptional guide.

"This is a male lemur, and I had to turn it into a female. I was plucking all the hair off its breast, and I think it shows in its face. There was no form signed on this. It was a forced sex-change operation."

He continued, "We just finished the koala bear. Had to replace its ears. We acquired two extra ears from Australia. I kept the best one to mount and kept the other for spare parts. Of course, I had to ask permission for that."

He pointed to the three-toed sloth. Its claws had spiraled out of control from disuse: "You can tell it's from a zoo. Obviously it's left-handed." Moving on, he said, "I don't know if it's a male or a female wallaby, but I gave it a baby."

He pointed out pages of legal documents and permits that

travel with the sea otter because it's highly protected under the Convention on International Trade in Endangered Species (CITES). Then he showed me the hippo, made entirely of wax. It sat in a huge wooden crate like a Christmas present in a fairy tale; its gigantic teeth hung down from its gaping mouth—stalactites in a cave. "Died in the National Zoo and was mounted by Brown, who was chief taxidermist here until the late 1950s," Walker explained. Apparently, Brown had yearned for it to die so that he could mount it.

Finally, Walker showed me the Patagonian hare, or mara, a creature so implausible it seemed dreamt up by the Dutch painter Hieronymus Bosch. *Dolichotis patagonum* has the front feet of a kangaroo, the back feet of a bird, and the ears of a rabbit; it is classified as a rodent.

Walker led me inside the colder of the two giant industrial freezers, which are alarmed. At eight degrees, it was thirty degrees warmer than Alberta in January, and he said, "This is where I go when I feel homesick." I shivered in my T-shirt and cotton skirt as Walker pointed to a dolphin, a clouded leopard skull, bats, and freezer bags filled with tongues, furry ears, and other extremities. Before he reached for the latch, he motioned to the midsection of what resembled a bloody snowman. It was Hsing-Hsing's torso—minus its pelt. I gagged. Walker's face lit up. He nodded, excitedly, and exclaimed, "*That's* a panda carcass!" The pelt was finally at the tanner's.

I asked Walker how he liked working at the Smithsonian. He shrugged. "It's credibility in a field where they don't give it," he said. Later, after he left Washington, he was more explicit: "If you are going to survive there, you have to work within that mentality. You get so caught up in people taking credit for this or that accomplishment. If I get recognition, I want it to be real . . . The secretary of the Smithsonian knew who I was. But in terms of respectability, the profession has a long way to go."

Later that day, Matthews brought me outside to see Paul Rhymer, who was sandblasting the okapi's manikin. A green face shield protected Rhymer's eyes; he breathed through a respirator while he scarred up the manikin to give it "tooth" so it would hold the precious skin without buckling. "Sanding alone would have been adequate, but we'll never mount another one of these again," he explained. Because supply companies could hope to sell only around a hundred okapi manikins at best, the Smithsonian team had cast a custom form in fiberglass using Akeley's methods. "Originally, we wanted to compete with this in the World Show, but we had so much snow, and John [Matthews] just had his baby," Rhymer said. He lamented his third-place chameleon. "It had wet paint, a fatal flaw. The pink one won," he said, sanding.

At six feet six inches, Rhymer stands above the rest, the other taxidermists joke. Both his father and grandfather worked at the Smithsonian. Mostly this fills him with pride; sometimes, however, I sense that it wasn't always so easy. "As a group, we're a little gun-shy about what people think of taxidermists. The way I survived was by making fun of myself," he said. Indeed, he calls himself "a big, bumbling, sensitive, New Age redneck." In the taxidermy world, Rhymer is, politically speaking, exotic. "I'm left of about ninety percent of taxidermists. John almost thinks I'm a traitor," he said.

He continued, "I've always had a pretty outward claim on my redneck roots. I'm a taxidermist and a good ol' boy, but I was also out on the streets protesting the first Persian Gulf War. I'm pro–gun control, and for a lot of taxidermists, it's all about guns and the NRA [National Rifle Association]. If you don't have a gun, you can't hunt, and if you can't hunt, then you can't have taxidermy. As a consequence, they see conservative politics as their ally, and mostly they are right. I own four guns. I'm okay with handguns, but I don't have one. If my wife wanted one because she didn't feel safe, I wouldn't have a problem with that. But a lot of taxidermists want them. They are very pro-NRA. It is very polarizing, and ninety-nine-point-nine percent of all taxidermists feel very strongly about this. It's not a southern thing. If I depended on deer heads for a living, I might be more ardent, but then I wouldn't be a taxidermist, because that's not my thing. I love the diversity, and birds are my favorite."

The okapi's pose, like every pose in the exhibit, was established by the concept people and architecturally rendered in a book of drawings called the "casebook." (The taxidermists had virtually no role in determining the content or script of the exhibit.) In this display, the okapi's ten-inch tongue would be reaching for a leaf on an artificial tree. "We sewed up the holes, turned up the eyes [and] ears, and made sure everything's fleshed out," said Matthews. "This isn't a fun job. It's hot out."

"That's all done from scratch," said Rhymer, lifting the respirator off his mouth to talk. "The way these muscles stack up in the brisket. The way the collar is shingled with a long cleft down the center."

"That's museum taxidermy!" boasted Matthews.

The okapi took "weeks and weeks and weeks" to preserve, but the most complicated mount in the new mammal hall was the orangutan. That is, the bald orangutan. That is, the ten-foot ape that arrived here from a zoo sans skeleton and carcass — the raw data Matthews desperately needed in order to sculpt an accurate form for the skin. Photographs would not do (two-dimensional; indeterminate scale); these taxidermists needed to wrap a tape measure around the torso and take calipers to the cranium.

If William Hornaday were around, he could have helped. After all, he spent weeks in Borneo, observing, measuring, and skeletonizing orangutans for *Tree-Tops*. Matthews wasn't leaving

Newington for the next four months except to sleep. He had to find the right size orangutan carcass for reference — without whacking one. But where? Suitland, Maryland, it turned out.

Suitland is where the Smithsonian's Museum Support Center (MSC) is located. The MSC is a state-of-the art storage facility; it contains thirty-six million natural history specimens (wet and dry) and collection items, more than any other museum in the world. The MSC has first-rate laboratories and a specialized library for advanced zoological research. It also had a two-year-old pickled orangutan.

The orangutan in question had died at the National Zoo and was floating in a four-by-ten-foot ethanol bath with a pickled porpoise and crocodile. Sopping wet, it weighed several hundred pounds. It had a long ventral incision across its stomach and chest, where its internal organs had been removed during its necropsy. Its head had been shoved into its abdominal cavity. Otherwise, it was "beautiful."

It wasn't bald. It had long auburn hair: fifteen inches on the back of the neck, five inches on the knuckles. Matthews glanced at its gorgeous cape with envy. So did Rhymer. Somehow, they convinced the museum to let them use this skin instead of the bald one. Then they hauled the carcass into a prep lab, where they took measurements; cast its face, feet, and hands in dental alginate (the stuff dentists use to make a mold of your teeth) and Bondo; and skinned it (five hours of emotionally charged work, because apes harbor viruses, and they also intimately resemble humans). After two grueling days, they returned the skinned carcass and skull to the vat (to preserve it for scientific study) and shipped off the skin to be expertly tanned. Nothing could be farther from Borneo or more ecologically responsible. The taxidermists were ecstatic.

Lab apes and hunted apes might as well be classified as different species. This one had been soaking in ethanol so long that its hands and feet were blistered and its face had become inelastic and distorted—something taxidermists call "losing its memory." Matthews spent two days "relaxing" its face until it "remembered" what it had looked like and wouldn't shift once glued onto the form.

Walker helped carve the artificial body. Rhymer retexturized its palms and feet, which were as smooth as sea glass, to give them some epoxy life/love lines. When the tanned skin arrived in Newington (long after my visit), they set its glass eyes (brown irises and "nicely dirty" scleras) and rebuilt its ear and nose cartilage.

Finally, the ape was ready for assembly. Using tricorner needles, two, sometimes three, taxidermists sat and sewed its eight-foot arm span; they sewed the seams down its legs and stitched up its ventral incision; then they sewed its head back on. Thirty feet of ape seams were meticulously joined. "We put thousands and thousands of stitches into it . . . an eighth of an inch apart," said Rhymer. As a finishing touch, they hid the seams with epoxy and paint and scrubbed off the excess with Windex.

I circled the lab until I reached Walker's station. He was disinfecting the bush baby in diluted Lysol. In the 1940s, bush babies were thought to harbor yellow fever. He shook his head, then said with disgust, "Hunted specimens are rarely diseased, because nature takes care of that. They have a real good system: it's called natural selection!" Then he wrung the skin, put it in a plastic bag, flung the bag into the freezer, and drove to the Hunter Motel for a chicken-fried steak.

In 1829, when the English amateur scientist James Smithson left America his vast fortune ($11 million or so in today's dollars) for "the increase and diffusion of knowledge among men" (apparently he felt snubbed by the Royal Society for rejecting one of his papers), the Smithsonian Institution became the first natural history museum to be scientifically organized. It was founded in 1846 and has since become the largest museum complex in the world.

Seven million people visit the National Museum of Natural History each year. Installing the new mammal hall took three years and involved around three hundred scientists, curators, production people, and designers. It cost $31 million and represented the most ambitious project at the museum in ninety-four years.

In 1998, an architectural firm began to renovate the West Wing, one of three wings that radiate off the museum's grand rotunda, preparing the way for the Behring hall. The West Wing has fifty-four-foot-high skylighted ceilings and terrazzo floors, the perfect setting for displaying mounted animals — or even administering life insurance programs for soldiers. During World War I, five hundred U.S. government employees subdivided the place with brick walls and got to work doing just that. Zoological displays weren't staged there again until the 1930s, when many of the cases were assembled by William Hornaday.

Renovating the West Wing was a tremendous job. Skylights were pried open, floorboards ripped out, and old mounts were discovered in the dusty attic. For two years or so, the museum was a construction site. To do their job, the contractors needed a storage area. Space is always at a premium at museums, but it was clear that something had to go.

One day the museum assembled a team of experts to walk through North American Mammals, a gallery of habitat dioramas similar to the AMNH's, to see if the 1957 hall was worth preserving. The survey team was divided.

Catharine Hawks, a conservator who has served as an adviser to more than seventy natural history museums, was on that team. She described the process to me one day by phone: "We were asked to walk through the hall and comment on the condition of the specimens. They said because of asbestos and arsenic, you can't move them. We said it's relatively easy, and it is." She went on: "It would have been easy to take down and move the foreground, the background, but I don't think that's what they wanted to hear. I wrote a memo at the time, saying basically it was possible to move the mounts. If they really wanted to preserve all of them, it could have been done. But it wasn't what they wanted to hear. I could see the way things were going. [The dioramas] weren't all sterling and stunning, but it *was* possible to preserve them in total. But I think the underlying plan was to have the space to do something else."

I asked Hawks to fax me the memo, and she did. It was addressed to exhibit developer Sally Love and said this:

> Removing the murals is a straightforward conservation project with little in the way of technical challenges. Even the presence of lead white ground is not particularly a problem, because done properly, cutting the murals into panels would be accompanied by very focused, at-source, HEPA Type I dust extraction. The same would be true if the plaster or any other part of the substrate were found to contain asbestos.

In 1999, the museum, disregarding Hawks's memo, began to dismantle North American Mammals. "The dioramas had been constructed as part of the building, and it was going to be outrageously expensive to preserve the background paintings," James G. Mead, curator of marine mammals, explained to me one day by phone. He paused, collecting his thoughts. He was very sad to lose them. "So . . . they . . . didn't . . . get . . . preserved."

I'm not particularly sentimental, but it seemed rather scandalous for a powerful institution such as the Smithsonian to trash its dioramas. Dioramas are irreplaceable; the Akeleys and Hornadays of the world are long gone, as are the intimate localities they painstakingly selected, then preserved for posterity. Some museums preserve their dioramas at all costs. In 2006, for example, following extensive documentation and conservation, the Canadian Museum of Nature in Ottawa transported nineteen dioramas from the 1950s and 1960s from one wing of its four-story granite building (also built in 1910) across an open atrium and reinstalled them on the other side. Remarkably, the museum remained open to the public the entire time.

Before North American Mammals was demolished, Mead and Hawks attempted to save the mountain sheep diorama, with its Canadian Rockies habitat and sheep personally collected by renowned paleontologist Charles Doolittle Walcott. The former director of the U.S. Geological Survey, Walcott had also served as Smithsonian secretary, and Mead called him a "museum man." The diorama didn't get saved. Neither did Life in the Sea. The mounts for both halls, however, were removed and stored in Newington, where museum officials said they'd stay until a new facility became available at the MSC. That didn't necessarily happen.

Take the eighty-nine-foot blue whale, for example. When a museum demolishes a hall, it hires outside contractors to do the work. As part of the contract, they are given salvage rights: that is, they own the stuff they remove—electrical wires, panes of glass, eighty-nine-foot-long blue whales. The whale in question was constructed in 1956 under the supervision of the whale biologist Remington Kellogg, who later served as assistant secretary of the Smithsonian. It had a huge fiberglass shell over a wooden structure and resembled an old aircraft. It dominated Life in the Sea for thirty-six years.

Although Mead knew that Life in the Sea would be replaced by the new Sant Ocean Hall, he didn't think the specimens would be destroyed. He had a good reason to think this. You can't just remove and sell a museum specimen; it first must be deaccessioned. In the museum world, deaccessioning is a formal process that requires certain paperwork and procedures. None of that had happened. But one day Mead heard, to his utter dismay, that the contractor had put the whale up for sale on eBay!

Mead was bewildered. Never in his thirty years as a museum man had he encountered such a ridiculous scenario: a gargantuan fiberglass whale on eBay. It might have been funny if the whale weren't such a treasured specimen. Mead wanted to keep the whale—at least its tail, head, fins, and flippers—for future exhibitions. Because it hadn't been deaccessioned, the salvage contract could have been nullified. "But everyone at the museum would have had to have agreed, and there wasn't an agreement," he explained, somewhat woefully. Meanwhile, the contractor, who had to take the whale off eBay because it was too big to remove from the building, heard about the dispute. He then filed suit for and was eventually awarded possession of "the object" (the whale). "It was his, and he was going to take it out. And we didn't get the tail, and we didn't get the flippers, and we didn't get the head. And I think the head, the tail, and the flippers ended up in a dumpster," Mead said.

"If the blue whale at the AMNH were torn down, the whole city [of New York] would protest," I said wishfully, remembering how the AMNH had given its whale a new navel when it renovated the Hall of Ocean Life.

"We loaned them our forms," Mead said. "That blue whale is a virtual duplicate of ours. The American Museum's is ninety-four feet—they stretched it, because they could then claim they had the longest model."

"Now they have the only one," I ventured.

"No. The National Science Museum in Tokyo has a life-size blue whale, and they are the only two in existence."

On Wednesday, November 15, 2003, the Kenneth E. Behring Family Hall of Mammals opened. People in tuxedos and evening gowns sipped cocktails in the museum's grand rotunda as acrobats rappelled down the gleaming marble walls—a dreamy ballet reminiscent of Cirque du Soleil. It felt historic to be present for the opening. A more elegant and distinguished group of people was unimaginable, and the renovation was stunning.

I scanned the crowd for John Matthews, Ken Walker, and Paul Rhymer, but I couldn't find them. In the center of the rotunda, however, I saw the famous Fenykovi elephant, which had been unveiled in 1959. (I had read somewhere that a top Smithsonian administrator had demanded that its anus be sewn shut so that it wouldn't offend anyone at a previous opening.) Everyone was loose and happy and celebratory, eager to see what hadn't been seen in this place for decades: something new.

Secretary Small got up onstage and welcomed everyone to this momentous event. While he spoke, my mind was filled with David Schwendeman's stories of the ribbon cutting for the Akeley Hall of African Mammals in 1936. How exciting it must have been to stand in that dark hall, listening to African drummers, while Akeley's dearest friends delivered heartfelt tributes to him. Then I remembered how the museum had decided to name the hall after Akeley instead of Theodore Roosevelt.

Small praised Matthews and Rhymer for their tremendous effort, then Behring—truly moved by the occasion—walked up onstage and addressed the crowd. Finally, we were all summoned to "meet our relatives" in the new hall, which bore only one name: Kenneth E. Behring.

It was sleek and modern, with bright lights and lots of glass: a Prada store filled with animals. The first thing I saw was a wall of framed animal photos meant to evoke my own family photos. I tried to smile, but I found the display somewhat patronizing, even for a kid. (I have a seven-year-old, and she knows that humans are mammals.) At the press conference the next morning, associate director Robert Sullivan told a group of reporters, "Once you free yourself from nineteenth-century-type displays, you can create odd juxtapositions." I thought he meant that figuratively, but the walrus was frightfully near the pink fairy armadillo, and the dolphin hung directly above the argali sheep. "Putting these guys on marble really elevates their status. We did that to treat them like sculpture," he said. And indeed, the European mole stood alone on a marble column.

A leopard crouched high in an artificial tree. I followed it into the Africa zone, the hall's centerpiece. It was organized around an abstract water hole that resembled a gigantic Corian sink. I spotted the dramatic tableau of two lions attacking a Cape buffalo. Then the sky darkened and thunder crashed and lighting struck (the "ooh factor"), and I wasn't sure whether I should run or grab an umbrella. The audiovisual thunderstorm went off every ten minutes (an amplification more than an evocation); I stayed for only one storm. Television screens embedded in the floor like rocks in a stream flashed images of leaves and water: *dry season, wet season; dry season, wet season; dry season, wet season.*

Blinding spotlights illuminated an abstract savanna. Xenon flashers flashed. Digitized animals crowed and growled and rustled for acorns. All 210 years of evolution (and its Discovery Zones) crescendoed to one cataclysmic big bang. The hall was very alive—so alive with the marvels of man that the animals seemed incongruous. "This hall is really about *us*," Sullivan said at the press conference. Although he meant mammals, the exhibits said otherwise.

A tunnel into which I could burrow tempted me, but not in an evening gown, so I skipped it. I skirted the hominoid footprints (high heels—clearly not a problem 1.5 million years ago). The human presence was so intense that I missed the tableau of a bat nibbling the toes of a research scientist (the "gross-out factor"). Instead, I trekked through an abstract rain forest and a refrigerated tundra (crackling ice, howling wind), until, finally, I found the taxidermists chatting with their wives near the primate case.

John Matthews had delivered all 274 mounts in time and under budget. Now he stood in the finished hall beaming, dressed in a tuxedo, his handlebar mustache waxed and groomed for the big event. Walker, wearing a black suit, had flown down from Alberta. He had run into Dr. Ruth, the sex therapist, at a preopening party and spent the night mimicking her: "You must remember to take off your pants. Hee, hee, hee!" Neither Small nor Behring had thanked Walker onstage, but he took it in stride. "I won't be acknowledged, but I'm glad to be here," he said.

"Hey, the orangutan!" I shouted, catching it out of the corner of my eye. The last time I had seen it, it had been a frozen skin in a cardboard box. Now it was combed out and glossy, clutching stainless steel poles in a stark glass case without a habitat. You'd think it had been shot in Borneo, except for its queer grin, which ever so subtly suggested the taxidermists who had mounted it. "That's the love child of John and Paul," Walker said, laughing.

I congratulated the taxidermists, who were filled with pride; took another peek at the Roosevelt rhino, the Tasmanian wolf, and the koala hugging a Lucite "tree"; and made my way out to the rotunda. The last thing I remember seeing was a hibernating metal squirrel.

After the opening, Paul Rhymer returned to the National Museum of Natural History's exhibitions department, where he works as a modelmaker, taxidermist, and bracket maker (someone who articulates skeletons). John Matthews was dispatched to Newington to dismantle the taxidermy lab that he had set up three years ago. The job involved figuring out what to do with the unused specimens. Some were in good shape; others were mangy and faded. At the onset, Linda Gordon had been told that the "keepers" would be moved to the MSC for storage, but that was no longer an option, so she and John had to decide what to do with the mongrel lot.

This was a shocking turn of events. Contrast the British Natural History Museum, which by law must preserve its specimens. In World War II, during the Blitz, the museum hauled thirty truckloads of stuffed animals (including its precious type specimens) to its annex at Tring for safekeeping. Likewise, in 1994, when the Muséum national d'Histoire naturelle in Paris built its phenomenal Grande Galerie de l'Évolution, it dug a three-story underground storage facility, the *zootheque,* to house the unused specimens, some of which were part of the Cabinet du Roi in the 1740s.

Here's what the Smithsonian did. First, it distributed the Behring and Martin specimens, which it had only recently acquired, to schools and nature centers. It saved several historic mounts, including a single Hornaday bison. And the rest, some preserved by Hornaday, Robert Rockwell, and other taxidermy pioneers, were hauled back to the National Museum of Natural History and, under a HAZMAT tent, broken down into scraps. "We saved a sample of the skin, skull, or skeletal elements inside

[each] mount to put into the scientific collections, and the rest of the mount—its stuffing or whatever it was—all of that was disposed of as hazardous waste," explained Gordon. "We sacrificed the skins for the skeletal material. It was a shame that we had to destroy them."

On several occasions, Catharine Hawks observed museum workers taking apart the animal specimens. "It was horrifying," she said. Sometimes Hawks would bring in Amandine Péquignot, a conservation scientist at the Muséum national d'Histoire naturelle, who was doing postdoctoral work at the MSC. One day she described those trips for me: "I was shocked. I saw [them cut up] a wild pig—a boar—also a big deer, a chimpanzee. I went there three times with Cathy, and every time I was very sad and upset. It was an opportunity to study.

"I was a little bit shocked at first because the condition of the specimen[s] was perfect. To see a whole specimen trashed, I imagined the taxidermists and the technique they used," she said, pausing to collect her thoughts. "You know they are dead, but it's like second death when you see them destroyed."

I asked her about something I had learned from Gordon—namely, that the specimens were loaded with arsenic and asbestos and the museum would be liable if someone got sick from them. "I don't think they did a mercury or lead or arsenic test on them," she said. "But even if they have arsenic, mercury, or lead, that's no reason to destroy [them]. There are different techniques to remove arsenic and also store [a specimen] in good condition . . . In the United States, if [something is] considered important, everything will be done to save it."

In September 2004, John Matthews's contract expired. He had hoped that someone—Secretary Small, perhaps, who had put a few final stitches in the fifteen-foot reticulated giraffe—might find another job for him. Gordon, for one, could have used his help with the scientific skin collection. But nothing happened, and so, after seven years at the Smithsonian, he left.

A year or so after the opening, I called Matthews, Paul Rhymer, and Ken Walker to see what they were up to. Matthews had been out of a job for two months when I reached him at home. He had joined the elevator union and was looking for work as a mechanic. "There's just no money in taxidermy," he said, setting down the receiver to calm his two-year-old son, who was crying in the background. "I'm burned-out on taxidermy," he said with resignation. "My interest has waned. I've had enough for now."

When I asked Rhymer about the mammal hall, he said, "In those speeches [at the opening], we were mentioned a couple of times. That's unfathomable. I've never seen a production person get the type of credit we did throughout the whole process. It will never happen again. They put us in front of newspapers and magazines. The secretary came by. He loved that place." His voice radiated enthusiasm; the opening could have been the night before. "I really feel we were part of history," he continued. "Not in that same Hornaday sense. We were really more production people than experts. I know Hornaday was highly respected; only the secretary was paid more. He was a heavy hitter. That's not happening for me and John. I'm making labels for bison mummies. I'm not bitching and moaning, but it's just not going to happen."

Of the three, only Walker was doing any real taxidermy work. He was back in Alberta, negotiating with Canadian customs to get them to release a walrus that he had hired Inuit hunters to kill for a client: Kenneth E. Behring. Alberta has comparatively relaxed laws regarding endangered species, but Walker needed money fast to cover importation costs. If it didn't arrive soon, the walrus would rot, and he'd lose face with the Inuit. "Million-aires never pay you!" he said.

I told him that I had spoken to Matthews. "I talked to John last week, and he said, 'I'm going broke slowly,'" Walker told me. "I would have liked to see him stay there, because he liked the security it offered his family. He had a pension and a little bit of prestige. But I wouldn't wish that job on anyone. As much as I have to fight for every dime, it was so nice to be home after that. I'm so glad it's over. It's so politically motivated . . . Politics change with fashion, but the laws of nature do not."

5

THE CHAIRBITCH

AT THE 2003 World Taxidermy Championships, the English bird judge Jack Fishwick told me about a sculptor who was arguably the best taxidermist in the United Kingdom—this, even though she became disillusioned with taxidermy years ago and now calls herself an "anti-taxidermist." Her name is Emily Mayer, and she lives with her husband, John Loker (an abstract painter), and any number of Jack Russell terriers in the Norfolk countryside, surrounded by dairy farms. With her spiky black hair, deep voice, and BITCH T-shirts, the village locals used to call her "that strange lesbian dog owner." Now they know her as a taxidermist who is vaguely associated with the arts. "Vaguely," of course, isn't quite accurate, yet it's not entirely wrong either. Mayer is at the very center of the art world and also on its fringes. It seems like a curious place for a taxidermist to be.

At least Fishwick thought so, and he is a savage critic. But when he described Mayer's erosion-molded rats, he practically fogged up his binoculars. "The realism is uncanny," he gushed. "I mean the *deathism*." I shrugged. Racing off to England to see rats—even exceptional ones—wasn't on my agenda. Then Fishwick leaned in and whispered that Mayer was Damien Hirst's taxidermist: the woman who repairs the sharks, preserves the grizzlies, assembles the skeletons, and casts the cow heads for his multimillion-dollar artworks. I asked for her phone number.

Mayer also happens to be an artist in her own right, with a degree from the Norwich School of Art and Design and a body of found-fragment sculptures the *Times* of London once compared to Ted Hughes's poetry. In Fishwick's words, "Anywhere you cut Emily's finger off, it will say 'art.'"

For years, Mayer was the only woman taxidermist in England. She was also the first female chair of Britain's Guild of Taxidermists, the professional organization devoted to promoting taxidermy in the United Kingdom. When I finally called her, she invited me to attend its upcoming convention in Nottingham. I knew that taxidermy had evolved differently in Britain, where it is a cottage industry with long ties to modern zoology, than in the United States, with its predominant hunting culture, and I wanted to meet the descendants of early British taxidermists, some of the country's most passionate animal lovers.

We decided to spend a few days at her house getting acquainted before the guild show. She'd tell me about herself and erosion molding, the technique she's perfected. The process is incredibly complicated (as I'd see on a later visit) but yields astonishing results. There's no manikin, since there's no skin to stretch over it. Instead, the inside of the animal is replaced with silicone (rubber); only the fur remains. Hirst likes the method because he can display animals submerged in water rather than toxic formaldehyde, and they won't rot or become tattered, theoretically eliminating the need for replacement tiger sharks.

Because Mayer herself is so edgy, people tend to call erosion molding cutting-edge. It's more accurate to say that Mayer has rediscovered a forgotten technique (the Smithsonian has used it on some primates) and has pushed it farther than anyone:

to the frightening point, in fact, where art is indistinguishable from life. Score one for taxidermy. Except for this: since erosion molding dispenses with the "derm" (and derm-less taxidermy is technically not taxidermy), taxidermists disdain her work as modelmaking. To Mayer, the distinction is semantic. "As long as you get the results, *who cares!*" she snaps with a dismissive air that belies how completely possessed she is by the absurd quest for utter realism.

Hirst once told me that Mayer is the only taxidermist who can "make it real." But real for Mayer—a perfectionist who is completely unsentimental about animals in art—is nothing like a diorama, with its idealized nature. Real is *really* real, and reality is unsettling, because it is often ugly and macabre. She and Hirst share this morbid fascination. Hirst's sectioned cows and bisected sheep are often nothing more than the cut-up animal, yet they are considered shocking. Encased in glass, they are the opposite of a diorama and yet convey the same powerful clashing of beauty and death. Mayer, like Hirst, loves to push the disturbance factor. As she puts it, "Animals die and kill things, and they lick their asses, and they shit. They just do stuff a taxidermist won't show. Taxidermists are all about the beauty of the animal. But I find beauty in *death!*"

If you met Mayer, you wouldn't doubt that. Ever since she was a kid, she's been wildly unconventional—not outright rebellious or disobedient, simply determined to pursue her own dreams. And beginning when she was twelve, one of her dreams was to be a taxidermist. Born in 1960, the Chinese year of the rat, Mayer grew up in Greenwich, when that section of southeast London was seedy and working-class and attracted bohemian artists such as her parents, who let her turn her bedroom into what she called her museum. Mayer, who is still a compulsive scavenger (and eBay fanatic), filled the tiny room with eggs, bones, and especially animals—living, dead, common, exotic, incubated, dissected, mummified, decomposed, fossilized, skeletonized. ("I was doing this before bloody Damien Hirst," she jokes.) She skinned her first mouse when she was nine and preserved—and ate—her first bird (a gull) when she was eleven, much to the disgust of her brother and sister. On a high school career form, she wrote "taxidermist, pig farmer, and jack-of-all-trades." "They thought I was taking the piss!" she says, using the Briticism for making a joke. "I was serious!"

She cares not a wink if people think she's mad; at least they remember her. "I can ring up people from way back in my past and say, 'Hi, I'm Emily the taxidermist,' and they go, 'Oh, right. Yeah.'"

The first time she rang me was to get my flight information, and it took me forever to figure out who was on the phone. The voice on the other end was so deep and gravelly from chain-smoking that I thought it was Jack Fishwick pulling my leg. It's only now that I'm not completely flustered by the words "Emily here." Before I hung up, I asked if she wanted anything from New York: bagels, perhaps, or an I ♥ NY T-shirt. She gave it a quick thought, then said definitively, "Novelty sunglasses with holographic rolling eyeballs."

I left New York for England on September 14, 2003. I caught the Norfolk train from London and took it to Diss, the closest stop to Mayer's house. It was balmy outside, and Diss station (a cement platform with an espresso machine) was deserted except for a man reading a newspaper. I paced back and forth in the fragrant heat, waiting for Mayer. Then I glanced up and saw a tall, imposing figure with short-cropped hair, dressed all in black, striding purposefully down the platform. With the heavy black work boots and black wraparound sunglasses, it was hard to tell whether the person was a man or a woman. He or she did not resemble a taxidermist. Then I saw the butcher knives glinting in the sun. It was Mayer, and the knives were her earrings.

She kissed my cheek in a way that was more London artist than rural taxidermist. I dodged the knives (she sharpens them). Unsure of what to say, I handed her the holographic sunglasses. She passed me the wraparounds, and when she did, I could see her elegant facial bones and huge, darkly expressive brown eyes. She led me to her silver Citroën van and lit a roll-up, then we drove to her house in each other's sunglasses.

She sounded tough. Every other word was "fuck" or "bloody hell." Yet her lips trembled when she spoke, as if she had just consumed a pot of espresso, and peeking above her boots were her trademark hot-pink socks. At the crossroads of two dairy farms, in the minuscule village of Guilt Cross, we pulled into a gravel driveway that led to what looked like a huge brick factory (seventy-six windows and fifty-six radiators): Mayer's house. This 1906 workhouse hospital originally treated poor boys with tuberculosis. In old photos, the yard is filled with consumptive patients lying on cots, getting some fresh air (a common treatment for TB).

Now it contains animal corpses for Damien Hirst and Mayer's other clients, who include grieving dog owners, the bad-boy celebrity chef Marco Pierre White (who once sent a three-foot pike here by chauffeured car), and the odd skeleton collector, bat enthusiast, or lobster freak. When Mayer bought the workhouse in 1995, it was being used to store grain for neighboring farms. After years of renovations, she and Loker have transformed it into two artists' studios, each with its own kitchen, bedroom, and freezer—one for meat ("domestic"), the other for carcasses ("Emily's").

I followed Mayer inside. The place was dark and cold, a maze of long corridors. Her five terriers went nuts, running frenetic circles around her. "That's Alice. Her father fucked his aunt, which makes her inbred," she said with a jarring bluntness. Visiting Mayer for the first time is something like being at the dentist's after he's given you "sweet air" and you're smiling as he drills your teeth. I went upstairs to unpack. My room had a view of grazing Holsteins. On the nightstand was a worn paperback by Nicholas Parsons, *Dipped in Vitriol*, an anthology of "hatchet art reviews." The cover had a picture of a smashed tomato on it.

After lunch, she led me to her two-story studio, called Flying Bear. Upstairs, in a minimally finished attic that resembled an art gallery, are her sculptures. It is a group show by a single artist. I glanced at her seven iridescent rooks (taxidermic) perched on a weather-beaten fence post, then examined her crowlike bird surgically assembled out of scraps of old leather and bits of rusty metal. The crow, one of her found-object sculptures, was abstract yet somehow conveyed more life than the taxidermy. Indeed, it revealed someone who is uncannily in tune with animals—not just their glossy coats but the inner movement of every muscle, tendon, and bone.

Downstairs is her workshop, the kind of job shop where you'd expect to see a carpenter turn wood on a lathe or a mechanic rebuild an engine. It's a well-organized clutter of paints, saws, tools, drills, credit cards (used as resin scrapers), and Frankenstein-like chemistry setups with heat lamps, funnels, thermometers, handwritten formulas, and plastic bins for rotting carcasses: erosion-molding equipment.

We passed bird skulls and death masks and boxes of mummified weasels and stoats that she used to pick off of hedgerows as a kid (some now hung on her bedroom door). Above a window hung a mummified cat, all dried up and sinewy, like something you'd see in the Egyptian wing of the Metropolitan Museum of Art. And lying on the floor was the glossy head of a black horse that looked as if it had just been axed off. I glanced at its teeth, slightly visible through slack lips. Mayer grinned but offered no explanation.

"Ugh! That's dead!" I shrieked when we came upon a sleeping foxhound. The dog was curled up near a radiator. It looked so peaceful, so alive, that I petted it to be sure. It was as hard as fiberglass. "I like things in repose," she said coolly. "I like that disturbance factor. If it had glassy eyes, then you'd know it wasn't alive." The calico cat, on the other hand, was obviously dead. One of her failed experiments (she keeps them), it had shattered like a broken plate; furry shards lay on her worktable awaiting reassembly. "I had more of a headache with that fucking pussycat than I needed. It was a bloody nightmare!" she groaned.

Mayer does preserve dogs and cats. She preserves dogs and cats for the same reason other taxidermists are afraid to: she enjoys the challenge of replicating the expression of an animal that someone once knew intimately. (And since her mounts satisfy pet owners, she doesn't get stiffed—another reason taxidermists won't mount pets these days.) Mayer's canines are so spot-on that they even fool live dogs. Her terriers actually curl up with the cast foxhound and fall asleep. That said, Mayer will preserve pets for only one of two reasons: as a humanitarian gesture for a bereaved pet owner who *absolutely* needs an effigy of *that* animal to remember it by, and, of course, for art.

Outside Mayer's workshop is a small annex with huge doors that she had installed to accommodate massive carcasses. That day the room was blocked with an orange barrier that said NO ENTRY. It was her current Hirst project, which she was bound not to show until it was finished. I was disappointed. As captivating as Hirst's sculptures are while on exhibit at the Guggenheim in Bilboa, the Tate Britain, or any of the world's other leading bastions of contemporary art, I was far more interested in the process of how they are made — the messy, complicated part that a museum would never show. I mentioned how frustrating it must be to work in secret for years. She shrugged. "There [are] times when I'm glad my tongue is tied so I don't have to talk about it — especially at parties. It gets exhausting, people asking what's the biggest animal you've ever stuffed. So I don't say I'm a taxidermist anymore. If someone asks what I do, I just say I'm a sculptor and I occasionally work with dead animals," she said.

Taxidermists are notoriously cagey, but no one is cagey like Mayer, whose favorite aphorism is "How can I tell what I think till I see what I say" (E. M. Forster). Fortunately, you can see just about everything Mayer has ever said, because she is a master archivist who has been documenting her own life since she was thirteen. Her JPEG files of her work for Hirst, for instance, are practically in real time. "I keep a record of my breathing," she said, exhaling smoke.

Then she led me into the kitchen, covered the table with scrapbooks and old photos, and launched into a show-and-tell that lasted for three days and nights, not unpleasantly, I might add, except that Mayer does not pause for food. According to her two assistants, David Spaul and Carl Church, she can survive on a diet of nicotine and coffee. That said, Mayer's kitchen is actually pretty normal, except for the wineglass shelf with the kangaroo head, the wall of cutting boards that also has a ferret leash (in its original package), and the flower vase with a beard of twelve white mice strung together. "I did that for Damien's Christmas party," she explained. "The theme was beards." She grabbed two beers out of the fridge and flicked a lighter she called "the Elephant Man" because it depicted a naked guy with super-enhanced masculinity.

When I flipped through one of her childhood scrapbooks, labeled "Twenty Years a-Growing," I could see that she's always seen the world from a slightly twisted perspective. An early Christmas wish list had "braces" (to look American), "Beano books" (a classic comic book series for kids), and "a real syringe." There was a self-portrait of her head wedged in a trap, and the transcription of a childhood dream in which she fatally conked a puppy on the head, then revived it with a saucer of milk. "My bible when I was eight," she said, handing me a musty copy of *Pets, Usual and Unusual* by Maxwell Knight. "It brings me back," she said, eyeing me to see if I was damaging the spine. Not only did she describe her pet squirrels, hooded rats, and ferrets—in some cases she could produce the actual items. With a magician's flourish, she lifted an aluminum Jell-O mold off the table, and there was the injured rabbit she had tried to save by suturing. "I'm not good at throwing things away," she said, cocking her head to the side.

Her mother, Irmelin Mayer, is from Berlin and was a theatrical milliner in London. Her father, Tomi, immigrated to London from Mauritius and worked as a scenic artist for the Royal Opera House in Covent Garden, painting backdrops for ballets and operas. "I've slept through more operas than you've been to in your entire life," she told me. Sometimes Tomi would bike home from work in his paint-splotched overalls carrying sugar cane he'd just picked up at a city market and say that he'd been to Mauritius. Other times, he'd bring home a finch that he had preserved in spirits at the scenic studios, and he and Emily would sit side by side in the kitchen sketching it. Both her grandfathers were physicians (one in Germany, the other in Mauritius). Her maternal grandmother was Lotte Pritzel, a well-known sculptor in 1920s Munich, whose erotically charged wax dolls inspired the Dadaists and the surrealist Hans Bellmer.

Even the poet Rainer Maria Rilke said that he was moved to write part of his favorite verse, *Duineser Elegien,* after seeing Pritzel's haunting figurines. Pritzel died in 1952, eight years before Mayer was born. Her flamboyance, however, was legendary. If broad-brimmed hats were in style, Pritzel wore a broader one. She smoked cigarettes in the subway, embarrassing her daughter, whom Pritzel called bourgeois. "The rebelliousness skipped my mother and hit me. I've just been a bit different. I don't like to conform to what's expected," Emily said, raising an eyebrow.

At twelve, Mayer yearned to dig her scalpel into something more exotic than city sparrows and pigeons, so she took a job at Amazon Pets in southeast London, cleaning cages and exercising dogs and sheep. The owner, a falconer and part-time amateur taxidermist, imported amazing creatures that Mayer found incredibly alluring. Soon he taught her how to train an owl to fly to a lure, and he gave her taxidermy lessons. With some convincing, he also gave her his "dead inventory," which she smuggled home and dissected for practice.

Around then, she and a boyfriend went ferreting (hunting) for rabbits at night. They'd trap them in a purse, kill them, and eat them or feed them to the dogs. Mayer is not opposed to hunting for the table, and she has killed marketplace pigeons and rabbits for taxidermy, but she refuses to kill an animal only for taxidermy. The Akeley concept of dispatching the perfect specimen in order to make the perfect mount and then try to resurrect it revolts her. "Just leave it *alive!*" she says with disgust. She disapproves of fur farms and believes that roadkill is the most ethical meat you can eat. Her own specimens come from veterinarians, zoos, other taxidermists, and a network of obscure specialists, including skeleton assemblers, ornithologists, and lepidopterists. The horse intestines she uses to repair Hirst's *Some Comfort Gained from the Acceptance of the Inherent Lies in Everything* (a cow cut up and displayed in twelve separate glass cabinets; 1996) are from John Warman the knacker, whose family has been in the slaughtering business since the early 1800s. And her rats and mice are mostly cat fatalities.

She literally will not kill a fly. Once when I was at her house, she had just made a "blood run" (a resin blood puddle embedded with dead flies) for Hirst's landmark sculpture *A Thousand Years* (a rotting cow head on the floor of a giant glass case that is outfitted with a bug zapper and real flies, which eventually get sizzled; 1990). When I asked Mayer if she had killed the flies, she shot me a daggerlike look.

At seventeen, Mayer realized that her fascination with dead animals was more than a morbid predilection, perhaps even something of a gift. It was 1977, and she was waiting for the school bus, when she saw a dog get hit by a car and die. She carried the dog to the owners and gently broke the news. They were grateful, and soon Mayer was hanging out with them on their porch, drinking port, smoking pot, and complaining about how bored she was in school. ("I'm a maker of objects; I'm not intellectual," she says.) She wanted to drop out and become a taxidermist. "Do it then! Stop going to school and do it!" said the man, whom she describes as a rebel from a wealthy family. And so she did just that and has never regretted it, although one teacher told her she'd never be a taxidermist without advanced courses in biology and art. "And so I proved her wrong; I refused to be discouraged," she said.

That summer Emily worked as an apprentice taxidermist at World of Nature, in North Yorkshire, a zoo and a private museum housed in a converted mill. There was a window through which the public could watch taxidermy—or, rather, what minimally passed for taxidermy. World of Nature, you see, had the whiff of a circus. The owner was a former strongman who got his animals—including his pet lion, Libra—from his circus world contacts.

At World of Nature, Mayer learned how to skin eyelids, ears, and lips. She discovered, after skinning a rotten tortoise, that she had the requisite strong stomach for the task. Mostly she learned what not to do: break squirrel noses to enhance their cuteness; mount snarling stoats with one arm raised (like a toy); or implant teddy bear eyes in fox faces.

One day after she was told to flesh an elephant with a blunt skinning knife, Mayer quit. She returned to Greenwich for a time, then moved to Norfolk, where she freelanced doing taxidermy for schools and fox-hunt kennels and hung out at the pub with the local plumbers and builders. Then her efforts started to un- ravel. Glass eyes looked "glassy"; dog noses, dry; cat ears, opaque (when they ought to be translucent). And the faces—the ten- der windows onto an animal's soul—looked hard, not soft and fleshy. Mayer grew restless; the task of merging art and nature never seemed more illogical or unattainable. So she did some- thing she had always found rather repugnant: she enrolled in art school. There she studied the energy of movement, discov- ering in sculpture what was missing in her taxidermy: her own interpretation.

It's as natural for a taxidermist to become a sculptor as it is for an actor to direct. Almost inevitably, taxidermists go the way of the nineteenth-century French animaliers (painters or sculp- tors of animal subjects) and cast animals in bronze. When Carl Akeley, Robert Rockwell, and David Schwendeman (briefly) each took up sculpture, they did bronze casting. To Mayer, however, nothing was more confining than what was essentially metal taxidermy. Until she met Damien Hirst, the only animal sculptures that inspired her were Picasso's assemblages.

Then one day she read about erosion molding. It was taxidermy in reverse: working from the outside of an animal in, dispensing with the derm. She explained the method to me using a dog as an example.

You take one dog, preferably dead, and position it in a way that you want the thing to end up looking. You can do it either fresh or frozen. Small mammals are better to do frozen, because they'll hold their shapes. Then you coat the dog's fur with silicone.

"What about rigor mortis?" I asked.

"It doesn't really last. Otherwise, people would die in really weird shapes, and you wouldn't be able to fit them in coffins, would you?"

After applying the silicone, you bolt a support-jacket mold around the coated carcass so it will hold its shape while the body decomposes, or "slips." The idea is to decompose the skin uniformly, so that when you remove the carcass from the mold, you are left with a hollow rubber shell that is the exact duplicate of the animal, with the fur embedded in it. A dog takes about a week to slip. It releases first from the belly, where there is a lot of bacteria. (The bacteria take longer to reach the ears, eyelids, toes, and extremities.) The smell is vile.

Mayer hand-casts every wart and freckle. So if a dog's belly has patches and splotches, she paints them into the mold. If it has one pink toe and three black toes, she casts each toe separately. Quite a bit of chemistry goes into erosion molding, because anytime you alter a batch of silicone resin to change the color, for example, or the tactility (the material's strength), the curing time may also change. Mayer has spent more than a decade fine-tuning the process. She knows how the material will react if changed by a tenth of a gram. "I can't have a piece for Damien discolor in five years," she says. "It has to be archival."

Her first erosion mold, in 1985, was for a pig farmer in Metfield, Suffolk (prime farm country), who wanted the head of his prized Berkshire-Peiron cross mounted as a memento. Mayer wanted to capture its fine details, but a pig's skin, like a primate's, has soft, hairless folds and wrinkles that would show imperfections if mounted conventionally. She suggested erosion molding but warned the farmer that she might "cock up." Mayer rarely cocks up. The pig was fabulous; the farmer was ecstatic. Then Mayer enrolled in art school and forgot all about erosion molding until Damien Hirst hired her to make a replacement severed cow head for *A Thousand Years.*

That was in 1998, five years after Marco Pierre White introduced them. The first animal Mayer mounted for Hirst was an upright grizzly bear posed in the Victorian style for *Last Night I Dreamed That I Didn't Have a Head* (Guggenheim Museum, Bilbao). (She used conventional taxidermy because the bear was too huge to erosion mold at that point in her career.) When Hirst went to Norfolk to inspect it, Mayer was expecting him to be "a right jumped-up little asshole that was really up himself." Instead, she found him to be "really straightforward, what you see is what you get kind of thing." While they were drinking beer in the garden, Hirst mentioned a concept similar to one he describes in his book *On the Way to Work* (2002). Mayer just happened to have a tiny plasticine cow on a cross that she had made, and she took it out to show him. Synchronicity! Hirst yelled, "Fucking hell! Fucking hell!"

For Mayer, beginning to work with Hirst was a turning point. The grizzly led to shark repairs, skeleton work, and eventually more cow heads for *A Thousand Years* (he changes them periodically). The pay was "phenomenal." Better yet, she got to live inside Hirst's mind during his meteoric rise to fame, when his controversial work was shaking up the art world in a way that may sound familiar today but was absolutely shocking then. One art critic described the Hirst phenomenon like this: "Each time he showed a new work it was as if some art-world Jack the Ripper had perpetrated one more outrageous crime." Mayer was stirred by the experience. She saw Hirst's work as a sophisticated version of what she had done as a child, and she saw him as a kindred spirit. "My heart went faster. My mind went *Flip, flip, flip: My God, he's right! Oh, fuck!* It's just about putting things together and not trying too hard to make them into a story. I've always been a maker of objects. Damien put them into a context. The pig cut in half—*fantastic!* You don't meet many people with that same fascination with dead things . . . He made it permissible to use that kind of language. He's allowed me to experiment to get the results he wants, and it's been a steep learning curve—an armory of techniques. It's been brilliant for me."

She dug up the original work order for her first severed cow head. It said, "Notes on head: real skin, eyes to look fresh, alive; exposed flesh on base of neck molded. In the round; to be displayed on its side." At that time, erosion molding was still nasty, trial-and-error work. She explained the risks to Science, Hirst's company in Bloomsbury. The company said, "We need this head, please!" It turned out to be the most beautiful severed cow head with an exposed bloody spinal bone imaginable. Other taxidermists would have driven it straight to Science. Mayer entered it in the 1998 guild show. It caused a minor sensation but won not a single ribbon. Everyone agreed that it was clever—clever, that is, for something that had been *molded.* Nevertheless, the guild published a photo of it in its annual magazine *Taxidermist* with this comment: "You can see it as part of a Damien Hirst show a year from now." The magazine thought it was a joke.

The guild show started that afternoon. The three-day conference was being held at the University of Nottingham, Sutton Bonington, an agricultural college, and Mayer was giving the death mask demonstration with a taxidermist from the National Museum of Scotland.

While Mayer packed, I flipped through back issues of *Taxidermist*. Articles by zoologists, museum taxidermists, and curators filled its pages. I read about preserving Mediterranean spurthighed tortoises, refurbishing antique giraffes, and casting lightweight rocks for dioramas. The guild members sounded serious, but they didn't seem to take themselves seriously. One contributor actually called taxidermists "pathetic."

The guild takes trips to fascinating places: museums and estates whose collections were amassed in the 1800s by wealthy enthusiasts, big-game hunters, and field naturalists who hunted on other continents for specimens to bring back to England. During the early 1800s, Britain dominated the race to acquire as many new species for its national collections as possible. Not only did the British collect specimens with imperial zeal, but they also formed brilliant theories about them. By contrast, their American counterparts were known mostly as specimen providers (hunters), with some important exceptions. England was also the place where artistic taxidermy advanced after London's Great Exhibition of 1851, the first world's fair. The guild members had giant shoes to fill if they ever hoped to live up to their forebears, the best of whom had been granted the royal warrant "Naturalist, by appointment to his Majesty the King."

That said, only England could produce such animal fanatics —and then turn them into enemies. You see, the early taxidermists who served science at the British Museum and the ones who prepared artistic mounts for public display were often bitter rivals. As a result, many private museums and stuffed menageries sprang up throughout England, each one as idiosyncratic as the person upon whose collection it was based. These are the places the guild likes to visit.

One year the guild visited the Walter Rothschild Zoological Museum at Tring. It's now a branch of the Natural History Museum, but in 1892 it opened as the private collection of the ardent self-taught ornithologist Lord Lionel Walter Rothschild, son of the banking magnate Nathan Mayer Rothschild, who gave him Tring for his twenty-first birthday. The baron used his vast fortune to hire hundreds of people to hunt for rare birds and butterflies throughout the world to add to his collection. He also liked to outbid the British Museum at auction. The baron was particularly fond of the most striking of feathered wonders, the bird of paradise, and he also loved tortoises. But he didn't just want to observe them; he wanted to own them — all of them. In the 1890s, he devised an unsuccessful plan to bring every turtle from the Galápagos Islands back to England, angering other naturalists who didn't believe his explanation that he was saving them for science. During the 1920s, his collection of 225,000 stuffed birds and live menagerie drew people from near and far.

In 1932, Rothschild, disinherited for eschewing banking in favor of birds, became embroiled in a museum acquisition that would make a gripping soap opera. Rothschild, who was being blackmailed by an ex-mistress, was forced to sell his beloved birds to the American Museum of Natural History for a dollar a bird, or $225,000. At the time of the sale, the baron broke down and wept; parting with the birds of paradise alone proved far more painful than parting with the mistress. The museum was unrelenting, but Rothschild got the last laugh. According to one account, when the AMNH ornithologist arrived at Tring to pack up the birds, he realized that none of them had been cataloged or labeled. There wasn't any need; the baron knew the Latin name of every bird by heart. When the crated birds arrived in New York, they filled an entire storeroom.

Rothschild died in 1937. He bequeathed Tring to the British

Museum, which owned it until it split with the Natural History Museum in 1963. Today Tring, the NHM's bird annex, contains the world's greatest collection of birds — nearly a million skins, including Charles Darwin's Galápagos finches (which he collected on his historic voyage on the *Beagle*), as well as 800,000 eggs and more than 2,000 nests. (It includes numerous stuffed dogs, too.) When the guild visits Tring, members get to go behind the scenes where all the scientific research takes place.

The guild also has gone to the Powell-Cotton Museum in Kent. Major Percy Powell-Cotton (1866–1940) was a rich hunter who survived a lion attack in Africa, then re-created other lion attacks at his home. Powell-Cotton hired the best British firms to preserve his kills, which he shipped home from Africa and Asia. He pioneered the diorama in England, eventually turning his house into a private museum where people could feast their eyes on the glorious scenes where he hunted.

However, the guild trip I thought sounded most exciting was the one to Charles Waterton's estate, Walton Hall, in West Yorkshire. Waterton is known as taxidermy's "eccentric genius." In the 1820s, Walton Hall, built on an island in a lake, was his Xanadu — the antithesis of a museum, with its storerooms of lifeless skins. Here all the animals lived harmoniously with Waterton as a landlocked Noah who communed with nature as only a Victorian British taxidermist could. He built stables so that his horses could converse, kennels so that his hounds could look out on the land, and cozy pigpens that absorbed warm sunlight — all while he, an ascetic Catholic, slept on the floor with an oak block for a pillow. At Walton Hall, birds could have sex in a starling tower that was cleverly hidden by tall yew-hedges, then raise their young on the lake where rowing was forbidden. What was so eccentric about that? But how else would you describe someone who once tried to persuade vampire bats to suck his toes as a means of bloodletting? Or who built a three-mile-long brick wall around his property to keep out poachers and their deafening guns, thereby establishing the first nature preserve in England?

Taxidermists knew Waterton as the fiery squire who pleaded with them to go outside and study animals in the wild. In this, he prefigured William Hornaday and Carl Akeley by nearly a century. Most other people knew him as the author of the Victorian bestseller *Wanderings in South America,* his remarkable, if discursive, account of his barefoot trek through Guiana, where he encountered the rarest, most colorful birds and beasts, which he killed and brought home. (The epilogue of the 1889 edition has a treatise on taxidermy.) Sometimes Waterton was an unreliable narrator, interchanging the names jaguar and tiger, chameleon and lizard, and puma and lion. But his vivid prose, painstaking mounts, and daring adventures—shooting deadly vipers, finding the curare used to poison arrow tips, and riding a thirty-foot caiman (perfectly safe if you avoid the teeth and tail)—provided Victorians with a glimpse of the marvelous unknown, a place they longed to see, if only from an armchair.

About taxidermy, Waterton said, "You must possess Promethean boldness, and bring down fire and animation, as it were, into your preserved specimen. Repair to the haunts of birds on plains and mountains, forests, swamps, and lakes and give up your time to examine the economy of the different orders of birds."

Waterton was antiestablishment in a way that is characteristic of all taxidermists—that is, he sided with animals over people, especially museum men, who tagged and labeled birds as if they were machine parts. Nothing depressed Waterton more than a beautiful bird badly mounted, something he called "a hideous spectacle of death in ragged plumage." His own birds blazed

with vitality, as they did in the jungle. No one could get a hummingbird's gorget to sparkle quite like Waterton. Yet even he
was capable of falsifying nature to make a point or stir up controversy. Take, for instance, his most famous mount — a "taxidermic frolic" — called the *Nondescript*.

In the early 1800s, whenever new species were brought back
to England, they were given two-part Latin names that typically
incorporated the name of the discoverer or the person who had
funded the expedition. Waterton despised binomial naming because it made the fascinating study of wildlife arcane and elit-
ist. To him, nothing was less truthful (or more self-serving) than
naming one of God's wonders after a person, especially if that
person was a rich collector or a hunter who knew virtually nothing about the species. He called binomial naming "pseudo-classical phraseology." Once, while flipping through a book of bird
plates with scientific names, he said, "I find that a hawk is called
the 'Black Warrier,' and that the Latin name . . . given it is 'Falco
Harlani.' Pray, who or what is 'Harlani'? A man, a mountain, or
a mud-flat? Is 'Black Warrier' a Negro of pugnacious propen-
sities?" His own system, called complimentary nomenclature,
used local names and characteristics to describe species. This
was a perfectly logical approach, except that Waterton made it
really confusing. Even his admirers had no idea what he meant
by names such as *Hannaquoi, Camoudi, Salempenta,* or *Coulaca-
nara,* each of which might refer to a bird, a plant, or a snake.

The *Nondescript* was even more perplexing. It was a hairy
little mannish ape that Waterton said he had procured in Guiana while hunting for specimens. The problem was that it was
just a head. Waterton had discarded the body in the jungle (too
heavy to carry), making it impossible to identify the riveting new
species. Eventually, he admitted making the *Nondescript* out of
two red howler monkeys that he had manipulated to resemble a

particular customs official. In the meantime, however, he used a picture of the *Nondescript* as the frontispiece of *Wanderings,* creating a buzz that kept the book in print for fifty years.

Waterton really liked only his own taxidermy, claiming that all other specimens were "wrong at every point." He refused to show any mount at his museum that he deemed inexact and unfaithful—which is another way of saying that he displayed only his own mounts. He snubbed every grand exposition.

That said, he was a good taxidermist—perhaps too good, for his taxidermy innovations, as heartfelt as complimentary nomenclature, were too tedious to spawn any followers. For Waterton, every feather, every strand of hair needed tending, a monotony for which he alone had the patience. His method for preserving quadrupeds for natural history cabinets was torturous. First he removed every claw and bone. Then he peeled off the entire skin and pared it down with a knife until it was paper-thin. Even the ears had to be split (inner and outer parts), treated, and seamlessly reassembled. He dispensed with all internal wires when mounting birds and used the treated skin alone, instead of the rag-and-sawdust method. He renounced arsenic. To anyone who found these methods mind-numbing, Waterton quoted Horace: "By laboring to be brief you become obscure." He obviously knew what he was doing, because nearly all his mounts, including the *Nondescript* (now at the Wakefield Museum), have survived, unlike his wearisome methods. A person would have to be insanely obsessed to actually rebuild a bird feather by feather. Yet in this, Waterman reminds me a lot of Emily Mayer.

Mayer is still racing around her house, putting clipboards, programs, and death masks and agendas into a box to take to the conference. I ask her what she is entering into the competition. "A dog in a suitcase," she says matter-of-factly.

She isn't joking. She explains with a steely empathy how over the years, she's seen plenty of dogs in suitcases. Someone's dog dies, and the owner, who has a parental attachment to the animal, can't bear to part with it. So the dog gets enshrined in a suitcase and is dropped off at the vet's with Mayer's phone number on it. Mayer's entry is a tiny erosion-molded terrier with closed eyes, set snugly in a small suitcase—an open casket of sorts. She calls the piece *Last Journey, Precious Cargo*.

Mayer joined the guild when she was nineteen and hardly misses a conference. This is her first one as chair, and I'm curious to see her in that role. A death-fixated anti-taxidermist who calls taxidermy "contrived" and "tedious" seems like the wrong person to lead the guild.

Mayer being Mayer, she has no intention of letting anyone call her "chair." Right after she accepted the post, she had a letter published in the guild journal renouncing the term. "I am two-legged and warm-blooded not four-legged and wooden," she explained. She also rejected "Chair Person" ("I deplore this kind of P.C."), and "Madam Chair" ("smacks of grey hair and tweeds"). "We are all of mankind so chairman is fine thank you. Chairbitch is OK too." This was Mayer's acceptance speech.

The two-hour drive from Mayer's house to Nottingham has innumerable roundabouts and T junctions; it's like driving a maze. Even so, Mayer can steer, smoke, and answer calls from Hirst's company, Science, simultaneously. Still, I keep thinking about an article I just read by a taxidermist who warned, "It is a known fact that when a taxidermist is driving a car at speeds of 50 mph-plus, the car often lurches to an abrupt and inexplicable halt. He then rushes from the car, sometimes running back 200 yards or more at high speed, and returns holding a dead bird." Luckily, we don't stop for roadkill and reach the Sutton Bonington campus at 4:30 P.M.

We check into a dormitory, which is next to the lecture hall where the conference is being held. I haven't stayed in a dorm since college, and I'm surprised by the musty smell and the grim sparseness of my room, with its faded curtains and bedspread and its fluorescent lights. On the bed is the room's single amenity, a disposable paper bathmat I'm supposed to bring to and from the showers—the communal block of showers I'll be sharing with forty British taxidermists for the next three days. Watching the small bed sink under the weight of my carry-on bag makes me long for the Crowne Plaza in Springfield, Illinois, with its sparkle and glitz, where the bathroom was mine alone and the closet could accommodate my evening gown.

We unpack and cut through the ivy-covered brick campus to register for the conference. I glance around for people carting stuffed pumas or grizzly bears, or perhaps an alligator packed in fake water. There isn't a hedgehog, a rook, or a stoat in sight. I think we are in the wrong place. Then Mayer leads me inside, where a disheveled man with the gruff, boisterous voice of a pirate (and the broken teeth and scraggly red beard to match) sits in a quiet hallway registering a woman's "bits and pieces" (a hare and a buzzard) into the juried competition. The man's name is Kim McDonald, and he is the guild's legal expert, the person whom Mayer relies on when she needs to know the legal status of, say, a tawny owl on eBay mounted before 1947 (legal) or a tawny owl mounted last month (a punishable crime). This area of the law is very complicated, because protected species vary from country to country, as do the fines. Although guild members are mostly good blokes who comply with CITES, some taxidermists do not. In fact, next to drug trafficking, animal smuggling is one of Britain's most persistent crimes.

British taxidermists have always had a fair share of forgers and smugglers among them, and over the years London's Metropolitan Police Wildlife Crime Unit has seized tens of thousands of endangered species being sold illegally as taxidermy, Chinese medicine, and luxury fashion accessories. One of the worst taxidermy crimes in recent history occurred in 2000, when London's best-known taxidermist, Robert Sclare, who runs the shop Get Stuffed in Islington, was charged with illegal possession of endangered wildlife. Sixty specimens were seized, including a stuffed tiger cub (less than a week old); tiger, leopard, wolf, and chimp mounts; gorilla skulls; an elephant foot and tusks; and rare lemurs and birds of prey. Sclare was found guilty on twenty-nine counts of permit forgery and twelve counts of illegally displaying animals. He was sentenced to six months in prison. When I told Mayer I wanted to visit the shop, she forbade me to do so, because that incident has given taxidermy a bad name.

Mayer stands in line, holding *Last Journey, Precious Cargo,* while the woman in front of her registers. "It's the first time I've done this," the woman says timidly. She needs to find a place to sleep, she says. "You can share a room with me," McDonald purrs, flashing a big, gap-toothed grin. Then he sends the woman upstairs to drop off her mounts for judging. When it's Mayer's turn, McDonald shouts with a brogue, "Bloody Chairbitch and you only bring one specimen! Go put a red dot on the *bloody* nose of your terrier!"

When the guild was established in 1976, taxidermy was floundering. It was an era of ecological awareness, and the big museums, having already plundered every jungle and ice floe for specimens, needed no more. So they began to ax taxidermy posts and shut down their workshops, sending their taxidermists off to find work at the big commercial firms, most of which were barely solvent, because hunting had dropped off, too. At the time, an American taxidermist passing through England called taxidermy a profession fraught with apathy and isolation. A group of British museum taxidermists, troubled by all this, got together and formed the guild.

In 1976, the guild may have had lofty ambitions, like those

of the World Taxidermy Championships, but the people trick-
ling into the hall now—museum, commercial, and amateur
taxidermists; people interested in modelmaking and natural
history; passionate ornithologists, lepidopterists, and skeleton
collectors; people who spend a great deal of time pondering
life forms—are exceptionally laid-back. (Had Charles Waterton
walked in here, I bet he would have preached fire and animation.) These people are, for the most part, Mayer's friends and
colleagues, people she relies on for specimens, reference, and
technical advice. At Hirst openings, Mayer is known as a taxidermist who is an artist; here she is known as an artist who is a taxidermist. She's known some of the guild members for more than
thirty years. They call her "wild," "artsy," and a bit "daft."

I think about all the changes Mayer must have seen since
she joined the guild in 1977: older museum taxidermists have
retired and died; younger taxidermists have quit taxidermy to
earn a living doing something else. Some of them are at the convention, including Derek Frampton, a former Natural History
Museum taxidermist who now uses his sculpting skills to make
props and robotic creatures for movies such as the Harry Potter series. He has also prepared study skins and dogs for Tring.
"Now I'm one of the senior members," Mayer says with a bitter-
sweet intonation. "At least they haven't kicked me out yet."

The turnout is low this year, only 40 out of 139 paid members (in 1990, the membership was nearly 300). Even so, the
group has a camaraderie that Mayer finds genuine and uplift-
ing. "I love the passion and the obsession—you know, the striv-
ing for," she says. "And I love the company." Because of this, and
because of the college campus, the show feels like a reunion. It
is as informal as a pub crawl. The ballot box is a plastic ice cream
container. The "trade show" is a trade stand (Jack Fishwick's artificial snow and resin icicles and a table of tanned pelts). The

nametags are totally unnecessary—everyone is chummy—but Mayer still growls, "Anyone without a badge is going to get a severe slapping!"

I wander around, listening. No one is talking about shoddy craftsmanship or how it's unnecessary to hunt animals for taxidermy—two topics that perennially come up at guild shows. Instead, I hear this:

"I've seen a bloke undress a girl with a bullwhip."

"I like a little pain."

"Her clothes were on with Velcro. She didn't have a wink on her. Most guys went up to inspect the body. You're talking twenty feet!"

While more people register, Mayer and I sit in the cafeteria, eating our dinner of lamb and potatoes. Unlike the WTC, with its religious revival overtones, there are no place mats with the NRA logo (indeed, many guild members oppose hunting, which in England primarily means foxes). No one says the Lord's Prayer. In fact, no one mentions taxidermy at all except to cancel tonight's slide show: "Given the late hour, we'll go to the bar and relax and have the slide show tomorrow."

The campus bar radiates blue like an aquarium. It has blue walls and blue tables and is lit with fluorescent sconces. It pulses with pop music—Sheryl Crow, the Rolling Stones. I find Mayer drinking pints with her mates, Jack Fishwick and her two assistants, Dave Spaul and Carl Church (both former welders). They exchange kisses, arms draped over each other's shoulders.

I pull up a chair next to Fishwick. The last time I saw him was at the WTC. He was wearing a baseball cap and binoculars and was almost arrested for birding too close to Lake Springfield's power plant. He told the cops, "You can't arrest me—I'm a judge!" They let him off. Taxidermy's British ambassador, Fishwick works for museums throughout Europe and judges international taxidermy competitions, where his ornithological expertise and unsparing critiques are legend. Even though he opposes hunting ("It's hard without a gun") and he believes that taxidermy is "not art," American and European taxidermists alike respect him (which for taxidermists, who are notoriously jealous, says a lot). Although I yearned to go back in time and watch herons (while reading Virgil) with Charles Waterton high up in a lofty tree, I was just as happy to be sitting here drinking pints with Fishwick. I love to listen to bird taxidermists describe birds, because their language is exacting and their observations are keen and passionate. Fishwick looks up, grinning, and says, "I've a tattoo of a ship on my stomach — see if you can find the mast." Riotous laughter erupts as I turn red and guzzle my beer, trying to regain my composure. The beer, however, gives me the courage to change the subject and ask Church and Spaul about Damien Hirst.

"He's cooked [dinner] for me!" says Spaul, beaming. "I get a big buzz out of just knowing that I've contributed to [his art]. I've signed it all — embedded in the plastic . . . It's just a big buzz!"

More people join us. Everyone is drinking pints. Mayer tells them that I'm a journalist writing a book about taxidermy, which puts me on edge. Taxidermists often distrust the press, and for good reason. They resent the media's morbid depictions and how the media tend to focus on unscrupulous taxidermists, such as Sclare of the Get Stuffed shop, rather than on those whose passion evokes that of the early naturalists, for whom taxidermy was a zoological tool. Because of this, I expect the conversation to become guarded. I am wrong.

These serious naturalists do not want to talk about the Linnean Society or Captain Cook's voyage in the *Endeavour*. Instead, they talk about their most bizarre jobs, and they play up all the blood and guts—something their American counter-parts would never do in front of a reporter. I'm surprised that they are being so explicitly gross around someone they've just met. I'm also surprised by my own reaction. Soon I'm laughing convulsively at stories I would have found repulsive a year ago: the menacing poodle made into a therapeutic rug to help rid a boy of his fear of dog bites; the man who asked to have his am-putated leg made into a lamp stand; the pickled terrier whose sunken eyes needed replacements. They chat about blindfolded taxidermy: eating the specimens!

The women are as raunchy as the men. Ruth Pollitt, then the National Museum of Scotland's skinner, is describing her job. "I do all of the measuring, pickling, tanning, and finish-ing of the study skins and some skins for exhibitions, from mice to elephants. I've worked on three thousand mammals in ten years," she boasts. This year alone, Pollitt has prepared 360 fe-lines for the museum's new Cats of the World Hall. That fact is astounding; I want to hear more. But Ruth is already on to an-other topic: the time she (and five others) skinned a giraffe in six hours. It was a highlight of her career as a skinner, and I sit with open notebook, eager to get it all down. But she's not talk-ing to me specifically; she's talking to the taxidermists in the room, two of whom work with her at the museum. So she says in-stead, with a huge grin, "Giraffes are very well-endowed." Loud laughter. My ears perk up.

Taxidermists can talk endlessly about animal genitalia, penis bones in particular. I was surprised to learn that certain mam-mals have bones in their penises, and taxidermists collect them as trinkets or curiosities. Even the Schwendemans and Mayer have raccoon baculums in their studios, which Mayer says are fertility talismans. (After the show, I gave a raccoon baculum to a friend who had unsuccessfully attempted in vitro fertilization, and she got pregnant the next month.) As it happens, in addition to penis bones, Pollitt collects testicles, kangaroo scrotums, and other sexual things. "I collect the testes. I put them on a metal tray and prepare them later. We keep the penis bones. We have a national penis collection. The National Penis Collection of Scotland," she says, pausing, everyone doubled over in laughter. "You have to watch your bollocks in that place!"

A sociologist might say that taxidermists are purposely lurid, because by making fun of themselves, it's somehow less hurtful when outsiders call what they do strange. I'm sure there's some truth in that, but I honestly think everyone in the bar that night was simply drunk and having a good time. And because most guild members get their specimens from natural death, that also eliminates the guilt factor. Still, I had made a great effort to come to England to attend this show so that I could learn something about taxidermy. I had high hopes of getting some real information the next morning at the death mask demonstration.

When I walk in, Peter Summers, a soft-spoken, self-effacing taxidermist with the National Museum of Scotland, is adjusting his latex surgical gloves. On the lab table to his right is a mangy black domestic cat—the demonstration victim. The method Summers is about to demonstrate is the one he's currently using at the museum for the Cats of the World Hall. Mayer, who hasn't done a death mask in fifteen years, will assist him.

Dressed in a black T-shirt with white handprints over her breasts, Mayer scans the place to see if everyone has arrived, then she introduces the competition judges. Everyone boos. Someone shuts off the lights, and Mayer sits in the dark, watching Summers through the holographic rolling-eyeball sunglasses. The first thing he does is deftly rub clay over the cat's face to flatten its fur. The idea is to capture a fresh imprint of its facial muscles. He says, "The next thing we're going to do is . . ."

"I'd reposition the *lips* now," Mayer interjects.

"I'd inject fluid into the *eyeballs* now," he continues.

He fastens a foam collar around the cat's neck to immobilize it while he skillfully drips plaster onto its face until it resembles a gargoyle.

"*Stop it!* Don't put any more on!" scolds Mayer.

"He's enjoying himself!" a taxidermist named Colin yells from the back of the auditorium. "No lumps in the plaster!"

"No one makes lumpy plaster but you, Colin!" Mayer shouts back.

"Peter makes lumpy plaster!"

Mayer reaches her finger into a jar of wave-and-groom hairdresser's wax that Summers is using as a separator (to keep the fur from sticking to the plaster) and works a little into her own spikes. Nobody is taking notes.

"I think it's dry," says Colin.

"It's *not*," insists Summers.

"You're making a mess," says Colin.

"Disaster!" says Summers with resignation. "I don't know what to say except sorry."

After the failed demonstration, Mayer's assistants, Church and Spaul, present slides from the WTC. I'm curious to hear a British perspective on an American show. They deliver.

Church: It's a big show and they take it very seriously. They're great people, but they haven't got a sense of humor, so I wouldn't joke with them.

Spaul: Food is cheap. Taxi's cheap. Go to Wal-Mart. I got really nice jeans for eight dollars. The bar is next to nothing. I gave up drinking for five years until I went there, and then I took it up again.

At the World Show, mammal judges use a checklist of 139 items to score a mount. Here things are far simpler and for a reporter an utter joy. The guild has one criterion for judging mounts: is it an acceptable standard?

Sable: yes.

Zebra: yes.

Sika: no.

In the end, Spaul wins Best Mammal, earning his accreditation (more important than a rosette because he has demonstrated that he can master the techniques established by the guild). Mayer takes second place with the dead terrier. Fishwick's kookaburra wins Best Bird and Best in Show. That night in the cafeteria, Mayer presents the awards in what can only be called a non-ceremony. "Your certificates are over there," she says flatly, pointing to a stack of loose papers. "Otherwise, it would take all night."

After dinner, Mayer says, "Happy drinking. See you at the bar." We all trudge to the bar. I'm starting to wonder whether I should have stayed at Mayer's house and read about taxidermy in the guild journal. As much as I love English beer, I hadn't come here for the pints. I had come to see if I could gain a deeper understanding of why people are drawn to taxidermy. I'm frustrated because the people in this room could provide insight into that question—if they are willing. I'm about to give up when someone points to a table near the bar, where a man with wavy silver hair, a long sharp nose, and piercing blue eyes is sitting nursing a pint. He has on a gray T-shirt and jeans, and in the blue glow of the blue bar, everything about him looks blue, including his skin. His name is David Astley, and he is one of the last living links to British taxidermy's glory days—and my last chance to connect the guild with the past. I grab my notebook, wander over to his table, and tell him about my research. He nods and invites me to sit down.

In the mid-1970s, before he was in the movie *The Great Rock 'n' Roll Swindle,* about the Sex Pistols, Astley was a taxidermist at Rowland Ward's, the firm established by England's most famous taxidermist (no relation to Henry Ward). Ward's mounted trophies for every elite hunter from Winston Churchill and British royalty to General Francisco Franco and a long list of movie stars. The firm also acted as an agent for museums and rich collectors, procuring polar bears, dugongs, and great auks (real and fake) for their dioramas and trophy rooms. Commercial firms such as Ward's flourished in England at the turn of the twentieth century. After World War I, however, only a few leading firms survived. Restrictions on the wanton slaughter of migratory birds, for instance, were starting to be imposed, feathered millinery was passé, and taxidermy was slumping. Ward's hung on until 1983.

Taxidermists often call Rowland Ward the British Carl Akeley. But if Akeley was Henry David Thoreau, Ward was Stephen King. He loved the sensation of the savage beast. His mounts were purposely terrifying. He had a gift for creating narrative tension by manipulating a predator's whiskers and spreading its paws to make the claws look like they could rip you to shreds. His open-mouthed snarl was peerless. From 1862 to 1890, Ward displayed groups of aggressive deer and leaping tigers (and a leopard poised to maul a dark-skinned toddler) at all the big European expos, where Victorians lined up to be shocked and entertained by his blockbuster thrillers. He died a rich man.

Ward called his London shop his "Zoological Studios" and "Gallery of Natural History." The public preferred "the Jungle." World-famous explorers, travelers, and sportsmen all gathered there to swap tales of stalking African lions or shooting Bengal tigers. In its heyday, Ward's received an order for sixty rhinos, dispatched during a single expedition.

Ward forbade photography in his shop (trade secrets, I as-

sume). His autobiography is incredibly scarce because he published only fifty copies himself. However, Pat Morris, the retired
University College London zoologist who would be giving the
guild show's closing lecture, spent twenty years gathering materials on Ward, which he wove together in a self-published monograph, *Rowland Ward: Taxidermist to the World.* And now seated
here in the bar is David Astley, an actual former Ward's employee.

In an old portrait, Ward, dressed in a long dark suit coat and
holding a craniometer and lion skull, looks professorial: the serious naturalist with stylishly tapered beard and mustache. Ward
quit school at fourteen to work at his father's taxidermy firm,
mounting bird illustrator John Gould's prized hummingbirds
and other famous specimens. At twenty-two, realizing the potential of tabloid taxidermy, he struck out on his own. His first
triumph was the McCarte lion, which killed its tamer in 1873.
Ward posed it in wounded agony, causing a sensation that would
launch his phenomenal career. Other effigy-like things followed.
He turned the hooves of Holocaust, the champion racehorse,
into inkwells, and rendered Cloister, another racehorse, into a
regal trophy head (now at the National Horseracing Museum).
London Jack, the dog that collected money for charity at Water-
loo station, was, after his death, stuffed and outfitted with bas-
kets to continue his benevolent duty. Lady Flora, the championship shorthorn cow, was a Ward mount, as was Brutus the circus
lion; Farthest North, an Eskimo dog Robert E. Peary took on his
foot expedition across Greenland; and, of course, the head of
Persimmon, King Edward VII's championship racehorse. Business was booming, and England never had to say goodbye.

In spite of the fetishism, Ward was considered a naturalist.
These were the days when taxidermy was taxidermy, no matter
what one had stuffed. A member of the Zoological Society of

London, Ward was granted the royal warrant "Naturalist, by appointment to his Majesty the King," which he used on his trade label to promote himself.

While Ward was establishing himself abroad, his firm was developing a prosperous sideline of animal furnishings. So imaginative was the firm that it is difficult to refrain from describing these accessories now. The firm turned crocodiles into umbrella stands, baby giraffes into high-back chairs (towering), and Siberian tigers into rugs. It made bowls out of lobsters, doorstops out of ostriches, garbage cans out of elephant feet, and inkstands out of rhino horns. Only at Ward's could a person buy "zoological lamps"—kerosene (later electric) lamps made out of eagles, owls, black swans, birds of paradise, and, on occasion, monkeys. Ward's elephant-foot liquor cabinets were especially popular with kings and rich hunters—rivaling even Rowland's brother Edwin's grizzly bear dumbwaiter (an upright grizzly holding a cocktail tray in its paws—an idea that Rowland would claim as his own). No one forged better great auks or dodos than Rowland Ward—or lied about them so convincingly. Surprisingly, the firm continued to turn rhinos and antelopes into ornamental bookends, lamps, and ashtrays up until the mid-1970s.

Ward died in 1912, but his studio thrived until the 1960s, when attitudes toward ecology shifted and orders such as the 365 tigers for His Highness the Maharajah of Cooch Behar dwindled, as did requests for "His" and "Her" elephant heads. When Kenya banned trophy hunting in 1977, the firm was doomed—and so was taxidermy.

By the time Astley arrived at Ward's, the firm—which once mounted lions by painstakingly removing and then implanting each whisker and eyelash individually, by hand—was sending out repair jobs with the glue still wet. Commercial taxidermy is never easy, but at Ward's it was becoming unbearable: low pay, long hours, sagging morale. "I got the sack for refusing to sweep the floor," Astley says, shaking his head. And so in 1983, Ward's shut down for good.

Today it's hard to find a former Ward's employee. Most of the people who worked for the firm are gone. They left no written records of their lives as taxidermists because, as Pat Morris suggests, they didn't think what they had to say about their profession was important. But here is Astley, and opportunity is opportunity, so I ask him to describe Ward's, and he's happy to oblige.

He lifts his head up from his pint, raises an eyebrow, nods, and begins to list several departments as if he's walking through them in his mind: elephant footstools, game heads, finishing work. Then he turns grave. I figure he's trying to retrieve the details; Ward's was, after all, England's most illustrious taxidermy firm. I glance down at my notebook to make sure I have plenty of blank pages. Then Astley starts to roll. He is bright-eyed and animated, a lively storyteller with a deadpan disposition. He speaks quickly, with increasing momentum. I'm not quite following what he's saying, but I write it all down anyhow, thinking it will make sense later, once I've had the chance to research Ward's myself back in the States. Astley launches into a long, discursive story about how the foreman of the big-head section threatened to murder him, as well as something he calls the passenger pigeon caper. (My notes are unintelligible and say only "fifty-pound ransom.") Astley talks and talks, and I scribble and scribble, hoping to uncover something substantial, until I realize that I've been writing for an hour or so about a deaf girl who worked near the Irish floor sweeper because she was immune to his drunken songs and who got too fat for the birdman and ended up dating the foreman of the big-head department, a liar and a petty thief, who soon left—as did Astley—for World of Nature.

As I walk back to my dorm room that night, I feel like a freshman who was just hazed. In the morning, someone pounding on my door jolts me out of a deep sleep. I climb out of bed, dizzy and disheveled, and crack open the door. It's the Chairbitch in her pajamas, a towel slung over her shoulder, heading for a shower with her colleagues. She tosses me my denim jacket (I forgot it at the bar), scrutinizes me, and growls, "Ugh! You look like something from out of a movie." Then she lets out a deep laugh that still haunts me today.

For all its frivolity, the guild show ends on a serious note: a lecture by Pat Morris, the leading authority on British taxidermy and, as it happens, a hedgehog expert.

Morris is tall, with thinning gray-blond hair. He looks stern, but he comes alive when he talks about taxidermy. He knows everything about the subject, and anyone who has ever seriously investigated the topic (doctoral students, curators, artists, historians, conservators) inevitably finds him, because his personal archive contains things that no one else in the world has — at least not all in one place. Sometimes he'll photocopy a deceased taxidermist's sketchbook for a library so that he won't have the only copy in existence. That doesn't mean he's exceptionally generous; he has a reputation as a shrewd barterer, using information as leverage to acquire mounts for his collection.

The guild is honored to have Morris as a member, and the other members sit in somber silence watching slides he has culled from his archive. What he shows us is essentially a history of neglect. For the first time in days, the guild members are silent — not a single wisecrack. Even Fishwick is quiet.

Mayer removes her sunglasses and watches as Morris shows mounts destroyed by natural causes (moths, beetles, sun); mounts ruined by accidents and fires; mounts dismantled because of "politically correct" museum policy; mounts bombed during World War II. He shows anthropomorphic foxes from the Great Exhibition of 1851, now sadly estranged from their historic context; distorted whales stored too close to hot boilers; and taxidermy collections quietly given away out of embarrassment, languishing in museum storerooms, or simply vanished. This is a taxidermy death knell.

It's also a fitting prelude to yet another loss, the auctioning off of Mr. Potter's Museum of Curiosities, an astounding collection of Victorian taxidermy. The auction is being held in two days, and the guild members are horrified to lose this "little bit of taxidermy history." No one is more aware of what the auction means than Morris. Victorian taxidermy is his area of expertise. In fact, he would have taught a course on the subject if interdisciplinary departments had been common early in his career, and if some of his colleagues didn't equate his passion for taxidermy with cruelty to animals. His love of taxidermy is actually an outgrowth of his deep appreciation for natural history, and he believes you cannot study the history of one without the other.

Morris has spent more than thirty years searching for old museum mounts. He asks how a museum could lose six upright polar bears or groups of fighting tigers. Where are these things? He's on the prowl for them. Sometimes he is bewildered by what he discovers. In the mid-1980s, for instance, he visited the Smithsonian Institution and found Hornaday's white setter on the scent of quail, called *Coming to the Point,* in the attic, on its side, dusty and forgotten. Unlike Hornaday's landmark baby elephant, at least it had surfaced, and Morris didn't have to wonder how a museum could misplace an elephant, of all things.

If given permission, Morris will go to extremes to authenticate a specimen. Once, in 1981, the dean of Westminster Abbey allowed him to x-ray the duchess of Richmond's three-hundred-year-old stuffed African grey parrot. He took the images in the crypt that contains the wax effigy of Lord Nelson, confirming that the parrot was indeed mounted using methods abandoned by the 1800s and therefore "one of the oldest surviving stuffed birds in existence."

Sometimes Morris's efforts are misunderstood, and he is called eccentric. However, not long after the guild show, the director of the Natural History Museum invited him to lunch, perhaps to placate him after the museum destroyed three Rowland Ward dioramas, works Morris considered the best they had in Britain.

And now he stands before Emily Mayer and the guild and says, "We're about to see another case of loss. On Tuesday and Wednesday of this week will be the auctioning off of Mr. Potter's Museum of Curiosities. The rumor is that quite a bit of this will go to America. This is a permanent loss to Britain, but so far no one has come forward to buy it *because it's taxidermy.*"

6

MR. POTTER'S MUSEUM OF CURIOSITIES

THE TRAIN FROM EXETER to Bodmin follows the English Channel past fishing hamlets and manor houses with seemingly endless hedgerows. On a sunny day, the jagged cliffs above the harbors live up to the region's nickname: the Cornish Riviera. But now rain and fog shrouded everything except the most colorful skiffs, and that was fine with me, because the weather seemed to come directly from the book I was reading, Daphne du Maurier's *Jamaica Inn*. The 1936 gothic romance, inspired by *Treasure Island*, compared to *Jane Eyre*, and adapted into a movie by Alfred Hitchcock (as were du Maurier's *The Birds* and *Rebecca*), seems to have defined Cornwall. Indeed, the Cornish still refer to the region as "Du Maurier Country," and looking out the train window at the dark sky moving in over the blustery moors, I could see why.

In writing the novel, du Maurier drew from Cornwall's history of wreckers and smugglers. She centered the book on Mary Yellan, a twenty-three-year-old "orphan" who moves to the Jamaica Inn, a gloomy old coach house, to live with her aunt Patience and uncle Joss. Joss, Mary soon learns, is the leader of a band of evil wreckers, who lure ships onto the rocky coast, kill the fleeing crew, and steal the cargo. One night she is forced to go on a run with them. The wreckers in the novel are sinister and cutthroat. The solitary inn is based on a real smugglers' tavern from the mid-1700s, which is now a resort that contains not only the tavern but other attractions, including Mr. Potter's Museum of Curiosities, my destination.

The Jamaica Inn is located on a barren moor, halfway down the Cornish peninsula, a promontory shaped like the bent, knobby finger of a witch. More than thirty thousand people visited the inn annually, a remarkable number given its isolation. They didn't all come to see taxidermy; most came to relive Cornwall's tangle with the wreckers, something the inn flaunts. On this day, however, dealers and collectors from all over the world were descending on the place for a two-day auction of what was billed as one of the most fascinating collections ever to come under the hammer. Nothing like Potter's would ever be available again: which is to say all kinds of sensational creatures preserved in glass domes and specimen jars, and great glass display cases, as well as the over-the-top anthropomorphic scenes for which Potter was famous.

One of England's oldest private museums, Potter's belonged to the era of the amateur nature lover, when museums were spirited jumbles, not the sober typologies they would become post-Darwin. Potter's verged on the freakish: random, cluttered, crammed to the rafters with curios and oddities, weird accumulations, and creatures that were stuffed, pickled, dissected, and deformed. And I was arriving just in time to see a world that had vanished long ago. The next day, it would be dismantled, and if the taxidermists at the guild show were right, this distinctly British collection of ten thousand artifacts (six thousand of which were taxidermy pieces) might be dispersed to America and Japan.

It was remarkable that Potter's had evaded the hammer this long. Nearly every museum of its kind — such as Charles Willson Peale's Repository for Natural Curiosities in Philadelphia, John Scudder's American Museum in New York, and Daniel Drake's Western Museum in Cincinnati (where John James Audubon briefly worked as a taxidermist) — had shut down years before. P. T. Barnum had bought Scudder's and Peale's museums in the 1840s and merged them into the Greatest Show on Earth. And Drake's Western Museum had morphed from a repository of stuffed birds, fish, and mammoth and sloth bones into a waxworks depicting Satan and other figures from hell. In England, William Bullock's London Museum of Stuffed Animals and the Lever Collection, both outgrowths of fabulous personal collections, had been auctioned off in the early 1800s. The Lever auction had drawn naturalists from every museum in Europe except the British Museum, which couldn't afford to buy the collection. The director of the British Museum wasn't going to make that mistake again; he was coming to the Potter's sale.

As the train neared Bodmin Parkway station, I reread du Maurier's description of the inn with uneasy anticipation:

> It was a dark, rambling place, with long passages and unexpected rooms. There was a separate entrance to the bar, at the side of the house, and, though the room was empty now, there was something heavy in the atmosphere reminiscent of the last time it was full: a lingering taste of old tobacco, the sour smell of drink, and an impression of warm, unclean humanity packed one against each other on the dark stained benches.

Then I exchanged du Maurier for the auction catalog. The cover featured a photo of a disfigured giraffe (circa early 1900s) with a gaping seam down its neck. State-of-the-art in its era, perhaps, the giraffe was oblong and distorted, as if someone had pulled its ears to stretch its face while it was drying. I discreetly slipped the catalog under my arm while I hailed a taxi, though I couldn't have been the only one with a copy of the catalog on the platform that day. According to Bonhams, the auction house in charge of the sale, more than a thousand catalogs had been sold.

The driver, a pleasant man with a Cornish accent, raised an eyebrow at the words "Jamaica Inn," and I felt like Mary Yellan when the coach driver tells her that respectable folk don't go there anymore. You could barely see three feet of the narrow road ahead, much less the green hilly farms it cut through, but the driver was a self-appointed Cornish ambassador, eager to show the sights to an American. "It would be lovely if you could see Cornwall, because it really is quite pretty," he said, squinting through the rain-streaked windshield.

That was an understatement. Cornwall's spectacular land-scape draws thousands of people every year. They come to see ancient stone circles, the Godrevy Lighthouse (which inspired Virginia Woolf's *To the Lighthouse*), and the Eden Project bio-spheres (the world's largest greenhouses), or maybe just to sit on a wharf sipping tea. But I was here to see taxidermy, and the driver did not hide his disgust.

"It was a Victorian thing," he said. "A bit gross, isn't it? A bit weird, don't you think? Those stuffed kittens in family scenes. Stuffed cats at the tea table."

I nodded sheepishly. The seventeen kittens at the tea table were nothing compared to the four-legged duckling with two beaks, three eyes, and four wings. I flipped through the cata-log, looking at the bizarre animals, each assigned a lot number. There was a pair of wandering albatrosses with ten-foot wing-spans (lot 308) and semihuman toads doing calisthenics (lot

167) — zoological wonders that would have delighted the Victorians — but I didn't bother to explain to the driver, thoughtful though he was, how crazy people were for this stuff back then, how the world was exploding with new discoveries and everyone wanted to live vicariously.

In 1861, for instance, the year Walter Potter displayed his first taxidermy case to the public, the French American explorer Paul Du Chaillu brought the first gorilla skins back to England, confirming the species' suspected existence and igniting what amounted to a gorilla craze. This was good timing because the public obsession with ferns was waning and the mania for aquariums hadn't yet taken hold. The revelations that tadpoles turn into frogs and leopards don't change their spots still riveted people's attention. Indeed, in 1861 it was still possible, if you absolutely had to, to squeeze all the known species onto Noah's ark — and that was fantastic.

We pulled into the Jamaica Inn. Rain streamed down the windshield and formed puddles in the gravel parking lot. A sign hung outside the entrance: "Come and absorb the atmosphere of a museum in Victorian times. Featuring the famous tableaux of Walter Potter, plus a murderous truncheon, a two-headed lamb, mummified creatures, the largest shoe in the world, a bird-eating spider, spittoons and opium pipes, a piece of the old London Bridge, a Victorian toy collection and LOTS, LOTS more." The driver shrugged and said, "It doesn't appeal to me whatever!" He pointed down the road toward Dozemary Pool, the spot where Sir Bedevere allegedly threw King Arthur's sword, Excalibur, to the Lady of the Lake. But at that moment, I was barely listening. I had stepped out of the taxi, my mind on Mr. Potter and his stuffed kittens.

Inside the Jamaica Inn, the Smugglers Bar, a dark slanty room that smelled like beer, was swarming with traders who knew one another from the antiques shops of London's Portobello Road. "We could have hired a coach," someone shouted. "There's a lot of money sitting here," another trader yelled, though you never would have guessed it from the scruffy people at the bar. But that was all camouflage, a strategy to downplay the seriousness with which some of the dealers went after their lots.

The collection, unusual as it was, wasn't nearly as eccentric as the people who knew every encyclopedic detail about it. People who knew, for instance, the complete history of Duplicate, the world-champion egg-laying Moray hen (she allegedly laid 462 eggs in one year). Or that the world-record 763-pound tuna (its massive glazed head was lot 571) had been reeled in after a nearly six-hour fight in 1933. Their business cards said it all: Ripley's Believe It or Not!, the Museum of Witchcraft, Ye Olde Curiosity Shop, Obscura Antiques & Oddities, Crime Through Time, and the Victorian Taxidermy Company. They were arriving en masse, in a downpour, and they were casing the joint with a complex mix of loss and schadenfreude, muttering, "How often does a Victorian taxidermy museum come up for sale?"

This was preview day. The next two days (September 23 and 24) were the actual auction. Yet television, newspaper, and radio reporters had already arrived in droves. Bonhams employees raced in and out of the coat-check room, now a makeshift office. They were prepared to take bids online; by phone, fax, or mail; through appointed agents acting for clients; and, of course, in person. People stood in line at the door, registering.

Not me. I knew that if I wanted to bid on, say, the scarlet ibis (I did!) or the bespectacled gentleman lobsters, I'd have to devise a clever strategy (a big distraction), and I wasn't about to go head-to-head with Ripley's Believe It or Not or Crime Through Time, not that *they* were after ibises or lobsters, per se, but someone in this room had to be. They hadn't come to this godforsaken place to leave empty-handed. Even so, in the commotion I heard, "That's all we do is sell stuff off. We don't value our own heritage."

Head auctioneer Jon Baddeley, specialist of all things "wild and wacky" (*T. rex* skeletons, Elton John memorabilia) and a regular on the BBC's *Antiques Roadshow*, was engaged in exotic problem solving: How to remove a one-ton elephant head from the first floor? Where to find a hotel with a helipad in quaint Cornwall? Was the rhino horn authentic? ("Absolutely!") A veteran with thirty-two years behind the podium, Baddeley called Potter's "one of the most unusual and eccentric collections ever to have been offered for sale." Yet, he said, despite phenomenal interest, no one had offered to buy the entire collection (for the owners' minimum price, reportedly £500,000, or roughly $800,000). With all the hype, I figured prices would be stratospheric. Baddeley said, "I sold an Alfa Romeo last week for five hundred fifty thousand pounds in ninety seconds. I've got to work harder tomorrow."

The inn was as dark and rambling as du Maurier's description, and its proud claim of ghosts seemed plausible. In the official souvenir guide, various specters, including that of murder victim Charlotte Dymond (d. 1844) and a dead man returning to finish his half tankard of ale, howl in the wind or walk through the cold walls of the du Maurier Restaurant. On this day, however, the only ghost likely to materialize was the taxidermist responsible for all this zaniness: Mr. Walter Potter.

Potter was born in 1835 in Bramber, Sussex, where his parents owned the White Lion Inn, a well-known hostelry. As a young man, Potter dropped out of the village school to work at the inn, eventually saving enough money to pursue his main passion in life: taxidermy. He began humbly enough with his deceased pet canary, followed by a family of his pet albino rats (lot

93), before advancing to dogs, cats, and common English birds. Soon Potter's parents gave him a loft above their stable to use as a workshop. But what to do with all those stuffed cuckoos, bramble finches, and nightingales?

Potter considered himself primarily an artist but was known as a naturalist, a term that covered a lot of ground in the early 1800s. Anyone who wanted to be a naturalist—from Charles Darwin to the lowly weekend egg hunter—was a naturalist. All you did was declare yourself one. Degrees were unnecessary; indeed, natural history wasn't even formally taught in school until the 1880s. Though by mid-century people had begun to specialize and call themselves botanists and zoologists, natural history was still the preoccupation of the passionate amateur driven by blind curiosity, and therefore it tended to be romantic and idiosyncratic—just like Potter's museum.

Eventually, Potter was able to support himself as a commercial taxidermist. However, stuffing dogs and cats for Victorian parlors would never satisfy his creative impulse. That would happen only after the Great Exhibition of 1851. Held in London's Crystal Palace, the fair celebrated progress: engineers, artists, and, of course, taxidermists displayed their finest work for a curious public hungry for science. If Potter attended (very likely), he would have seen the dramatic realism of Newcastle ornithologist John Hancock's gyrfalcons in action poses. His raptors captured the "jizz" (a birding term that means the general impression and shape), a significant breakthrough. Some displays audaciously featured "group mounts" of several animals posed together—a bit too much art and real estate for British museums. But nothing thrilled more than the taxidermic adaptation of Goethe's fable *Reinecke the Fox,* a comic depiction of the fable reenacted with semihuman foxes. As ridiculous as foxes dressed as small people may sound, the painstaking care Herrmann

Ploucquet of the Royal Museum in Stuttgart had used to manip-ulate his foxes' facial expressions raised the taxidermic bar, and the Victorians, always mawkish, were smitten. They loved Plouc-quet's foxes. They gazed at them for as long as the crowd al-lowed. Indeed, they felt "indebted" to Ploucquet and his clever foxes, which overpowered just about every other taxidermic dis-play at the Crystal Palace that year—except, of course, for an-other of his entries, a frog shaving another frog, a display that Queen Victoria herself found amusing.

Known (without irony) as the grotesque school, Plouc-quet's style became very popular, as taxidermists henceforth transformed animals into little humans: crows playing the vio-lin, squirrels as Romeo, kittens at the gristmill, and frogs doing all sorts of things—sitting for a portrait; lying in a hammock; doing the cancan; and dressed as barbers, longshoremen, ped-agogues, drum majors, duelists, bootblacks, King Lear, and, of course, taxidermists. Montagu Browne's famous late-nine-teenth-century manual *Practical Taxidermy* has a section devoted entirely to "mirth-provoking characters." His advice is succinct: use frogs. His second choice is monkeys: "not half so funny" and more cumbersome to mold.

After the exhibition, taxidermy blossomed. Professional col-lectors and taxidermists had finally overcome some of their ear-lier technical blunders, and it became easier to preserve natu-ral things. The ranks of professional taxidermists soared. More taxidermists meant more information, published in all sorts of pamphlets and manuals, which were widely read. Taxidermists began to model clay under skins to replicate muscles, folds, and wrinkles, and their mounts, though still gross approximations, became, if not lifelike, frightfully alive. Upright grizzly bears flaunted claws as long as tusks and fang-filled snarls; "roaring" lions had bubblegum pink gums and impasto tongues. "The days of birds on 'hat-pegs' stiff-legged long-necked and staring round-eyed, at nothing . . . [have] passed away forever; and only in dreary museums, far behind the age, where funeral silence obtains, and where the dust of mummified animals rises to awe and half poison the adventurous explorer, are these 'specimens' to be found," declared Browne.

Soon every middle-class home had an ornamental mount on display. Tailors and milliners regularly sought out the local taxidermist for feathers or whole birds to incorporate into their wares. Even certain hairstyles incorporated stuffed humming-birds. Eventually, a whole subeconomy of trade-skin dealers and wildfowlers sprang up, which served taxidermists by offering hundreds of thousands of skins for sale at auction and at Lead-enhall Market in London. The price list in a 1904 taxidermy manual shows that every living species had potential as home décor, including the ivory-billed woodpecker and the passenger pigeon, which may help explain their eventual demise.

By 1880, every town in England could support a part-time taxidermist, and taxidermists began to specialize to distinguish themselves. Rowland Ward became known for savage trophies, pets, and fake dodos; Peter Spicer for fox masks; John Cooper for fish.

Here's how Potter started. In 1854, three years after the Great Exhibition, Potter, barely twenty, was flipping through his sister's hand-colored book of nursery rhymes, *Peter Parley's Present*. In it, he discovered an illustrated version of the popular poem "The Death and Burial of Cock Robin" and in a burst of passion knew what to do with his storehouse of British birds. (The story in a nutshell: Cock Robin is struck with an arrow, bleeds to death, and is buried by his animal friends, who mourn the great loss.) Seven years later, Potter exhibited *Cock Robin* at the White Lion Inn, causing a sensation. The five-by-six-foot mahogany case contains ninety-eight British birds in a reenactment so fastidiously rendered that a few feathered friends actually shed glass tears. The bereaved birds walk in a sorrowful cortege through a tiny graveyard and up a sloping path toward Bramber Castle and Church. (Potter often painted local scenes as backdrops.) Every character is here: the parson, the clerk, the sparrow who shot the fatal arrow, the fly who watched him die, the fish who caught his blood in his dish, the beetle who made the shroud with his needle, the dove (chief mourner for his love), and the bull as bell toller, because, of course, the bull can pull. Three pall-bearing robins stand near the tiny blue coffin, while a cuckoo, a nightingale, a goldfinch, a hawfinch, and a bramble finch mourn in the treetops above, "a-sighing and a-sobbing when they heard the bell toll for poor Cock Robin."

From then on, Potter was besieged with commissions to stuff deceased pets, and he never had to work as a plumassier (someone who works with plumes), or a natural history agent (a purveyor of egg drills, entomological collecting tins, botanical papers, and other collecting supplies), or, oddly enough, a hairdresser—all jobs Victorian taxidermists listed on their trade labels to supplement their incomes. But stuffing other people's dogs and cats (quite a few are in the museum) did not satisfy him. And so, thanks to the fame of *Cock Robin*, he began to create other taxidermic masterworks, starting with the nursery rhymes *The Babes in the Wood* and *The House That Jack Built* and ending his career with the feline extravaganza *The Kittens' Wedding* (twenty kittens in black morning suits and cream-colored brocade dresses attend the nuptials of a dashing bewhiskered couple).

The attention to detail is insane. In *Rabbits' Village School* (lot 44), forty-eight newborn rabbits, each with its own writing slate, sit in an 1888 schoolhouse. A group of lapine scholars practices penmanship using inkwells Potter cut out of chalk (a rabbit cries when he blots his book); a female schoolmistress teaches her young rabbit girls how to knit (one bunny has turned the heel of a sock); a naughty bunny attempts to cheat off his neighbor, who is furiously working out a math equation, while the master checks another bunny's sums; and the little scholars learn about the Westminster Bridge as one eager bunny in the back waves his paw, hoping to be called on.

Potter had a dry wit. Most of the tableaux mock and mimic Victorian society or contain subtle jokes. In *The Kittens' Wedding*, the feline parson has his prayer book open to the wrong page, and a male guest sits in the back of the church, scowling at the bride's choice of groom. In *The Guinea Pigs' Cricket Match*, the band strikes up a song; one guinea pig musician can't tear himself away from the game, and the furry little conductor seethes on hind legs.

Potter wasn't a traveling or field naturalist who left insular England to find exotic new species on other continents. He never strayed far from home. His pleasures were simple, his habits metronomic. He loved to garden and was warden of Bramber Church. Every night he wandered into the inn's bar at precisely 9:50 P.M. for his daily pint.

In a circa 1880 postcard, a dapper but baggy-eyed Potter sits outside his museum, now a quaint stone cottage across the street from his house. He has a hooked nose and a bushy white mustache that extends below his chin in two long columns, and he's wearing a boater (a stiff straw hat). Lush foliage surrounds the museum, the arched front door is flanked by two flower-filled urns, and a sign above the windows says OPEN DAILY.

In his lifetime, Potter stuffed innumerable English birds and the occasional tusked rabbit (lot 462), but his raison d'être and the museum's main draw was his anthropomorphic tableaux.

Potter died in 1918 at age eighty-two, having seen British taxidermy rise to its pinnacle of popularity and then fall to its near-deepest depths. By 1914, after industrialization and hunting had resulted in the near extinction of numerous species and the destruction of their habitats, people stopped collecting. Taxidermy was unfashionable; only the big firms, such as Rowland Ward's and Edward Gerrard and Sons, survived. In addition, natural history in general no longer belonged to the passionate amateur (to which taxidermists have always belonged) but instead had become the exclusive domain of the specialist (scientists, curators, and "concept people"). Taxonomy was the guiding principle museums used to organize their zoological collections; evolution was transforming everything. And to be a taxonomist, or any scientist for that matter, required training and expertise. Although these changes were necessary for science to progress, they kind of spoiled the fun, at least from a Victorian perspective. By the end of the nineteenth century, as Lynn Barber notes in her fabulous book *The Heyday of Natural History*, museums would become (more or less) like they are today: highly specialized and rigorously organized, with collections so vast and varied that they couldn't all possibly be shown to the public. So the layperson was barred from the inner sanctum. As Barber eloquently puts it, "Once the heart is hidden away, a museum's public rooms begin to seem rather lifeless—in Victorian terms—vulgar, rather than rational amusement." Only at places like Potter's could one experience nature as if through a kaleidoscope.

When Potter died, the museum passed to his daughter Minnie Collins, then to his grandson Walter Collins, who kept it alive despite the fact that many other taxidermy collections went on the market in the 1930s or were destroyed in bonfires. When Walter Collins died in 1972, the museum was sold to Anthony Irving, founder of the House of Pipes, which is how it acquired its

opium pipes and spittoons. The museum was resold the same
year and moved briefly to Brighton (next to the Palace Pier)
and then to Arundel in Sussex, where it was set up in a mock-
Tudor house.

In 1986, the museum was for sale again, and Jamaica Inn
owners John and Wendy Watts bought the entire collection and
moved it to the inn. They spent the next seventeen years restoring
the collection, supplementing it with mounts preserved by other
Victorian taxidermists. (Gerrard's wrinkly, walleyed trophies—a
black rhino head, a tiger, a polar bear, a lion, a puma, and a giraffe—fill an entire wall.) Back in yet another inn, Mr. Potter's
Museum of Curiosities looked implausibly unaltered.

Now the Wattses had decided to retire and let their son,
daughter, and son-in-law run the inn. That was the reason for
the auction. This new generation of owners appreciated Potter's
taxidermy but wanted more space for bedrooms, christenings,
and wedding receptions. "If someone wanted to have a wedding
here today, we couldn't do it because we are fully booked," explained Kevin Moore, the Wattses' son-in-law, at lunch that afternoon in the timber-beamed du Maurier Restaurant. "Something had to go."

At first the Wattses tried to keep the collection intact by selling it as a single entity. They advertised it to all the national museums and on numerous Internet sites, hoping that the Victoria
and Albert Museum (V&A), which featured *The Kittens' Wedding* in its 2001 exhibit "The Victorian Vision: Inventing New
Britain," or some other big museum would step in and buy the
core cases. Moore gave eleven radio interviews in the United
States, Canada, and England. CNN and NBC both covered the
sale, along with, of course, the BBC and dozens of British publications, including the *Spectator, National Post, Times, Daily Telegraph, Independent, Financial Times,* and *New Statesman.*

"We tried to sell it as a complete unit, but we didn't get one offer," Moore said. "We didn't see the Natural History Museum or the British Museum. No correspondence from the V&A. We would have been happy with that. We probably would have accepted a reasonable offer . . . in order to keep it all together." At this point, Moore turned a bit flush. "Figures have been kicked around by the press but not by us."

The Death and Burial of Cock Robin had the highest presale estimate: £5,000 to £7,000. Everyone wondered who would buy it. Would *Cock Robin* actually leave the public view? Would it leave Great Britain for the first time in 142 years?

Pat Morris had arrived the day before to lend support to the Wattses, who were understandably nervous, wondering if perhaps it was a mistake to break up a collection that they had rescued from a similar fate. The guild members said it was an honor to attend the auction with Morris, and I did feel privileged to tour the place with someone who had served as an adviser to the museum and had spent decades collecting, archiving, and researching Victorian taxidermy. Morris was famous here; the Bonhams press release described him as "a leading authority on taxidermy in the U.K."

Morris led me up a narrow staircase and into the museum, where we vanished into a compartmentalized version of the natural world. I followed him through a maze of crooked corridors packed with hundreds of domed birds, each more vibrant than the next. Tropical butterflies pinned to boards like patterned wallpaper, jars of zoological horrors floating in spirits the color of Kool-Aid, and fantastic typologies of hawkmoths and minerals and sea horses and nautilus shells covered every surface. Horns and trophies lined the walls and rafters. Birds with outstretched wings too huge for domes hung down from the ceiling.

Just about every craze I had read about (and plenty of others) was represented in this room, each some obsessive attempt to understand—or, really, to accumulate—the natural world. Spiders, scorpions, and corals; dragonflies, African beetles, and migrating monarch butterflies—all were meticulously arranged in glass cases like rare jewels. Floating in jars of spirits were dissected frogs, grass snakes, a porcupine, a sea mouse, and a lungfish. There was a bisected rabbit head and a kitten with two bodies. I couldn't believe you could actually buy this stuff, but you could. And people would, the next two days.

Victorians may look uptight in photos, but they flocked to tidal pools to collect sea anemones, shot and stuffed owls, foraged for ferns for fern albums, robbed nests of eggs for oology cases, and netted butterflies and pinned them to corkboards. Each year came some exciting new fad.

All these marvels existed at Potter's in one form or another. Random and cluttered, lacking wall text and any open space at all, Potter's was the exact opposite of the Smithsonian. I wondered whether contemporary museums had perhaps become too scripted ("Come Meet Your Relatives!") or whether I was enjoying something here at Potter's that I was supposed to be too sophisticated to enjoy. If I ignored some of the conspicuous add-ons (tribal weapons and military memorabilia), it was possible to envision England as a nation of self-taught naturalists. The power of these relics to prompt the imagination was as strong today as it had been 150 years earlier, and I kept asking myself how that was possible.

Normally, Morris has a measured walk and a serious demeanor. In here, he grinned like a kid, and his gait had some spring in it. He'd been in here hundreds of times, and I could see why. To be surrounded by the "freaks and fancies of nature" (Charles Waterton, 1825) was incredible. It's hard to stay composed when surrounded by curiosities that are horrific and beautiful at once.

There was a "reverse taxonomy" to it, a randomness that was

both naive and playful. Victorian bird mounts, Morris noted, were often formed with near-total disregard for ornithological exactitude, and birds from three different continents were often grouped together to show off their colors and plumage, as opposed to their species relationship. Distorted and often mounted without support wires in their legs, these domed creatures did not convey a bird's real anatomy. A group of Potter's Australian and South American birds, for example, resembled Christmas tree ornaments, with bodies unnaturally bent at the neck and outstretched wings resembling the fans of a flamenco dancer.

By the mid-1800s, serious ornithologists grouped complete bird families together as a sort of three-dimensional field guide. The great hall at Calke Abbey in Derbyshire, for instance, has extraordinary bird cases filled with gannets, auks, puffins, owls, hawks, ducks, pheasants, and species likely to be seen near the estate. However, your average Victorian—the type of person likely to visit Potter's—wasn't interested in a scientific investigation as much as an exotic escape from his drab existence. Yet Victorian enthusiasm for nature was a serious hobby, a passionate pursuit.

This might explain the odd pairings. They weren't haphazard—Potter was as purpose driven as any Victorian—but his gift for merging spectacle with science to entertain his customers was superior. Thus the seal cub with the greater kudu skin and elephant soles; the beagle head with the lamb skeleton; the two-faced kitten with the goldfinch and immature flycatcher. I couldn't quite wrap my mind around Potter's *Californian Curiosities:* a horned toad, a tarantula, a scorpion, a centipede, a deformed calf head, and, of course, ostrich and springbok skins (lot 130). But the magic of this place was that I didn't have to. For all the Victorians' moralizing, nothing in here was didactic. The whole point was to marvel.

"He collected freaks!" one trader gasped, astonished by one of Potter's deformed specimens. "You won't see this again!" another dealer said, racing from case to case.

Potter was fascinated by freaks. He got them from a local farmer. We encountered his two-faced puppy with three eyes and two mouths; his two-faced kitten with four eyes, two faces, and two mouths; his three-legged duckling (with, of course, a corncrake and a starling) — all mounted in the late 1800s at the end of his career. The Victorians loved the distorted and the macabre; unwrapping mummies and public dissections were popular forms of parlor entertainment. So, apparently, do we.

The more ghastly the specimen, the larger the pre-auction crowd. Nothing drew more people than the Siamese twin fetal piglets in lime green formaldehyde. I edged over for a closer look. Two pink snouts (or was it a single snout with four nostrils?) were pressed against the bell-shaped glass in surreal symmetry. Four shriveled pink legs were crammed into the jar's base. Rumors circulated that prop seekers for the Harry Potter films were after the conjoined swine, and the tension mounted among traders who lusted after only the pickled piglets. Factions were forming. They sized up each other's reserves. They walked past the Siamese swine feigning indifference.

Thankfully, except for a mummified hand, the museum had no human specimens. It sounds crazy, but the Victorians did preserve people. According to a *New York Times* article about "El Negro" (an African man preserved in the 1830s by two French taxidermists, displayed in a Spanish museum, and then buried in Botswana in 2000), human preservation was not uncommon: "To stuff and exhibit a dead person, one taxidermist advised . . . 'it is necessary to make a circular incision around the fingertips and peel back the skin as if it were a glove.'" One preserved human is the British economist and philosopher Jeremy Bentham (1748–1832), who donated his body to University College London. This is Morris's old haunt. Morris called the specimen "Old Bentham" and said that I could find him seated in a chair in a big armoire in the main building of the South Cloister—except for his head, which was replaced with a wax replica after some students played soccer with his real head (at least according to the guards who unlocked the armoire for me). His real head is taken out only for ceremonial dinners, to satisfy the clause in the economist's will requiring his presence at such events.

Although Potter's freaks sent shivers down his guests' spines, the anthropomorphic scenes delighted them. Morris smiled drolly when he came upon Potter's tableau *The Happy Family* (lot 55), a zoological fantasy for sure. Here Potter created in taxidermy what you'd never see in a forest: barn owls and a falcon adoringly watch mice play; a cat (a robin perched on its head and a mouse on its back) reclines with a dog under a shady tree; a rabbit cuddles with a stoat. The scene is cloyingly sentimental and surreal, but what it lacks in realism, it makes up for in heartfelt affection.

I still hadn't seen *The Death and Burial of Cock Robin,* and Morris and I squeezed through the crowd to find it. The case is huge, far bigger than I had imagined, and utterly filled with birds. It is dazzling. Seeing *Cock Robin* in person is a lot like viewing a famous painting that you have only seen in photographs—the *Mona Lisa,* for instance. Up close, the avian mourners look pitiful. The owl (spade in talons) seems particularly distressed by seeing the vandalized bones of one of Cock Robin's relatives.

I felt like a schoolgirl gazing into Lord & Taylor's Christmas windows: how easy it is to become lost in these glass-encased wonderlands. I tried to burn it all into my memory, because there'd be no second viewing. But when I remembered that I was looking at birds at a funeral, which is really very silly and morbid at the same time, I quickly moved on.

Squirrels are something I know something about because I see them all over New York City, but I had never seen squirrels drinking port or dueling to win the affection of a female squirrel. Potter's squirrels drink booze. They smoke cigars. They gamble and play cribbage.

I wandered over to *The Upper Ten* (aka *The Squirrels' Club*) and its companion piece, *The Lower Five* (or *The Rats' Den*). Potter chose the names, which come from a popular Victorian song, to show how aware he was of his era's rigid class distinctions. *The Upper Ten* is a Victorian men's club where squirrels drink port and play poker in a dollhouse of decadence. Things are far cruder in *The Lower Five,* where fifteen large brown rats ("the riff-raff") smoke and gamble in a ramshackle public house; a rat bobby in hat and cape has burst in to interrogate the rodents. I laughed out loud, knowing the British traders wouldn't mistake my laughter for politically incorrect glee. Instead, I was sure they were sizing me up as part of the competition.

Each case took years to make, and that's because Potter was an uncompromising taxidermist, especially when it came to coat color. When the exact right skins did turn up (red squirrels from nearby Winston Park; kittens from Wards Farm in Henfield; rabbits from a breeder in Beeding; rats supplied by old stuffed Spot, Potter's dog [lot 238]), he'd replace his cardboard templates with actual fur. Morbid as this process may sound, a 1977 museum catalog says that he never killed anything specifically for the museum, though a nearby farmer periodically killed large litters of kittens and gave Potter first dibs. Interestingly, Potter banned black cats (dead or alive) from the museum because they were associated with witchcraft.

An artist who visited Potter's as a child had returned for the auction. He peered at the squirrels, overwhelmed by the strange hold they had on him. "All that beauty and horror—how you really love it and are repulsed by it at the same time," he said, shaking his head without taking his eyes off the case. The fact that the players were squirrels or kittens mattered little to Potter or to other Victorians, who affectionately imbued animals with human characteristics (pathos, humor) without irony or detachment. Imagine Beatrix Potter, for example.

In *The Postmodern Animal,* an academic book about animals in contemporary art, Steve Baker describes the exact opposite condition: *anthropomorphophobia,* a fear of being overly sentimental about animals. In fact, he uses the term to describe Emily Mayer, because artists need critical distance to maintain an edge. Victorians would have scoffed. For them, anthropomorphism was good and rational, the most pious way to identify with God's creatures. To see oneself as separate from nature, now *that* was something to be afraid of!

Nevertheless, at the guild show, Phil Howard, a taxidermist with the National Museum of Scotland, had told me that because Potter's humanistic mounts were something *beyond* nature, they trivialized taxidermy and contributed to its tawdry reputation. He's not alone in that belief. Many sane people find kittens dressed as tiny brides vile and exceedingly strange (in fact, it feels ridiculous discussing them now). For Victorians, however, attributing human characteristics to animals was a form of endearment. They were obsessed with knowing, for instance, whether animals were happy. They wanted to discuss the very goodness of animals. For Morris, the transference of human characteristics onto birds and mammals is "the basis for much of what we recognize as the British love of animals."

I wandered around, as disturbed by the two-faced lamb as I was captivated by the dealers sizing it up. "It's a shame that [the collection is] being broken up, because we're never going to have the opportunity to see it again," one trader remarked. And in the next breath: "But there's plenty to go around. We don't intend to go home empty-handed." Downstairs, auctioneer Roger Tappin registered Peter Blake (the artist who designed the Beatles' *Sgt. Peppers Lonely Hearts Club Band* album cover) and dozens others. During the lulls, Tappin was composing lines to "sing" for each lot. The pitch style the auctioneers used to sell the Alfa Romeo the week before, for instance, would never move the 111-pound conger eel (lot 252). This one was catchy: "The wandering albatrosses will fit onto the roof rack." "There's a good one for the lion," he said, grinning. "But you'll have to wait until tomorrow. An auctioneer always tries to save some of his gold."

Nearby, head auctioneer Jon Baddeley was in between television interviews when I went up to him and repeated the words of the trader upstairs: "It's a shame that it has to be broken up." I tried not to sound indignant.

"Collections are living things," he explained. "All these things will end up in international museums and institutions. As you break up one collection, you form other collections."

The phone rang and rang, people asking if Bonhams was prepared to handle the complicated transactions that are required when endangered species cross international borders. In England, any specimen collected before 1947 is considered an antique and can be freely bought and sold within the United Kingdom (although some species such as parrots require special licenses). But in the United States, the same species can't be traded without proper certificates, permits, and inspections administered by the U.S. Fish and Wildlife Service. Species protected under the 1900 Lacey Act, the 1918 Migratory Bird Treaty Act, and the 1973 Endangered Species Act are scrupulously monitored by Fish and Wildlife Service agents, and an extensive paper trail and inspections are required for every importation. For instance, whereas magpies are like rodents in England, in the United States they are protected species, which can't be traded. The same rigorous laws used to prevent animal smuggling apply to 125-year-old antique specimens. Nearly six months after the auction, several Potter cases arrived in Port Elizabeth, New Jersey. They were transported to a bonded warehouse in Kearny, New Jersey, where Fish and Wildlife Service agents dismantled them, confiscating several illegal specimens (a loon, a snipe, and others). After a complicated process of signed wavers, ownership of the birds was transferred to the U.S. government.

Emma Hawkins, a dealer of "all sorts of wonderful things," mostly Victorian taxidermy, arrived at the Jamaica Inn from Edinburgh, Scotland, and had a look around on preview day. She needed to inspect the condition of items (mostly the large tableaux) before she committed herself to certain lots for her clients. The dealers who buy and sell taxidermy for other people provided me with yet another perspective of this eccentric world. On the one hand, they seemed to recognize the historic value of the collection. On the other hand, they were most eager to buy and sell it off. Still, I was grateful to hook up with Hawkins, because she was meeting two hard-core taxidermy dealers that night to strategize over dinner, and she invited me to join them.

A year earlier, Hawkins had heard that Potter's was for sale, and she offered the Wattses a significant sum for the entire collection. She wanted to relocate Potter's to Edinburgh and had a building in mind in which to house and maintain it, but her offer wasn't accepted. Hawkins typically avoids auctions, but Potter's was unique. According to Christopher Frost's *A History of British Taxidermy*, 95 percent of all taxidermic mounts from the Victorian era have disintegrated or are of poor quality: motheaten, lumpy, scraggly, threadbare. Potter's mounts, preserved with a secret arsenical formula that died with Potter (typical!), hadn't lost a patch of hair or feathers. They were, in the rarified world of taxidermy collectors, remarkable.

"To have and to hold," she chirped, a British Holly Golightly. At thirty-one, Hawkins was far younger than the seasoned traders at the Smugglers Bar, but she posed a serious threat because of her unusual tastes, shrewd tactics, and ample resources. "I won't drink tonight so I can keep my eye on the ball," she said without the hint of a smile. Hawkins learned the art of the deal from her father, a jeweler. She discovered the love of taxidermy at home, under a horse-hoof candelabra. Her grandfather was a big-game hunter, and over the years her relatives have given her taxidermy as gifts: at twelve, a giraffe head and neck from the 1890s ("I still have it, and it's in fantastic condition!"); at fifteen, a polar bear head on a shield (to hang above her bed). Ever since she was a child, she has seen the "true delight" in taxidermy.

Typically, when Hawkins shows up at a client's door, the person is expecting "a mad old woman on the verge of death," not a vivacious brunette with a Prada handbag, a silver necklace strung with seashells, and gold Chinese slippers. "Everybody thinks I'm strange," she said. "I prefer to be strange than normal. I saw a card once that said, 'I was normal until it drove me crazy.'"

Hawkins scanned the museum, annotating her catalog. Then we climbed into her red Mercedes van and drove to Fowey, the nautical village where Daphne du Maurier lived and wrote. The drive wound past picturesque harbors and lush rolling hills. For Hawkins it was all beside the point. She was meeting Errol Fuller, author and illustrator of books on extinct and rare birds, and Rob Chinnery, owner of the Victorian Taxidermy Company in Leamington Spa. When we arrived in Fowey, I found the last vacancy in town—in a guesthouse run by a red-bearded man with a red ponytail, who resembled one of du Maurier's Cornish wreckers. When he opened the door, he had a live parrot on his shoulder, a shocking sight after so many days among dead things.

Hawkins checked into the Marina Hotel on the wharf and began riffling through her Bonhams catalog, frenetically writing notes in the margins as she called clients to confer. She had a strategy. It involved her fiancé, who was on telephone standby in Edinburgh. The plan was simple: She'd bid at the auction until her lots reached the price she and her fiancé had agreed on beforehand. When the price climbed above that, she'd set down her paddle, and he'd take up the bidding remotely by phone. Hawkins would watch from the sidelines, feigning a lack of interest. The strategy, fairly common among serious auctiongoers, requires a poker face. Hawkins has one with dimples.

Whereas Hawkins was here to purchase taxidermy for clients with unusual tastes, Fuller was motivated by his own obsessive habit. Fuller has been collecting Victorian taxidermy since he was fifteen. His house is crammed with taxidermy cases, dinosaur fossils, and prehistoric skulls. There's practically no room to walk. Some of his treasures are exceptionally rare, such as a case of 350 hummingbirds ("appalling" but "beautiful, because of their colors, not faded at all"). He has an ichthyosaur in his living room and an ammonite in his bathroom. One of Rowland Ward's lions that used to belong to Eton College resides in his garage, where he keeps his overflow. But his prize possession is Charles Waterton's saki monkey (a South American species), which was "lost" for 150 years. Fuller found it in an antiques shop in Greenwich. "I'm going to be buried with it!" he said. An amateur boxer turned painter turned self-taught natural historian, Fuller is the author of *The Great Auk* and *The Dodo*. "Mostly I've written about extinct things—mostly bones or stuffed ones," he explained. "It's my inability to cope with death. I think it starts with that—just like the Egyptians couldn't cope with it. You can't look at that fox. That individual fox tolls for thee."

The fox comment is very Victorian, and in some ways so is Fuller. He's a passionate amateur like Charles Darwin or John James Audubon, but instead of traveling to exotic locales to shoot, stuff, and study, say, Galápagos finches, Fuller visits far-flung museums, where he tracks down every known dried skin and plume of the extinct birds he's investigating, which he reproduces in paintings, formulating theories of substantial scientific merit along the way.

Fuller's obsession with extinct animals is extraordinary. When he wrote *The Great Auk,* for instance, he spent six years chasing down every great auk skin and egg in existence and had to drive a taxi to finance the book. His book on the dodo, a species that vanished in 1690, was far less grueling to research, because hardly any dodo skins exist, plus "all the known skeletons came from the same swamp in Mauritius."

"Have you carved up everything without me?" Fuller said to Hawkins as she walked into the restaurant. "She thinks she's outgrown me," he said to me. "She was the greediest little child! Emma tried to buy the whole lot!"

"I wouldn't buy taxidermy there that *wasn't* Potter," she said.

"Most people hate taxidermy for bogus reasons. They think it's disrespect for the dead creatures and that you are promoting it," said Fuller.

"Taxidermy connotes the taint of bad taste. Why is that?" Fuller's girlfriend asked.

"Quality affects it," offered Chinnery.

"It's like pickling your grandmother!" said the girlfriend.

We sat down to dinner, but instead of menus everyone held up auction catalogs. Images of distorted baby giraffes greeted the waitress. Fuller explained that the auction had no "reserves"; that is, Bonhams had not established a minimum price for each lot and therefore was willing to let it all go — whatever happens, happens. That fact was exciting yet sad.

Fuller flipped through his catalog, pausing at the duck-billed platypus (lot 182), and said, "I was thinking how badly I wanted that platypus thirty years ago. I would have given anything for it. We'll probably go home with nothing, and the Americans will go home with it."

"Very beautiful," said Hawkins with a demonic grin that concealed what she was admiring in her own catalog. Fuller yanked the catalog out of her hands. Hawkins yanked it back. Then Fuller's girlfriend threatened to snatch it so she could eat in peace. "We don't need a neutral referee!" Fuller snapped. "This is war!"

"I'd put three grand on that elephant head," said Chinnery.

Chinnery, no slouch in this absurdly narrow world, restores Victorian cases and resells them to a highly specialized clientele. One of his customers is his accountant, Mark Godfrey, who was seated at our table. Godfrey's business card didn't say ACCOUNTANT; it said TAXIDERMY COLLECTOR: HUTCHINGS OF ABERYSTWYTH and depicted two barn owls.

Chinnery and Fuller decided to go in on a lot together. They said they hadn't seen any "serious" people at the preview, and therefore no one would have the same combined diversity of their interests. It buoyed their spirits, but they kept their lot to themselves.

Then Fuller glared at Hawkins. "Stay off of my list!" he warned her. "Otherwise, I'll break your heart on something else!"

On the walk up the steep hill to my guesthouse, I realized

how tired my eyes were from all I had seen. Mr. Potter's Museum of Curiosities was amazing. But by the end of the auction, the exhibits would be crated up and packed into vans or into shipping containers destined for Britannia tankers bound for other countries. As I made my way up the hill, I felt depressed. I had hoped that someone would rescue the collection at the eleventh hour, but now that seemed improbable. I knew the general public might find the collection distasteful (the dealers were ahead of the curve; taxidermy wouldn't be considered hip and trendy again for another two years), but some smart curator at some big museum had to know what was at stake, which was, in the words of Richard Taylor, deputy librarian at the art college in Dartington who had launched an unsuccessful campaign to save it, "an absolutely unique, irreplaceable collection, and a national treasure."

Half a million pounds, the Wattses' rumored minimum price for the entire collection, was unremarkable when compared to what a large museum might pay for a single Dutch masterwork, Pat Morris remarked. I wished someone would make a last-ditch offer that Bonhams and the Wattses couldn't refuse. And it had almost happened. Damien Hirst reportedly made a one-million-pound offer for the entire contents. He wanted to merge Potter's with his own sculptures to form his own museum of curiosities. But his offer had reportedly been rejected because he had missed the August deadline for single offers. Hirst published a letter in the *Guardian* in which he called the sale a tragedy. He owns a house in neighboring Devon and brought his kids to Potter's all the time to watch their faces light up. He said that Potter's had meaning only if it was kept together.

The next morning, Hawkins and I climb into her van and leave Fowey's old port behind. The auction will start in an hour, barely enough time to make the drive, which winds through quaint towns where no one—except Hawkins, who is in high gear—appears to be in any hurry. She still has to finalize lot prices with her boyfriend, and she's jumpy, fumbling for her cell phone with one hand while keeping the other one on the wheel. I try not to focus on her driving and look out the window instead. Shafts of sunlight stab through a huge white cloud—an incredibly dramatic sky over a breathtaking landscape of granite cliffs and green hills. Hawkins couldn't care less. But now her cell phone is dead, no reception, and she starts to lose it while barreling down the winding road. "I can't believe this!" she fumes. "I've got to readjust my game strategy! I've got to call some people! You've got to make sure you're making the right decision for your clients."

Things only get worse. Another snag: a car crash in our lane. Thankfully, her cell phone reception is restored. Suddenly stuck in traffic, she feverishly phones her banker to make sure she's liquid should Bonhams call to verify funds. But alas, the bank's computers are down, and Hawkins, in a near panic, convinces the bank manager to vouch for her. Then she clicks off her phone, bellowing with delight, "I love a bank when [its] computers are down!"

She calls a client to confer on a lot. "Darling, you're a star! You looked brilliant! Bye, gorgeous!" Then she calls her boyfriend. "At least my boyfriend and banker are on call."

At 9:49, the Jamaica Inn's parking lot is packed. The sun is blinding, bright white, and blue Bonhams flags, hung high on poles, snap in the wind. Hawkins calls her boyfriend one last time: "Lot 66. The scarlet ibis. Eight hundred fifty pounds." Then she clicks off and strides into the tavern. The du Maurier Restaurant, with its timber beams and rustic crockery, is now an auction hall, brimming with three hundred or so people seated in rows of white chairs, as at a wedding, with paddles instead of fans and people instead of kittens.

Rob Chinnery is pumped up. He grabs Hawkins and says, "I want a word with you!" Pat Morris stands around in a tie that says WISCONSIN PEREGRINE FALCON SOCIETY. Jamaica Inn owner Kevin Moore wipes his wet brow with the back of his hand. His small, dark eyes dart around the room, and he says, "I'm nervous. I had three hours of sleep last night." Meanwhile, seated in the back, is Andy James, vice president of Ye Olde Curiosity Shop (est. 1899) in Seattle. He's after a church made out of corks and two-headed monstrosities (he'll have to outbid Crime Through Time). He relates the information British traders most fear: "Bonhams says there's been more interest internationally than locally."

Hawkins and Chinnery emerge from their huddle. They stand, strategically, in the middle of the room, directly behind the seated crowd, where they can make eye contact with each other and also be seen by the auctioneers. "We're fired up! You're going to see some action!" Chinnery says to me.

Standing under a wagon wheel behind a podium flanked by a jungle of potted plants, from which emerge a polar bear and a stiff-faced tiger with a tongue that looks like spoiled meat, is Jon Baddeley. He is wearing a gray sport coat with a red Bonhams lapel pin and a blue tie. The sharp white sun and the black wood interior create a blinding chiaroscuro, obscuring the television simulcast of the first lot: the oil portrait of Walter Potter. Potter's portrait is a profile — as if he can't bear to face the crowd. The wide brushstrokes give him the saturated appearance of someone wearing makeup. He is radiant, with his bushy white muttonchops and thick tuft of silver hair, and this suddenly feels to me like a surreal wake. Finally, after a few tension-filled minutes, the auction is about to start. Baddeley, composed and smiling, grabs the mike and, in a steady voice that doesn't remotely evoke a sideshow barker, greets the crowd with words that will never be spoken here again: "May I welcome you to Mr. Potter's Museum of Curiosities."

POSTSCRIPT

In the end, the auction raised £529,900 ($874,335), far less than Hirst's million-pound offer. Hawkins bought *The Guinea Pigs' Cricket Match*, the scarlet ibis, a skinned rabbit floating in formaldehyde, and several other lots. Fuller snagged *Athletic Toads* and *The Squire and the Parson After Dinner* (those gentleman lobsters). And Rob Chinnery paid £23,500 ($38,775) for what turned out to be the most expensive lot sold at the auction: *The Death and Burial of Cock Robin*. Four years after the sale, the Wattses reportedly threatened Bonhams with a lawsuit for failing to notify them of Hirst's offer, and the Walter Potter Foundation had been established to attempt to reassemble the exhibits.

7

IN-A-GADDA-DA-VIDA

I LIKE TO THINK of Damien Hirst as a very rich Walter Potter and his exhibits as a contemporary museum of curiosities—places where people encounter the most shocking and
distorted forms of nature: sectioned cows, pickled sharks, glass-
encased skeletons, and giant mosaics made entirely of butterfly
wings. People are willing to spend millions of dollars on a single
Hirst sculpture. In August 2007, he sold a platinum skull stud-
ded with 8,601 diamonds for $100 million. Nevertheless, he can
create a sense of wonder (or repulsion or fear) in the minds of
his viewers only if what he presents is convincing—at least per-
ceived to be genuine. And for that he employs scores of artists,
including "the woman behind the dead animals": Emily Mayer.

A year or so after the Potter's auction, Mayer invited me
to the Tate Britain for the opening of "In-A-Gadda-Da-Vida."
The name is from the psychedelic rock band Iron Butterfly's
monstrously popular album of 1968. Apparently, Iron Butterfly's lead singer, Doug Ingle, was too stoned to say "Garden of
Eden," and that title came out instead. It was a great name for
the Hirst show because it, too, was a garbled Eden, one in which

the themes of fear, desire, sex, death, and decay collided to form unsettling tensions.

When I arrived in Guilt Cross, Mayer was in the yard combing a collie that looked as if it had been coated in aspic. She was using a fork to extract silicone from its fur, which was an incredibly tedious process because the fork kept bending out of shape. "I've got to finish the collie and then get on with the dodo skeleton," she said, dipping the fork into solvent, which smelled like nail polish remover and cut through the cloying smell of silage and manure from the surrounding dairy farms. In addition to the fork, Mayer used a horse-hoof-trimming knife and a gynecological tool she called "a nasty instrument for taking smear samples from women." "I think this is a better use for it," she said indignantly. I groaned. One minute she's crass, and the next she's Mother Nature, looking up at the rooks swooping overhead (as she was now doing) and talking about global warming: "I have an issue with people saying animals are pests. I think the biggest pest on earth is *us!*"

On the train to London the next morning, Mayer considered how people would react to the huge slabs of beef she'd molded for the show. "I wonder whether or not they will think it's real. If anyone asks, [Hirst is] going to say they are real and changed every day. How important to the work that is, I don't know." It's very important, in fact. For Hirst, realism (or the illusion of realism) is what differentiates his work (and taxidermy, for that matter) from representational art and gives it the provocative edge he is famous for. His skeletons, sectioned cows, and bisected pigs are genuine, and to see them in a museum (out of context) is intentionally disturbing, exciting, and sad. The floating tiger shark, for instance, was inspired by the movie *Jaws,* because he wanted to show something "real enough to frighten you."

The Tate Britain is not very scary. We arrived an hour before the opening. Mayer dressed up looks nothing like Mayer in her grimy work clothes. She has on a green suede bolero jacket from France with a spider brooch on the lapel, mod blue mirrored sunglasses, and trim "city leopard" spotted pants. I followed her to the service entrance, where she handed me a badge that said TATE CONTRACTOR, FLYING BEAR LTD. I put it on, and we glided through security. Attending a Hirst opening as a contractor was nothing like attending it as a curator, art dealer, or critic. I felt like one of his artistic stagehands—the artists and technicians who work behind the scenes, enabling Hirst to put on his show.

And what a show he puts on. We walked under two rotundas, lit purple and yellow like a chic dance club, and into a hallway where Hirst was sitting with his crew. When he saw Mayer, he shouted, "Drum roll for Em-i-ly!" Everyone pounded on the table as Mayer approached Hirst, who hugged her. Reporters and television cameramen hovered around, waiting for interviews. People slapped Hirst on the back in a congratulatory manner. It felt as if we were backstage at a West End theater production on opening night, with Hirst the leading man. He was wearing brown-tinted sunglasses, a long sweater-coat with dragons embroidered on the back, and taut green leather shoes that looked reptilian. He has spiky salt-and-pepper hair and is half a head shorter than Mayer, who playfully hopped on his lap before she took off to chat with friends.

"She sounds like a man!" he said, smiling, as I opened my notebook. I laughed out loud. I considered what I knew about this man who had transformed himself from a working-class lad from Leeds into one of England's wealthiest men. He was born in 1965. He didn't know his birth father, and the father who raised him (a car salesman) left when he was twelve. He never forgave the Catholic Church for turning its back on his mother (a former florist with an artistic bent). As a kid, Hirst's childhood bedroom was an animal laboratory where he, like Mayer, bred and raised butterflies and other creatures. He is a Gemini ("I want to fucking share everything with everybody and have a party for the rest of my life") who loves the Beatles song "Two of Us." He has an insatiable fear of death (a love of life, really) and a terrible curiosity about life forms, especially how animals look when taken apart and reassembled. He once said, "I just like rotting." He is an exceptionally brilliant namer, juxtaposing complex titles with simple images. Among the best is *I Want to Spend the Rest of My Life Everywhere, with Everyone, One to One, Always, Forever, Now* (a Ping-Pong ball floating in the air above a spray gun and a glass stand). A known prankster, Hirst once got sued for wagging his penis at a Dublin restaurant. Now this art star was sitting directly across from me. My time was limited. I jumped in: Is taxidermy art?

"Yeah. I think anything done well is art," he said, and gave an example—cooking, I believe. "If you want to go from point A to point B, it's all about *transport*. Great transport." He paused and continued. "I just want to create things that look real. I think art is about life. You want things to reflect that—killing things to look at them. For me it's a love of life to explore it on the fringes. It's why kids take toys apart. It's a morbid fascination. It shouldn't be."

> Q: A lot of taxidermists don't consider what *they* do art.
>
> D.H.: They spend too much time creating hunting trophies and not enough on what they do. They should be more like Emily. I love her. She's brilliant. She's the only one who can create a sense of fantasy. She's the only one who can do what she does. She is on *that* level.

Q: Could you do what you do without Emily?

D.H.: I think I'd do it differently. I used to use real cadaver
  animals. If it looks real, that's all that matters.

Ever since Hirst won Britain's coveted Turner Prize for contemporary art in 1995 for *Mother and Child Divided* (a cow and
a calf sawed into twelve parts and displayed in separate cases),
the *New York Times* says the press has disparaged his work. This
show, which also contained work by two of Hirst's former Gold-
smith College classmates who rose to fame together in the early
1990s, was no exception. When I got home, I downloaded the
reviews: "banal" (*New Statesman*); "This is not just paradise lost,
but paradise never conjured in the first place"(*Observer*); "You
can expect more in fact from the average truck driver" (*Guardian*); "Its real themes are pompousness, vacuity, big budgets,
shot bolts, and the flogging of dead horses" (*Financial Times*). I
wasn't brandishing the knife of a critic, however, but the magnifying glass of a child.

Yet, even I had trouble imagining that what I encountered in
the first gallery was truly Adam and Eve. Lying head to head on
two hospital gurneys were Eden's first man and woman—Damien
Hirst style—with exposed, hyperrealistic genitals (prepped for
surgery) visible through fig-leaf cutouts in blue surgical paper
that covered their bodies. *Adam and Eve Exposed,* a one-liner
the critics vilified, honestly didn't move me one way or another.
Then the bodies started to breathe. Their chests rose and fell,
rose and fell. I gasped, uneasily, then I went over to see something undeniably dead: a six-legged stillborn calf.

In His Infinite Wisdom reminded me of a Walter Potter freak
—the conjoined pickled swine, actually—only supersized and
strangely beautiful. Pristine and fleecy white with large black
spots, it languidly floated in a glass tank as if in a cloud. The

critics loved this unaltered (or so it seemed) piece for its power and simplicity. I figured the calf had been simply dropped into formaldehyde, but when I told Mayer that, she laughed. "Well, actually, quite a lot was done to that," she said, explaining how it had been frozen for fifteen years before she had defrosted and rehydrated it, then shampooed and fluffed it up. I wondered why it was considered art and not natural history. If the calf were displayed in South Kensington at the Natural History Museum, would it then become science?

Hirst's first formaldehyde piece, *Isolated Elements Swimming in the Same Direction for the Purpose of Understanding* (1991) — thirty-eight Plexiglas boxes, each one containing a fish—looked like science masquerading as art, a direct attempt to blur those boundaries. Similarly, the floating shark in *The Physical Impossibility of Death in the Mind of Someone Living* (1991) was Hirst's rendition of a "zoo that worked." "Because I hate the zoo, and I just thought it would be great to do a zoo of dead animals, instead of having living animals pacing about in misery, I thought that's what a natural history museum is really," he once said in a catalog. Even the sectioned cows evoked pathos in Hirst's mind: "I never really thought of them as violent. I always thought of them as sad. There is a kind of tragedy with all those pieces. I always did them where their feet don't touch the floor. They are floating things."

Mayer and I circled the exhibit. Everyone from Hirst's inner circle was here: Frank Dunphy, his business manager and accountant; Rungway Kingdon, the tall bearded Mauritian who owns Pangolin, the foundry that casts Hirst's huge bronzes; his assistants and independent contractors. At any given time, Hirst employs more than forty artists and technicians to do his behind-the-scenes work. Many of them were here in this room. They cast the resin pills for the stainless steel medicine cabinets (sixteen thousand pills in one piece), design the graphics for the pharmaceutical logos, and saw the sheep. People are often surprised to learn that Hirst doesn't paint a single spot on his signature spot paintings. Yet his name is on them all, just as it would be, Mayer explains dismissively, if he were Frank Lloyd Wright and she were Fred the bricklayer.

We chatted with the "butterfly ladies," the women who make his floor-to-ceiling mosaics of intricately patterned butterfly wings. Intense and radiant, these giant panels evoke a cathedral's stained-glass windows — macro-versions of Potter's pinned butterflies, only incomparably powerful. I asked the women if, after a year or so of pulling wings off them, they still enjoyed butterflies. "Sadly, no — not that much," Rose, a bubbly blonde, replied.

While Hirst's butterfly paintings move people with their beauty, his fly paintings (giant canvases coated with gobs of dead flies that resemble gooey raisins) fill them with dread. In the next gallery, Will Sheer, the artist who made Hirst's fly painting *Night Falls Fast,* stood in front of the huge black monochrome. A Hirst staple, the fly paintings represent a plague of sorts — Eden falls to desire.

"Will made this," boasted Sheer's girlfriend.

"We hatch them and kill them with fly spray. They die and we scoop them up, and they get mixed up with resin and stuck on the work. We paint them into place. We do it by the liter. There must be two hundred liters [of flies] in each piece," he explained.

"They stink!" said the girlfriend.

"I got used to the smell. They smell like moldy cheese," said Sheer.

Finally, Mayer and I headed over to *The Pursuit of Oblivion,* a crucifixion in a butcher shop. Only this butcher shop was in a gigantic fish tank filled with provocative props. What was being crucified was Mayer's sides of beef, which hang from meat hooks above a butcher block. The molded slabs with yellow marbling looked exactly like what you'd see in a butcher shop before the meat is cut into steaks. The butcher block did not; on it was a human skull, knives, a nautilus, and a frying pan filled with brains. An umbrella and strings of sausage dangled from above, swaying in the clear water of the fish tank like plankton.

The sculpture was Hirst's homage to a Francis Bacon painting called *1946*. Bacon, the Irish-born Parisian exile, who died in 1992, has been Hirst's hero since he was sixteen, and I could see why. Bacon was captivated by slaughterhouses as "the absolute place of death": meat suspended as if crucified; meat with contorted mouths screaming in agony (he also painted monsters, bloody carcasses, crucifixions, and decomposing heads—consider Hirst without bathos or tropical fish). Bacon's shock tactics were meant to evoke the horrors of human existence. He painted *1946* at the end of World War II. As Bacon once famously said, "Well of course we are meat, we are potential carcasses. If I go into a butcher's shop I always think it's surprising that I wasn't there instead." Hirst is more minimal: "Animals become meat. That's abstract."

I stared at the swaying meat. Tropical fish darted around a skinned cow head. British art critics called the piece chaotic and heavy-handed. The viewers that night were riveted, though not disturbed or even perplexed. Still, they were not without curiosity. Mostly they wanted to know if the meat was real. Even Hirst's dealer, Jay Jopling, owner of London's White Cube gallery—someone who knows Hirst's sleight of hand—gazed into the tank, mystified. "You just would *never, never, never* know," he said.

"That's fabulous! Amazing!" people cried.

The tank gargled. An eel twined around a fractured human skull, evoking a medieval apothecary. "That's a small shark, I believe," said a spiffy woman.

Another person said, "I don't know how it doesn't poison the water. All the bits and pieces. The water's completely clean. I think it's a model. Is that real meat? It might have algae or something?"

The week before, when Mayer delivered the piece, the museum staff thought it was a kitchen delivery. A scuba diver had to dive in and arrange the props. The gallery floors (directly above the Tate's library) had to be reinforced to support the weight of the massive glass tanks. "The last time I saw it, the water was murky, and the [cow] head was floating up to the top," Mayer said, smiling with pride.

I went back to see it a second time. A young man with sideburns and closely cropped hair stood inches from the glass. He admired the sculpture. He admired the beef. The man was Martin Gilder, and he knew the cut intimately, knew it better than an art critic. Gilder happens to be the owner of Martin's Meats, a large meat wholesaler and slaughterhouse and farm, which supplies the carcasses from which Mayer makes her replicas. If anyone here could discern art from life, it was Gilder the butcher. I asked him to critique it.

He shook his head. He flashed a big smile and examined it with the trained eyes of a master craftsman. Was it believable? No, he said, the color was off. But just slightly. "Needs to be redder. Should look wetter—even in water it looks dry." He laughed. "It's above average. It's what you call a very high confirmation; it's almost double muscle. It's graded a 'u-plus-one'—one is fat content. You could eat it, but it would need more fat to taste good."

He went on, "If you went back thirty or forty years, this wouldn't be shocking, because even a small village had a butcher shop and an abattoir. People are so far removed from how meat comes to your table. They see it beautifully packaged in supermarkets and don't associate it with animals anymore. What gives it away is the way it is hanging—all carcasses hang the other way around, because it's the way the meat pulls down from the hind legs and becomes more tender. Also, the neck would be much darker and redder."

Before Hirst's crew headed to a nearby pub, Mayer looked at the beef one last time: "I'm a little scrutinizing but happy. I love the way the fish are interacting with it." She bought the exhibition catalog. Hirst signed it:

> For Emily.
> Keep it real.
> XXX
> Damien Hirst

It was great to attend the opening with Mayer and to meet Hirst. But I still hadn't seen Mayer work. Another year went by. Then one day, the phone rang. It was Mayer. Her two terriers, Alice and Gus, had been mysteriously poisoned and died. (No: she buries them. Always.) She was deeply disturbed by this and also very sad. Then she said, "I have another cow here at the moment that I'm working on. And two cow heads that have to be cast as well." She invited me to watch her work. She sent me a link to help me find a cheap flight.

She was 372½ hours into the cow when I showed up in Guilt Cross. It was the week before Christmas. Half-finished Hirst projects lay everywhere: resin blood puddles, a fish skeleton in a vise, and two cow heads in the boiler room. But the first thing I saw when I stepped inside the workshop was a seven-foot-long black-and-white Holstein suspended from an I-beam. Its head drooped down, limp and lifeless. Its tongue stuck out comically from lips that were soft and black and fringed with stray whiskers. The cow looked dead—freshly dead—which it was supposed to be. Its glossy legs were artificially bent at the knees as if it were genuflecting or begging for mercy. Its chest cavity was split open. You could see its guts, its blood-red rib cage, its glistening milky yellow fat. It was horrific. It was beautiful. It was a hanged cow.

"How the hell did you make this?" I asked, unable to move for several seconds as I gazed at the most stunning, and the most terrifying, piece of art I have ever seen. It was the most alive dead replica imaginable, which of course sounds silly.

"You can see inside the cow—all the ribs and everything. That's all fake," she said. "You want to believe it's a cow in there and not just a black hollow cavity." Her tone was admonishing, as if I should know what the fake innards of a fake dead cow were supposed to look like. She lit a roll-up and thoughtfully inhaled. I stared transfixed.

Mayer had no idea what the client intended to do with the cow once it was finished, and I didn't pry, because I found it far more disturbing here in Mayer's studio than it would ever be anywhere else, especially a gallery or a museum where glass panes might separate it from me. Glass panes are barriers, which say in effect, "This is staged." Glass panes anchor a piece (and us) to the museum, a cultural authority, legitimizing it. Moreover, the glass separates us from death; it's a distancing element, providing safety, comfort, and, perhaps more important, a sense that someone is in charge of this death, someone with a respectable title that is not "taxidermist," such as "conservator" or "curator" or "philanthropist" or "scientist." But in here, in Mayer's workhouse studio, in this dark, wintry, isolated Norfolk farm country, the cow was eerie and surreal. There was no glass partition separating me from it, and I shivered with excitement and fear.

It was her fifth erosion-molded cow and her best. It is incredibly difficult to erosion mold a cow. Every scrap of anatomy must be preplanned. If she miscalculates, say, the catalyst times for the resin, the cow might cure improperly, and the fur is irreplaceable. The attention to detail is staggering. You can look up its nostrils and see bumps and hair. You can peer into its mouth at its pink-and-gray-ribbed pallet. Its big brown eyes are bloodshot near the irises; its fur-fringed ears are soft and translucent; its teats and asshole are embarrassingly convincing. All of that has to be worked out before the cow is slaughtered.

"Everything is fake except the hair, *obviously*. It's essentially a fake cow with real hair," Mayer explained.

The hooves?

"The hooves were cast with everything else. There's pink inside so you have that glow and depth and it looks like a living thing rather than a lump of solidness."

The teeth?

"I just cast the teeth in when I cast the whole cow. You can see the negative in the mold in the boiler room."

The eyes?

"They need to look fresh like it just died. I like them a little more glazed over."

Mayer still had to reattach the cow's head, fine-tune its face, and hide the seams. She also had to make fake intestines, because the work order called for guts to spill out of its body. Color photocopies of purple and yellow cow intestines lay all over the studio; she'd use them as a guide—like a high-tech paint-by-number—only instead of paint, Mayer would use a mixture of resin and flock (wool fibers that give it texture). She compared the process to painting on glass.

For this job, however, color photocopies alone wouldn't do. Mayer would need fresh reference, so she had the slaughter-house open up a cow and photograph its hot intestines spilling out onto its hooves. The intestines were then frozen and deliv-ered to her studio. Now she booted up her laptop and clicked on a file name, calling up the slit-open cow spilling guts. Then she clicked on another file (I'll spare you). She took a drag on her cigarette; the smell of smoke kept me from throwing up.

"Obviously, we didn't want it sitting on its ass, because that would look totally stupid!" she said with a snarl, clicking JPEG file after JPEG file. No, it was to be bent at the knees. But cows' knees don't bend ("Obviously!") unless you cut the tendons. With typical Mayer relish, she showed me where she cut them. "I just put a scalpel . . . I just cut them from the insides just like a tiny old nick." The tongue had already been sticking out, but "I persuaded it a bit more."

Here's how Mayer cast the cow's body. Once the frozen cow was posed and coated in silicone inside and out (she intubated it and poured rubber down its throat), she bolted a thermo-plastic support jacket with ribs over the outside of the body to hold the cow in place while the flesh rotted and the rubber cured. Once it had uniformly decomposed, Mayer pried off the jacket, peeled off the silicone, and implanted all the precast anatomy.

"You can do things most women never would," I said.

"I can do things most *men* can't do!" she said with a loud laugh.

While I was there, she worked for hours and hours reattach-ing the head, never pausing, not even for food. (Luckily, I found a pillowcase full of dried apple slices hanging on her husband's door and snuck upstairs periodically to eat.) By day three, I started to fidget and ask questions. "You could be doing this yourself in galleries and making quite a splash," I said, crunching numbers in my mind.

"Well, I couldn't, because I don't think of the ideas, do I? And if I went and showed this as a piece of art in a different context or whatever, I'd be like stealing, wouldn't I? I can't do that. I wouldn't want to anyway."

The next afternoon, Mayer suggests we visit the big commercial dairy farm across the street from her house. She wants to observe cow noses, eyes, tongues, and topknots in order to perfect her facsimiles.

A ceiling of gray clouds hovers over us as we walk to the huge milking sheds. They smell like manure and wet hay. "It reminds me of my childhood in the country," Mayer says. She is wearing a blue fleece jacket, black leather clogs, and torn jeans splotched with paint. When we pass the birthing field, Mayer spots a still-born calf lying on the muddy ground. She stops to examine it with the unsentimental eyes of a scientist or a veterinarian. The industrial sheds, covered by corrugated cement-composite roofs, contain rows and rows of Holsteins. "Metal would be too noisy for them, wouldn't it?" she admonishes. I, her reluctant apprentice, nod sheepishly.

We walk along the side of a shed. Mayer narrates what she is seeing; she is teaching me how to look at cows. They are post-card perfect, black with wonderful white spots, tagged and numbered (yellow clips in their ears), wearing electric bracelets that monitor their milk production. They poke their bony heads through the fence, grazing, staring up at us with huge brown eyes. "They have great faces," she says excitedly. "When you start looking at them, each one is different. That one has bluish eyes. They've got different topknots—curly, straight. That one's kind of worn-out, really." Then she does a very un-Mayer-like thing.

She gets all gushy, talking to the cows as if they were children. She grabs some hay and waves it under their pink and black nostrils, trying to get one to stick out its tongue for a photo. "I want to see your tongue, baby! Taste some hay!" she croons.

"That one's got a really short face compared to that one, which is long and broad," she says. I check out their faces. To me, they look alike, but I'd never say that to Mayer. So I look for variations: 00676's nose is more well-defined than 00758's, and 500211 has amazing wrinkles above its eyes. 00749 (mostly black) has a blue tongue. "That one has an orange nose, and that one's really pink. And that one is concave between the eyes," she says.

She gives a cow an "Eskimo kiss," rubbing noses with it. The cow's bony head is three times as big as hers is. "It's called Ray! Look! Look at the pink on that nose [00636] versus the orangy pink on that one [60075]! They can lick right up their nostrils. Look!" As if on cue, 60075 sticks its tongue up its nostril. Mayer bursts out laughing.

She leads me farther along the side of the shed. "Look how fat that gray one's nose is. It's like a boxer. It's quite narrow behind the nose, and the nose is broad, like it walked into a wall." Occasionally, she turns back to make sure I've noticed everything—all the nuances that enable her to excel at her job. "That one has a face like Alice [her late terrier]: she has a funny undershot jaw—the lower jaw is too far forward. Look at the shape of their bodies. I love cows! Look at how bony that one is! It's almost like a skeleton with the skin just hanging over it."

She pets the bony one's nose with the back of her hand. "They're friendly but don't like to be touched too much. The more you look at them, the more you can see. Some are really pretty, and some are quite brutish-looking. She's quite cute.

"I just want it to stick its tongue out for me, and it's gotten all shy," she says. The cow sticks its tongue up its nostril. Mayer snaps a photo. "You've got a ridiculously pink nose, don't you?" she gushes, extending her hand to another grazer. "*Somebody lick me!*"

000021 is an archetype: the perfect specimen, almost a cliché. "That's a beauty," Mayer says, eyeing me to make sure I've noticed all the variations—variations taxidermists live for and I am only now just beginning to perceive. "There! Are you seeing the differences now?"

8

KEN AND THE IRISH ELK

WITH ITS OIL-RICH PRAIRIES, cattle ranches, and mechanical bulls, Alberta, Canada, is often compared to Texas, only it is
much, much colder. In the 1960s and 1970s, Edmonton, the prov-
ince's capital, was like Houston: a boom-and-bust town founded
on light oil, which was discovered just south of the city in 1947.
Then, in the 1980s, the big petroleum companies moved their
headquarters to Calgary, much to the dismay of Edmontonians,
who also never got over losing their area code to Calgary or losing the distinction of having the world's largest shopping mall
to Minneapolis. Nonetheless, in spite of what some locals call its
huge inferiority complex, Edmonton doggedly clings to its nickname: "City of Champions."

Of all the champions ever to have come from Edmonton,
none is more famous than hockey star Wayne Gretzky. Gretzky
won four Stanley Cups with the Edmonton Oilers and is considered the greatest hockey player ever. He retired in 1999, the
same year, as it happens, that Ken Walker took his first Best of
Show with his timber wolves. Other taxidermists accused him of
coming out of nowhere. "Out of nowhere?" he exclaims. "I was
a commercial taxidermist for fifteen years before I competed,

and people would say to me, 'You came out of nowhere!' If you take a real good commercial taxidermist and open up his mind he's gonna win."

Ken was telling me this as we pulled out of Edmonton International Airport. We were in his pickup, a Toyota Velocity, driving northwest to his acreage in Alberta Beach. The highway cut through snow-covered prairies; the dim sun hung low in the sky; the gusty air was crisp and filled with swirling snow. "This is what I missed so much in DC," he said, his alert hunter's eyes scanning from side to side.

It was a balmy ten degrees that day in February 2005—not icy enough to plug your radiator into one of those parking lot heat boxes that keep Edmontonians' engines from freezing. I shivered in a down parka and heavy snow boots and slid the .410 automatic shotgun, which I had been sitting on, to the edge of my seat. A box of empty .270 casings lay on the armrest between us. Birds seem to recognize the roar of his engine and fly off the moment he approaches. Even the local animal rights activist keeps his distance. "He's kind of creepy," Ken said.

Ken hadn't trimmed his beard or cut his hair in weeks and superstitiously vowed not to until the World Taxidermy Championships in two months. His wife, Colette, called him "Grizzly Adams," and it wasn't an exaggeration. If he wasn't wearing a camouflage baseball cap that said NORTH COUNTRY TAXIDERMY and a shirt emblazoned with the Smithsonian logo, I might not have known it was Ken—until he started to ramble in that dazzling Ken-like way. I didn't believe everything he said (Theodore Roosevelt shot and had someone preserve a porter on safari?), but I loved his unbridled enthusiasm, how he glided from topic to topic, equally excited about everything that entered his mind. First he mimicked Dr. Ruth, then, without pausing, he went on and on about a mammoth dug up recently in

Japan. "I want to be the guy who puts the thing together!" he exclaimed.

A stand of frost-covered conifers caught his eye. "Killed my first moose with a bow and arrow right here in these trees," he said. "My only moose with a bow and arrow!"

The landscape was a vast expanse of white, blank as a sheet of paper. Ken noticed every track that marked every ditch and hill. "Saw a white wolf here this morning," he said, scanning shoulder to shoulder. "There's been a big cougar hanging around my place."

Then on to another topic: "As a big fan of Red Skelton, Howard Stern doesn't do a lot for me. If the only way to get attention is to shock people, then you better move to another town. The only way you shock someone with taxidermy is with the harshness of reality. A lion disemboweling a live zebra—that can be portrayed through taxidermy. You can do a doe killing its fawn with its hooves—that's the harsh truth."

He drove in silence for a few miles, then proclaimed, "Animal rights people are like streakers. It's a fad!"

Ken was consumed with the upcoming competition. He was entering Re-Creations again and was the big favorite. Some of his rivals had already dropped out; others had switched categories. "The *world* isn't ready for a Best of Show Re-Creation," he said, boasting that he had already written his acceptance speech. "I want to talk about Carl Akeley and the legacy that he created," he said. Sometime later he added, "People like Carl Akeley and myself lived in relative poverty at the start. He lived in a shack, and so did I. Reading his autobiography made me feel complete." Then, with a smile as broad as Alberta, he exclaimed, "I love how his two wives fought over him!"

This year Ken was pushing himself. Instead of re-creating something exotic such as the giant panda, he was resurrecting one of the most majestic and mysterious beasts ever to have roamed the earth: the prehistoric *Megaloceros giganteus,* commonly known as the Irish elk.

Irish elk weren't actually elk at all, and they weren't exclusively Irish. Taxonomically, they are classified as deer, giant extinct deer—the largest deer ever, except for the cervalces, which lived fifty thousand to ten thousand years ago. Irish elk were so regal and strange, in fact, that they seem almost mythical, like fantasy creatures dreamt up by the French primitive painter Henri Rousseau (1844–1910). So removed are they from our world that people who encounter their mounted skeletons in the National Museum of Ireland (which has the largest collection: 10 complete skeletons and the remains of 250 animals) often mistake them for a strange type of dinosaur or a moose. The reason they are called Irish elk is because their skeletal remains turn up primarily in lake sediment under peat bogs throughout Ireland. Their actual range extended from Ireland to western Siberia and parts of Asia.

Irish elk were designed for endurance: they were machines of incredible strength and dominance. Mature bucks stood seven feet at the shoulder and weighed nearly a thousand pounds. They had huge chests, colossal shoulders, lithe legs for speed, and strong bodies. But their most distinctive feature was undoubtedly their antlers. This stag had a massive rack—a twelve-foot spread from tine to tine—the largest antlers of any known deer, living or extinct. Nature's ultimate status symbol, these palmated billboards advertised great authority and power and sex (mostly to other deer). For centuries, people have lusted after these antlers. Nineteenth-century fossil hunters dredged every peat bog in Ireland looking for them; kings hung them in castles; people used them to decorate gateposts and bridges, hunting lodges and baronial halls.

These glorious beasts mystified even Ken, who has spent countless hours hunting whitetails and elk, imagining life in the early Holocene era, when Irish elk roamed. Science is still untangling their story: how did such a resilient species—this stag of all stags—manage to survive the Ice Age, then abruptly die out? Their demise seems like a parable for our own imperiled wilderness.

Ken called his re-creation a ten-thousand-year-old headache, and he was right. Resurrecting an Irish elk would overwhelm even the most passionate paleobiologist. For a taxidermist in isolated Alberta who'd quit school in the eleventh grade, it posed an incredible challenge. That's primarily because Irish elk exist only in Paleolithic cave art, in fossilized remains, and in Seamus Heaney's poetry. Taxidermists strive to copy nature exactly, but how do you make a microscopic duplicate of a species that vanished from the earth seventy-five hundred years ago?

Ken's been fascinated with Irish elk since he was a kid. He's seen taxidermic models that he believes are wildly inaccurate: moose with supersized antlers. He's seen museum mounts unnaturally erected to exaggerate their huge size. He's never seen a convincing model, so now he was determined, by obsession and sheer unbridled will, to make one himself. As he put it, "The reason I do it is because I want to see it. If somebody else does it, I can never be sure that they did it right. You know, I wanted to do my own research. I wanted to be *absolutely* sure that it was the right size and color and everything else, so I picked it because I wanted to see what it would look like if it was done like *I* believe it should be!"

Ken's devastating urge to see an Irish elk is hardly unique. Ever since the first Irish elk skull was discovered in county Meath in 1588, naturalists, fossil hunters, anatomists, geologists, climatologists, archaeologists, evolutionary biologists, paleon-

tologists, biomechanical experts, kings, princes, poets, and folk-
lorists have all had a burning desire to know what they looked
like and how they behaved. One reason museum models vary
from elk to elk is that biologists revise the species' phylogenetic
blueprint every few years as they get closer to unlocking the
mystery.

Ken works alone in the middle of snowfields. He has no access to a university's vast resources or a museum's scientific specimens—nor is he a part of those worlds. He couldn't simply
waltz into the Page Museum at the La Brea Tar Pits, for example,
and borrow their megaloceros. And he wasn't going to Chauvet
or Cougnac to study cave art. (He had to settle for photographs
and diagrams.) Nor, for that matter, did he have $30,000 for
real antlers. (He was using fiberglass replicas.) However, few biologists have had the type of intimate contact with wildlife that
Ken has, the years spent in the wilderness hunting bears, sheep,
elk, and deer and then reproducing them. Fewer scientists still
are in regular contact with the type of unofficial animal expert
Ken trusts more than anyone for reference: Canadian trappers.
What Ken lacked in academic credentials, he'd have to supplement with his hands, his eyes, and his feet.

He'd also read every book and article he could find, including studies by famous scientists such as Stephen Jay Gould, who
published a landmark essay about the species in 1974. He'd
compared that essay with the latest DNA analysis of fossilized
remains done by University College London biologists in 2005.
But you can't see coat color in DNA sequencing. Ken *needed*
to see coat color. He needed to see coat color like Carl Akeley
needed to replicate Africa and Emily Mayer needed Yorkshire
terriers to look as if they had died an hour ago. The process of
making an Irish elk, it turned out, was a lot like the old fisher-
man's quest in Ernest Hemingway's *The Old Man and the Sea,*

and now I was heading to Alberta Beach to watch Ken wrestle with prehistory.

Alberta Beach has two seasons: *Sea-Doo* (Jet Skis) and *Ski-Doo* (snowmobiles). During Sea-Doo season, the population hovers at around eight thousand; during Ski-Doo season, that figure drops precipitously, to about nine hundred. At this time of year, Alberta Beach looks like a blue-collar resort town coated in snow, which is basically what it is. Hand-lettered signs advertise fireworks, murals of the Chinook and Inuit adorn storefronts, and the dollar store is appropriately named the Loonie Bin.

We passed an alpaca farm and contemporary log homes with vast yards of grazing horses. Finally, we pulled onto an isolated gravel road and followed it to the end. Ken's house is a brown contemporary wood-frame surrounded by fenced-in snowy fields that in the summer take eight hours to mow. Colette does the mowing—with a riding mower. On its seventeen and a half acres are llamas and horses, a Swedish Haggelund (a military surplus vehicle that Ken rides for fun), and a barn where Ken does his own tanning and keeps his carcass freezer (extraordinarily well stocked). "It's coming down to the wire for me," he said, killing the engine. "If I have to stop now to make money, I won't finish in time . . . The home and the family should come first, but . . ."

Before we went upstairs for dinner, Ken took me on a tour of his house. It is wood paneled and filled with wildlife paintings and books, animal bedspreads, animal photographs, animal coffee mugs, and, of course, lots of taxidermy. ("It's art, and everybody has art in their house," says Colette.) The finished basement is Ken's terrain: half recording studio (keyboards, piano, amplifier), half trophy room (polar bear, alligator, nutria, white foxes, wolverine, raccoon, tarantula). He showed me the

Siberian tiger he mounted as a birthday present for Chantelle, his daughter. Then he pointed to his son Patrick's snow leopard (another present from Dad). "That's my saber-tooth," he said, handing me a photo. "I can do a far better Irish elk."

Upstairs in the kitchen, Colette was calling the kids to dinner. Colette is a bank teller in Onoway ("Oh, no way!"). She has straight brown, feathered hair and warm brown eyes. Patrick was in the den watching a documentary about Koko the gorilla. Chantelle was looking through the kitchen window at Dalai Lama, one of her "riding llamas." The kitchen is big and bright with large windows overlooking the farm fields and, beyond them, the barn. On the yellow Formica countertops are a panda cookie jar and a panda coffee mug; the floors are blond wood. It smells like home cooking.

As it happens, Colette and Ken met over a meal. Colette was waiting tables at Boston Pizza. Ken showed up and ordered a pie. She's been serving him deer and moose and bear ever since. When the kids were babies, Colette used to help Ken by sewing linings onto bear rugs. "I hate sewing with a passion," she says. "Now I work for a living. I don't need to do taxidermy." Even so, almost everyone around here defines her by Ken's celebrity. "I just went to a funeral, and I was talking to my cousin's wife. This is *my* family, and she says, 'Oh, you're Ken the taxidermist's wife!'"

Colette, who is allergic to deer hides and does not hunt, is the pragmatist of the family, the person who arranges Ken's paperwork at competition time so he can bring endangered species into the United States. CITES permits take three to six weeks to process; without them, Ken won't clear customs. Border crossings are always stressful for the Walkers, and Ken is virtually helpless when it comes to filing permits and arranging inspection times. Colette calls him a zoo animal: cage him in, and he won't perform. "If he has to do the paperwork, nothing else will get done. It's all me, and because I don't know a lot of what he does, it's hard. So I have to call [the U.S.] Fish and Wildlife [Service] and get papers organized and whatnot, and then I have to do the Canadian part of it, and if they're not kept up, they expire," she says with a laughing-to-keep-from-crying grin. "For the Irish elk, all we'll need is our provincial papers, so that'll be an easy one. But I don't think that's all he's taking."

In spite of the financial hardship that comes with having a championship taxidermist for a spouse, the Walkers never want for fresh game. Sometimes, however, Colette needs other things, too, such as milk and toilet paper. One competition time, Colette discovered that she had run out of everything. When people in New York City say they have nothing to eat, it generally means they dislike what's in their pantry. For Ken and Colette, it means the cupboard is empty. As she put it, "No vegetables, no potatoes, no rice, no soup. Yeah, okay, we can eat roast after roast after roast and steak after steak. But you do need the milk and the bread and everything else in between, and there was nothing, and I actually had to call his mom and say, 'You know, there's no more shampoo. There's no more soap. There's no more toothpaste, no more toilet paper, no more paper towels. Nothing left in my cupboards!'"

It's not that Ken lacks work. Right now he had an entire safari in his freezer that needed mounting, and the Get Stuffed shop in London recently hired him for a gorilla. But those weren't megaloceros. "I don't care about money. That's my problem," he says, shaking his head. For that reason, I'd wanted to stay in a hotel, but Ken wouldn't hear of it: "It'll cost me more in gas to pick you up. And I've seen you drive. You don't want to drive on ice."

For dinner, Colette was preparing elk—a roast from one of

the white elk Ken had shot and skinned at a game ranch south of Edmonton in order to make his Irish elk. Normally, when a customer orders meat from a game ranch, a butcher will prepare the meat, but Ken insisted on shooting and skinning his own elk. He needed the incisions to be properly made so that when he joined the pelts, the seams would disappear. Irish elk were massive, so Ken needed three white elk skins to make the cape of a single Irish elk. It took Ken and two other taxidermists six hours to skin four elk and a deer. They arrived at the game ranch at nine A.M. and were back in Alberta Beach, skinning out elk hooves and ears, by five that evening.

Re-Creations is a tricky category at the WTC. For years, the National Taxidermists Association refused to recognize its legitimacy. In Re-Creations, for instance, you can't use an elk to make an elk; you have to use a different species. Otherwise, it's not a re-creation. For the same reason, you can't make a prairie chicken out of a prairie chicken or a lobster out of a lobster. You can, however, use a chicken to make an eagle or a lizard to make a snake. Irish elk weren't actually elk; they were deer. Their closest living relative is the fallow deer, a much smaller species, with which it shares 90 percent of the same DNA. So it's perfectly legal for Ken to use an elk to make an "elk" that was a deer.

It's a good thing he wasn't competing with a vulture or a domestic cat, because Colette was now serving us hot slices of roast re-creation *Megaloceros giganteus*. This competition mount was heavenly.

Dinnertime, as it happens, was when Ken's five siblings used to ask young Ken about taxidermy. They found his approach to nature baffling and told him so. They said that someone who loves animals should not kill them. It became a Walker family refrain. "They had a mindset that I should not kill things. My mindset was *totally* different," he says.

Ken owns four guns. He believes that gun control is like communism: "great on paper." "In Canada, there aren't enough noncompliance laws. There aren't enough prisons to arrest us all," he explains. If it weren't for hunters who manage animals, he adds, species would be depleted by farmers (who find them a nuisance), by indigenous people (who sell them for food or Chinese medicine), or by developers (who destroy their habitats). "Tree-huggers use toilet paper. The biggest predator is the newspaper," he reasons. In 2004, for instance, black rhino hunting was reopened in Namibia: $150,000 a rhino, something Ken believes is good for the species. "Take away the value, and you take away the animal," he says.

Scientists believe that the Irish elk's antlers may have had something to do with their extinction. Exactly what that was, however, has been confounding people for centuries. One aspect they agree on is this: an astonishing amount of fuel is required to grow hundred-pound antlers in four months every year. One theory contends that the ecology of the land changed, becoming too densely forested for a hulking species adapted for life on the open plains. Another suggests that the elk's antlers "over-evolved," becoming too massive for its five-pound skull to support. Still other theories say that climatic changes and habitat loss from early humans (who also may have hunted the elk) made it impossible for it to find the phosphorus- and calcium-rich plants it required to regenerate new antlers every year. As a result, the species developed a type of osteoporosis and died out. This is the theory that most scientists adhere to today.

The first naturalist to write about the "large and stately beast" was Thomas Molyneux (1697). Molyneux got the story half right. He knew the elk had vanished from Ireland, but the idea that a species could go extinct was heretical at the time, and therefore unthinkable: God would never snuff out one of his own creations. Even Thomas Jefferson, a great fossil collector, would have to be convinced of something as controversial as extinction. Instead, Molyneux hypothesized that the elk was alive somewhere. Indeed, he claimed that the species had migrated to North America (where animals shrank), and people there called them moose.

The French were among the first to accept the concepts of both extinction and evolution—but they found these ideas mutually exclusive. The two leading naturalists of the late eighteenth and early nineteenth centuries, Jean Baptiste de Lamarck and Baron Georges Cuvier, were archrivals. Lamarck believed in evolution but not extinction; Cuvier believed in extinction but not evolution. Cuvier, the founder of vertebrate paleontology, was a "catastrophist." He theorized that animals dispersed and became extinct due to apocalyptic floods, earthquakes, and other global environmental disasters. An eco-soothsayer, Cuvier claimed in his four-volume *Research on Fossil Bones* (1812) that the Irish elk had died out during the last "great freeze" along with the mammoth. Recent radiocarbon dating of skeletal remains, however, has proved that the Irish elk survived the big freeze and lived with prehistoric humans into the early Holocene—three thousand years after the ice sheets receded, around seventy-five hundred years ago. Humans, it appears, may have done this beast in.

The Victorians found the Irish elk a most perplexing creature. They believed that its ever-evolving antlers were a liability and cited the elk as an example to disprove Darwin's theory of natural selection. Undaunted, Darwin said that the elk's antlers were not weapons but "splendid accoutrements" for attracting mates. In 1974, Stephen Jay Gould confirmed this theory: although the antlers did intimidate rival suitors, they were pri-

marily three-dimensional aphrodisiacs used to lure females to
the male's "lek" (a patchwork of territories it had staked out).
Then, in 1996, Gould retracted that conclusion: giant deer *did*
use their antlers in combat after all.

In 2004, a team of University College London biologists re-
vised this portrait once again. They examined the DNA of the
fossilized remains of two Irish elk from two widely different extremes of its geographic range (one discovered in the Ballyna-
mintra Cave in Waterford, Ireland, the other in Kamyshlov Mire
in western Siberia) and confirmed that its closest living relative
is the fallow deer, not the red deer as previously believed. All of
which brought these scientists, and now Ken, back to mating.

If the Irish elk was essentially a giant fallow deer, one can as-
sume that it mated like a fallow deer. The fallow deer is one of
the few species in which females, which tend to travel in herds,
select their mates. Back to the antlers. Female fallow deer lust
after stags with impressive racks, and alpha stags mate with as
many females as possible, often fathering thirty to one hundred
fawns a year. Ken described the situation like this:

"A fallow deer, when he ruts, during the mating season, has
an area of ground he calls a lek. And what happens is, they flash
their antlers and they attract cows like a harem onto this lek.
If another buck or bull comes into that lek, they will force it
off . . . There's a confrontation, and they do a display, like a rit-
ualized dance. The Irish elk is no different. He would use his
horns to attract the females in and his body size to push his rivals off. *That's the way it had to be.* Natural selection favored big
antlers and heavy bodies. Only the biggest, widest-antlered bulls
would actually mate, so their genetics would always go in that
direction."

This was the stag that Ken was re-creating. I was thinking
about all this the next day when Ken and I drove to his studio to

see his Irish elk in progress. Ken's studio is on an unpaved road next to the trailer where the Walkers lived up until six months ago. Approaching it, we saw an unkindness of ravens taunt a bald eagle, and a coyote dart over a hill just as Ken pulled over and lowered his window.

The studio is about the size of a two-car garage. That day polar bear feet, patches of kudu and wildebeest fur, and Kenneth E. Behring's skinned walrus head and tusks—all frozen solid—were scattered around the yard. We passed them to get to the door, which said WALKER STUDIOS. "I don't know if it's the best thing I've ever done, but it's the most fantastic," Ken said by way of prelude. "I want people to go ballistic, to feel they are going crazy, seeing something they can't believe is real." Then we entered the Holocene.

Past a wall covered with taxidermy awards, past shelves of reproduction prehistoric skulls, was a massive hulking form covered with plastic sheeting. "She's kind of suicide blond now," Ken said, peeling off the plastic sheets. He hadn't modeled its facial features yet, or set its large amber eyes, or cast its small ears. And the blond pelts that he had described the night before at dinner—now stitched together to form a new animal—were held onto the form with long upholstery pins. But it was 100 percent megaloceros, which is to say the most masculine stag imaginable. Back at the house, Ken had shown me a few photos. They didn't come close to conveying its imposing scale and grandeur: its huge chest, its colossal shoulders, its powerful hump.

"It's starting to look like a real animal now," he said, walking over to a sawhorse that held a roughly nine-foot rack. The antlers weren't real. They were a fiberglass model that Ken had had custom-cast for $3,500 at Prehistoric Animal Structures, a local company that makes fake dinosaurs. (Later, he bought another rack, a thirteen-footer, from Taylor Studios for $5,000. Eighty-five hundred dollars in antlers quickly depleted the Walkers' savings. Nonetheless, the one anatomical feature you can't sacrifice when making an Irish elk is antlers. The family would recover when he sold the elk, preferably to a natural history museum. His asking price: $75,000.)

"I'm not into antiquities. It doesn't do me any good if they look like antique antlers on top of a live elk," he said, lifting the nine-foot rack off the sawhorse and walking over to his imposing buck. When he held the antlers above the elk's head, I could sense the animal's magnificence. I could imagine it standing high above the grassy plains, its antlers radiating sunlight like a beacon.

Ken had a buck on his sweatshirt and another one on his baseball cap. He circled his elk, looking for flaws that the World Show judges would catch, such as exposed seams. When you sew three animal skins together, even longhaired bulls, imperfections will emerge. Each leg may have up to ten different hair patterns. As in fine tailoring, the hair separations must align, or you'll lose points. "To impress the judges, sometimes you have to help them decide if you should win, and craftsmanship and attention to detail is one way," he explained.

Ken is nearly six feet tall. The elk was three feet taller and about as hairy. Ken groomed the elk's neck mane, applying Dippity-Do to every strand. He combed its tail (deer have tails; elk have stubs) with a wire dog brush. "Kind of cool, huh? I've used one hundred twenty-five yards of fire-line [thread] in that. I've got to be out of my stinking mind!" he said, shaking his head and smiling.

Before he put on surgical gloves to texturize the antlers, he handed me stacks of reference. Then he spent the next two days describing how he would make an extinct animal so alive that "people who have studied these things their entire lives would believe that it is real."

This is how he did it. First, he had John Matthews, who was still employed by the Smithsonian at the time, measure their Irish elk skeleton for reference. If Ken used that diagram, unaltered, to make his own elk, it would be a template. Ken would never use a template that he hadn't drawn—even one derived from the Smithsonian specimen—because the articulations might fall short of his own exacting standards. Today most biologists say that museum-mounted skeletons are unnaturally erect to emphasize the species' size, and Ken agrees. "I'm really fussy about my articulations. A lot of times I don't agree with the way a skeleton is rearticulated, so I go to anatomy books to see where the scapulas are supposed to sit and how straight the legs should be to hold the weight of those animals. Obviously, an animal that weighs one thousand pounds isn't going to hold his legs half hunched, because it is too stressful. There are references to physics in the whole thing."

He had no carcass to cast or erode. He was working from the inside out: skeleton, muscles, skin, fur. He redrew the Smithsonian skeleton, bone by bone, onto plastic sheets, which he cut out and reassembled like a giant jigsaw puzzle. When he was done, he had a flat skeleton. But he still wasn't ready to carve the form.

Ken is a gifted sculptor. He can shape rippled muscles with unerring accuracy by eyeballing diagrams or flat pelts. To do this, however, Ken had to know how an Irish elk's muscles behaved in motion and at rest. Fossilized remains, skeletons, and DNA sequencing don't show an animal's soft parts—its musculature, fur patterns, and humps. In fact, because fatty tissue does not fossilize, the Irish elk's hump wasn't officially confirmed until Stephen Jay Gould's study. He also needed to know how the animal behaved and sounded. But that data must be obtained by observation. How could he get it?

Fueled by a fierce curiosity, Ken posed the same questions asked by people such as Gould and the famous nineteenth-century British anatomist Sir Richard Owen: What kind of adaptations would enable an animal with a five-pound skull to support one-hundred-pound antlers? (Answer: incredibly powerful neck vertebrae and large muscles and ligaments.) What kind of form would a creature with massive dorsal spines (the third, fourth, and fifth spines are each a foot long) have? (Answer: a broadly raised area at the shoulders.) And so on.

For clues, he studied Paleolithic cave art: seven caves throughout Europe, particularly the Chauvet and Cougnac caves in France, whose megaloceros paintings are considered most accurate. Ken was collaborating with prehistoric humans, the first animal artists. "It's like comparing the Bible to yesterday's newspapers," he explains.

To someone who isn't a paleoarchaeologist or a taxidermist or Gould, the twenty-five-thousand-year-old icons resemble stick figures, static silhouettes. But Ken saw all kinds of clues in them. He saw how the animals looked in life and in death. He studied how they were shaded to determine their fur patterns. He believes that they were mostly light-colored, except for dark swaths along their humped backs, down their briskets, and ventrally, along their stomachs. He believes that they had short ear manes and dark throat manes and that their slender, pointy-snouted heads were disproportionally small and never held bolt upright, as they are in museums' mounted skeletons. He explained his scientific method as simply and as directly as a taxidermist would: "Two different caves. Two different time periods. One animal." He was using ancient reference to make an elk that looked as if it had rubbed off velvet four weeks ago. "There are

some things I'll have to guess at, but it's an educated guess: dark
animals have dark eyes; light animals, light eyes. It has to be scientifically sound—my interpretation of fact. Why would three
generations of cave painters paint the same animal?" he asked.

Once he had answered these questions, he put a second
sheet of plastic over the flat skeleton and drew on the muscles,
so you could see the bones underneath. Imagine the human
anatomy section of an encyclopedia where each layer of anatomy (the skeleton, the organs, the muscles, the skin) is on a separate sheet of Mylar. The sheets are then sandwiched together
to make the body.

Finally, he took his knife and started carving the form out
of big foam blocks. He carved muscles that flexed and muscles
that rippled. He carved tendons that contracted and tendons
that were relaxed. "It's like mixing a cake, a dash of this and a
pinch of that. You know, you have to feel the consistency in your
hands," he said offhandedly. "My take is half-cooked, and I'm
still inventing the rest of it. A lot of people don't like the way
I work. They want to know exactly how they can get my results
without taking chances. There've been a lot of happy experiments in my shop."

I asked if he'd devised the method. "I don't think so. From
the moment there was Styrofoam, people have been doing it."

After he carved the body, he cast the head and the hooves
(moose) in polyurethane foam and ordered custom fallow deer
eyes. Now he had to do the finishing work: texturize the antlers,
cast the ears, and sculpt the nose patch. I sat in his studio for
about a week, watching him, thinking about what Gould and
all the other scientists, and even the great Irish poet Seamus
Heaney, would think if they walked in here right now and saw
this stunning beast. Frozen in mid-trot, it was crossing a creek
to drive off a rival bull that was approaching its harem. Its small

slender head was low and upturned, its nostrils flared. Its left foreleg was aggressively raised. Its hump and fringy mane were shaded as in the Chauvet cave paintings. I stood and stared at it for a long time, overwhelmed by its ability to evoke confrontation and tension. I let its presence pull me into the Holocene with the same brutal magic and tragic force that the French writer Charles Baudelaire said made dioramas as concentrated as theater. Then I imagined the conversation that Ken might have with Gould if this were a different era and the leading taxidermists and the most imaginative scientists were colleagues (or fierce rivals!) — coconspirators who shared a love of and curiosity about animals and, indeed, preserving them, so that someday, when they are gone, there will be a lasting record.

Ken has a gift for sculpture and for music. He could have, for instance, earned a living as a singer, but he doesn't like to be around drunk people, and he hates cigarette smoke. In 1993, he worked as a Roy Orbison impersonator, performing at clubs around Alberta. He was so spot-on that he received top billing over "Marilyn Monroe" and "Frank Sinatra." He got the job when a scout for Starz and Legends saw him sing "Only the Lonely" at a karaoke competition. The scout asked him to sing "Crying." He nailed it, and the company hired him on the spot.

Ken is always comparing taxidermy to karaoke; he is equally talented at both forms of mimicry. In fact, he is so good that his male rivals often try to get him disqualified from karaoke competitions because they claim he's a professional. Women swoon when they hear his imitation of Ian Gillian from Deep Purple. He's won several competitions with "Dream On" by Aerosmith because his voice can reach its super-high refrain: "Dream on, dream on, dream on." But his Roy Orbison is extraordinary.

Orbison was the crooner of all crooners. His falsetto was as distinctive as Irish elk antlers. His lonesome ballads pierce your heart with a tenderness and longing that would be utter camp if it weren't so genuine. The Beatles idolized Orbison. So did Bruce Springsteen. During his life, Orbison suffered several personal tragedies, so he knew a thing or two about loss — about people who vanish and don't come back. "They asked Roy Orbison how he wanted to be remembered, and he said, 'I just want to be remembered,'" Ken told me.

One night Ken, Colette, and I piled into Colette's pickup and went to a bar. It was in Stony Plain, thirty miles east of Alberta Beach, a place called the Stony Plain Hotel. Colette was meeting some friends here. It was cold and icy — an ordinary mid-February night in Alberta. We wore jeans and sweaters and heavy snow boots. A yellow sign outside said KARAOKE. We walked inside. There was a long wooden bar already decorated with shamrocks for St. Patrick's Day. Albertans with muttonchops and cowboy hats or wearing black leather pants and T-shirts sat at tables loaded with pitchers of Labatt's. The beer was cheap. Everyone was smoking.

Colette's friends were chatty and laid-back. Two of the women had been best friends since they were eight; they'd vowed to marry brothers one day, and they had. The brothers sat next to their wives, drinking beer. Karaoke started at 10:30. We sat down and ordered a pitcher. Ken looked preoccupied, as if it were a distraction to be here tonight when the World Show was only weeks away. But it was evident that he was going to sing.

He flipped through a binder of titles; there were thousands of songs. I wondered which one he'd choose. Then the MC, a skinny rocker with a beard and long black hair, walked onto the linoleum dance floor, turned on the teleprompter, grabbed the mike, and led off with "Lay Your Hands on Me" by Bon Jovi. He flailed his head this way and that, his long black hair slashing the air like a cat-o'-nine-tails. When he finished, an attractive blond woman sang "Like a Little Prayer" by Madonna in a voice so angelic and calm it was comforting.

At the Stony Plain Hotel, people could momentarily escape the isolation of winter in Alberta, with its off-season poverty and alcoholism. Here it was possible to imagine yourself a star in Montreal or Vancouver. That is, unless you struck up a conversation with one of Colette's friends, Pete. He wasn't moved by "Bon Jovi" or "Madonna." He preferred to talk about Alberta.

"Is Alberta beef on the menus in New York?" he asked me. I had not heard of it. "While you're in Alberta, have a prime rib or a T-bone," he advised. "It's ultimate. It's fine, not a coarse meat. Have a charbroiled beefsteak. And you've got to ride a mechanical bull. The women love it! Go to the Cook County Saloon. There's also one at Cowboys." Pete talked and talked. He talked through Shirley's rendition of "You Sexy Thing." He talked while Shirley's boyfriend belted out "Brick House." "D'ya eat buffalo yet?" he asked. I shook my head. Then: "Men are really men here. They aren't sly dogs like in Toronto and the States. Hardworking. Driven. Rednecks, but tolerant. Strong, too."

Finally, it was Ken's turn. He got up on the dance floor and grabbed the mike. He stood far from the teleprompter and began to sing. It was an old rock classic by Stealers Wheel, "Stuck in the Middle." I hadn't heard the song in years; listening to it now made me feel nostalgic. "Well you started with nothing and you're a self-made man," he sang, holding his hand out by his side for ballast. His voice was rich and even-toned and had the unmistakable high tenor of Roy Orbison. It was thrilling to hear it. When Ken was finished, everyone applauded. He nodded and sat back down as "Axl Rose" took the mike and sang, "I used to love her, but I had to kill her."

"After I won my first Best of Show, no one ever treated me the same," he said, reaching for the binder. He flicked through the pages. The song lyrics were in plastic sleeves so they wouldn't get beer stained. I yearned for Roy Orbison, one of his lonesome ballads: "Crying" or "Blue Bayou." Orbison seemed like the perfect singer for Ken to imitate because of the daunting challenge: few can knock off Orbison's three-octave range. The MC said, "Ken's going to kick us up with some good old classics. I haven't had this tune in years. 'Come a Little Bit Closer' by Jay and the Americans."

It would drive a person crazy to name every animal species that has vanished from the earth. The number is incomprehensible and rises daily. The 2006 United Nations Convention on Biological Diversity reported that species are going extinct at a rate one thousand times faster than in the past. The Audubon Society's WatchList of threatened birds now includes 214 species, a 10 percent increase from 2002. The *New York Times* reports that 40 percent of all mammal species in China are endangered: pollution, hunting, and uncontrolled development are decimating them. The world's last two Yangtze giant soft-shell turtles — the largest known freshwater turtles — are unlikely to mate: these two symbols of health and longevity, ages eighty and one hundred, live in separate zoos. Cuvier the catastrophist was prophetic, yet who could have predicted the global meltdown that is defrosting the polar ice caps, scorching Arizona, and flooding New Orleans?

When I thought about Ken's endeavor to breathe life into an Irish elk, it seemed profound and important. This didn't make me happy; it filled me with dread. Taxidermy has come full circle. As more and more species become extinct due to global warming and other human factors, dioramas, sadly, have regained their original purpose: to freeze nature in its most glorious moments for a public that yearns for it yet is watching it disappear. Perhaps in the future, taxidermy will be mostly re-creations — re-creations of animals that have perished because of man.

As Ken drove me to the airport, I felt sad for all the taxidermists, from William Hornaday on down, who had something to offer science but who had to compete in shows for recognition. Ken called it credibility. You could also call it dignity.

9

I STUFF A SQUIRREL

FOR A LONG TIME, I had been thinking about attempting a mount. Next to competing, Ken Walker said the best way to learn is to actually preserve something, so one day I decided to roll up my sleeves and get my hands bloody.

Although I love birds, I wanted to mount a mammal — something suitably small and relatively easy, something ubiquitous and easy to observe even in New York City, where wildlife seems incongruous and irrelevant. The animal would have to be legally procured. It would have to have a tough, pliable skin, nothing delicate like a rabbit or with translucent parts like an opossum; nothing with a thick layer of subcutaneous fat like a walrus or with stink glands like a skunk; nothing politically incorrect like a baby seal.

One of the most common mammals in the eastern United States is the eastern gray squirrel (*Sciurus carolinensis*), a rodent with a year-and-a-half life span. I wanted to mount one. I wanted to make my own form from scratch using the soft-bodied technique — the method whereby you make an artificial body out of bent wires wound with excelsior (slender wood shavings) and padded with tow (chopped hemp fiber) and cotton. I figured if I could stomach skinning and fleshing, I could mount something. I was less convinced that I could give it the vital spark taxidermists always talk about: the magic part, requiring discipline and obsession and reverential love. Taxidermy's objective is clear yet impossible: to create a counterpart to life itself.

"Bad taxidermy is easy, I grant, but we are not discussing stuffed monstrosities of any kind," William Hornaday wrote in 1883. You have to know everything about an animal to capture its essence in a mount, yet you needn't know a thing about it to detect even a tiny flaw—and everyone knows what squirrels are *supposed* to look like. I had seen mounts at the World Taxidermy Championships with exposed seams, lopsided ears, or unnaturally angular shoulders; whose eyes were too closely set; whose bodies were truncated or hollowed out into planters or whatever. Whenever I encountered these horrors, I felt deeply disturbed. No wonder people find taxidermy creepy.

You'd think the proliferation of taxidermy schools in America would raise the standards—and they do to a certain extent. However, no formal training has ever been required to become a taxidermist, which adds to its idiosyncratic appeal. All the famous American taxidermists entered the trade circuitously or by apprenticeship. Apprenticeship seemed the most authentic way to go, and for an unskilled, unartistic New Jersey native who fears unleashed dogs, it was truly the only option. However, before I asked the Schwendemans if they would teach me, I considered my alternatives.

I could have enrolled in a taxidermy school. The Academy of Realistic Taxidermy in Havre, Montana, seemed a good choice at the time, but its beginner course required a tetanus shot and eight weeks in a dormitory with a roommate. I could have gone it alone. Darin Flynn's *Mounting a Fox Squirrel* video, which I had bought at the WTC, was tame enough, but he used a premade foam manikin; I wanted to make mine from scratch, using the method Walker had on the bush baby at the Smithsonian. It was because of him, in fact, that I had bought *The Breakthrough Mammal Taxidermy Manual,* another false start. It contains a how-to section on small mammals, with photos of flayed squirrels turned inside out like leather gloves. When I saw their sunken eyes and exposed organs, I slammed the book shut and never opened it again.

The Wildlife Artist Supply Company in Monroe, Georgia, sells a prefabricated squirrel-mounting kit specifically for the aspiring taxidermist and a choice of 125 squirrel manikins, each striking a riveting pose: climbing a tree, hanging dead, sitting upright with a nut, barking. The kit costs a reasonable $24.95 — a compelling alternative to formal education — but where would I do it? In my parents' garage? In my publisher's conference room?

An apprenticeship seemed the best way to go. I needed mentors, I decided, and when the Schwendemans agreed to teach me, I was overjoyed (and a bit nervous).

Bruce can mount a squirrel in two 14-hour days if he does nothing else, but David insists that when a taxidermist rushes, it will show in his work. "People can erect a shopping center in less time than it takes to mount a deer head," says Bruce. He compares the intricate craft to bookbinding or restoring an old flag; no two mounts are alike. We agreed to pace ourselves and work in discrete phases, and in the end, the squirrel took six months to preserve. "Geez, you had to choose a squirrel," Bruce groaned when I first mentioned the idea. "Why couldn't you choose something easier like a bear? How'd you talk me into this?"

We never discussed when we would start or who would "dispatch" the squirrel — or how. I wasn't in a hurry. I wasn't sure I had the stomach for taxidermy. The tools alone — eyehooks, brain spoons, and toe probes—made me shudder. I could barely watch Julia Child filet a fish on TV. And I certainly wasn't going to shoot anything. For one thing, up until fairly recently, the only trigger I'd ever pulled was at a boardwalk arcade. For another, I have awful eyesight.

Before we began, David urged me to study my specimen, and like all good taxidermists, I started to identify with the species, imbuing squirrels with human characteristics (neurotic little New Yorkers, always impeccably groomed). On my way to work, I observed their nervous, jerky behavior in a lush community garden on Twenty-fifth Street. On my way home, I watched them scamper, then freeze (always clutching a nut, their beady little eyes transfixed) in front of the Clearview Cinema on West Twenty-third Street. At home, I kept my binoculars near the window to watch them race across wires or leap like monkeys from branch to branch. My visits to the American Museum of Natural History become more pointed. In the Hall of North American Mammals, I made my way down a dark corridor to the squirrel diorama to admire their plump, fleshy bodies. I even began to study them in storybooks I read to my daughters. Squirrel Nutkin and his brother Twinkleberry would never hold weight as taxidermic reference at the Smithsonian, but Beatrix Potter's illustrations nicely capture the idiosyncrasies of the species.

My daughters, innocent accomplices, picked up on my interest and began to point out squirrels wherever we went: the playground, the schoolyard, the Halloween parade. The only people who make a concerted effort to watch squirrels in Brooklyn Heights are crazy people on the Promenade. I was paranoid that one of my neighbors would ask why we were so infatuated with squirrels and my older daughter would say, "My mother is going to *stuff* one." In fact, she saved that information for both her elementary school teacher and the executive director of the

Brooklyn Heights Association, who asked pointedly, "And how do *you* feel about that?"

Looking back on it now, I realize that I devoted too much energy to studying their behavior and not enough to their anatomy. I could have, for instance, assembled a squirrel skeleton first to see how the thing is constructed. At the time, however, it seemed perfectly reasonable—or, more likely, vainly presumptuous—to simply observe.

To prepare my mind for surgery, I'd walk over to Frank's butcher shop in the Chelsea Market to look at the huge skinned carcasses hanging in the window. Then I'd pore over old taxidermy manuals from the 1800s. Montagu Browne's *Practical Taxidermy* (originally published in 1878) was the most highly respected in England. In America, Oliver Davie's *Methods in the Art of Taxidermy* (1894) and William Hornaday's *Taxidermy and Zoological Collecting* (1891) were considered the best of their era. Both manuals include scientific diagrams and illustrations; the authors' motives were linked more to science than to sport. I bought the Davie book at an antiques shop and read the section on mounting small quadrupeds. But it was Hornaday, whose chapter "Treatment of Skins of Small Mammals" I had photocopied at the AMNH library, who ultimately bolstered my courage. He wrote, "There are few circumstances under which a determined individual finds himself thwarted in his desire to remove and preserve the skin of a dead animal. In nineteen cases out of twenty the result hinges on his disposition. If he is lazy, a thousand things can hinder his purpose; if he is determined, nothing can."

I was determined but squeamish, and I related my fears to the Schwendemans. All David said was, "We have plastic bags in case you have to puke."

• • •

One day in late November 2003, I stop in at Schwendeman's Taxidermy Studio to see when we will begin. Bruce hands me a plastic bag from Target; inside is a frozen lump, which smells like blood and wet fur. "That's your baby!" he says, smiling. "Tomorrow we'll get the body out." He pauses, looking at me, then quickly adds, "I'll be right here to help you. It might be fun."

Fun is what I feared; nausea is what I expected. Fun would mean I had crossed some unspoken threshold; I had become too immersed in the subject and gone bonkers or lost my journalistic objectivity. Bruce then explains step one: skinning. We'll make a ventral incision from the chest bone to the anus, then skin the squirrel from the posterior end to the head, carefully removing the skin by snipping the membrane that connects it to the muscle, or meat. Eventually, we'll disarticulate (cut the ball from the socket) the hind and front leg bones from the pelvis and shoulder, respectively. Then we'll skin the head and the neck, severing the ear tubes, eyelids, nose, lips, and whisker pads from the facial bones without mangling anything; "split" the lips and eyelids; skin the paw pads; and finally extract the long tailbone from the tail. When we are done, we'll have the raw body with the head attached, skinned. The drama will begin tomorrow morning and take roughly two days.

Now I am truly nervous. Now what I fear is far worse than a bloody dissection: contracting Lyme disease, rabies, Rocky Mountain spotted fever, Bang's disease, bubonic plague, ringworm, cat scratch fever, sarcoptic mange, or any number of taxidermy's health hazards. I've read about them in *Stuffed Animals and Pickled Heads*, a book about natural history museums. The Carnegie Museum of Natural History's annotated bibliography on taxidermy lists even more hazards, from exposure to toxins in pesticides, insect repellents, and fumigants, to asbestos and arsenic poisoning, parasites, and carcinogens found in formaldehyde and other preservatives. Entry number 681, a bulletin put out by the South African Museums Association in 1980, urges all museum workers to treat every zoological specimen as if it harbored a potential disease. For no physiological reason, I start to feel itchy. I scratch my head. I can't wear my wool hat. As much as I don't want the squirrel to have been killed in vain, I desperately want to back out.

"I'm wearing surgical gloves," I say. David shakes his head and laughs. "Wimp!"

On April 30, 1883, the Society of American Taxidermists assembled in New York City for its third and final exposition. This last gathering featured a model workshop called "A Taxidermist's Sanctum: The Proprietor at Work." Never before could the curious outsider see the macabre tools and strange setting in which the taxidermist, as if by magic, simulated life. The model workshop, a period room of sorts, had this disclaimer: "The taxidermist's shop is for work, and not for visitors, and only the chosen few are admitted to the presence of half-mounted birds and beasts." Things haven't really changed. Few taxidermists—and even fewer museums—would ever allow the public to see a mount in progress, because people tend to freak out when they see a dead animal turned inside out, especially if that animal is named Fido or Mittens.

But now, on the day before I am going to skin a squirrel, David, as a rite of passage, wants to take me to the most forbidden place in the workshop: the cellar. More specifically, he wants to show me his macerating bison skull. Bruce forbids him. "It's too smelly!" Bruce insists.

The old man won't budge. "She's got to get used to the smells if she's going to be a *tax-i-dermist,*" he says with the persistence of a badger. "Let's go look at it!"

The banister to the cellar was once the mast of a sailboat. It is bowed and polished smooth. At the bottom of the steps, the

rank odor of putrefying bison emanates from a galvanized bath-
tub. "That's macerating, rotting. It's one of the worst smells you
could ever imagine," David says, turning on a faucet to agitate
the gamy, tepid water, which makes it even more repulsive.

"You had to stir it up!" Bruce shouts. I retch and gag.

"Oh, you sound like one of my daughters . . . and my son!"
David howls, grinning. With his knobby hands, he lifts the skull
out of the tub. The meat easily peels off the bones. He'll scrape
the rest off with a toothbrush. It buoys his spirits.

Bruce shakes his head in disgust and walks over to a big
plastic industrial bucket filled with saline pickle for tanning
small animals. Tanning breaks down the skin's oils and stiffens
its meshed fibers so the hair won't fall out. "That's where your
squirrel is going to go after it's skinned," he says. "Smell it! Put
your head in there!" Bruce is a big guy with a booming voice.
He's not joking.

Reluctantly, in the name of journalism, I lower my face into
the blue bucket, my gag amplified in the confined space. At the
bottom I see a jackass penguin slated for a touch-me exhibit
at Jenkinson's Aquarium in Point Pleasant Beach, New Jersey.
Through several inches of pickle, the penguin looks distended
and bloated, as if it had drowned. (It actually died by swallowing
its nest material. When it was necropsied, the aquarium found
a long stick in its gullet.) The penguin smells less rancid, more
fishy and pungent, than the bison skull, but I gag again.

An animal can last in pickle indefinitely. The Schwendemans
once pickled a porcupine for twenty-two years. This penguin's
been in pickle for a month or so, which is average. Tomorrow
Bruce will mix three gallons of fresh pickle using a secret family
recipe.

"While you're used to the smells, I'll show you the freezer,"
Bruce says, and we trudge through the basement, which is strewn
with coarse salt, to the walk-in industrial freezer. It is so crammed

with bagged carcasses — some have been in there for years — that (thankfully) there's no room for us (although Bruce does keep an ax inside in case he gets trapped). The furry arm of a four-hundred-pound black bear dangles from a garbage bag; its long claws are as sharp as knives. The bear is already fleshed and salted (salt inhibits bacterial growth, which would make the hair loose). It's too large to tan here, so Bruce will ship it to a California tannery in a leakproof UPS box marked GREEN SALTED HIDES. Tracking a bear — or any specimen, for that matter — is complicated and requires special permits and tags. Every animal in the shop, including my squirrel, is tagged and numbered. This bear's ears were tagged by the U.S. Fish and Wildlife Service at a weigh station during New Jersey's recent bear hunt. To track the bear further, its lips are tattooed and its skin is punched and coded with an awl. If one skin gets mixed up with another skin, federal authorities could potentially close down the shop.

The basement is crammed with dusty deer heads, heaps of caribou and moose antlers, tanning drums, rusty tools, jars of sand, artificial snow, mica for bases, various bones and teeth, driftwood, aquarium stones, seashells, stoneware crocks, and galvanized tubs. There is a darkroom, where two polyester lamprey eels are posed mating. Past a pile of old patterns from which Mum-Mum made ear liners is a shooting range where local hunters and Milltown police officers used to shoot for target. It's coated with dust, but I can make out the rusted iron stars clothespinned to a wire, which we follow to a back wall that is pitted with bullet holes. A sign says:

SHOOT AT YOUR OWN RISK
Range Prices
.2 cents per shot rifle
.2 cents shot pistol, includes ammo

"I don't think Mum-Mum ever shot for target," Bruce said. "That would have been too wasteful. She only shot for necessity—rats, muskrats, that kind of thing."

Our basement tour fails to make the impending dissection more palatable. I want to race home, eat a salad, and soak in a hot bath. "It's not that gross; you'll see. You don't attack it like a . . . ," he says, pausing. "Even butchers are delicate in how they do things. It'll be fun," he adds consolingly.

The next morning is the day before Thanksgiving. I pull up to the shop. The air is brisk, and the sky is filled with high wispy clouds. The sycamores that line Main Street are bare, and an American flag hangs from nearly every house. Through the plate-glass window, I see Bruce setting up his window display, an eastern wild turkey (mounted) and two human skeletons (fake).

Bruce, in a denim apron and jeans, has a backlog of projects to finish before Christmas, and the workshop is filled with half-mounted birds and beasts. I sit at the worktable, which is strewn with scalpels, knives, poultry shears, scissors, razor blades, a sharpening stone, and a thawed Milltown gray squirrel shrouded in paper towels. Attached to the squirrel with a rubber band is a bank deposit slip on which is written "Milltown Squirrel 9/10/03 DJS. Drowned. OK. Juvenile. Female."

Bruce wipes the blood and condensation off the squirrel, prepping it for skinning. "I want this to be a nice specimen for you," he says, placing it on newspaper in front of me. The squirrel, when I inspect it, is nothing like the plump squirrels in the AMNH diorama. It is bone thin and has a mangy tail, a bloody nose, and a stained bib. Its cloudy, sunken eyes are (thankfully) shut, and its meager whiskers need mascara.

"Only one tooth?" I ask. Bruce points out its other brown incisor. Then he says, "When he's pickled and washed and fluffed, you'll be surprised."

"If it's really nice, I can enter it into the World Show," I hear myself say. It's a joke, but Bruce says why not.

When David shuffles in from his nap, he explains how he had baited a trap for groundhogs (they were eating his tomatoes) and caught two squirrels instead. "I let one go, but this one I'm fed up with," he says, settling into his rocker.

"What kind of trap?" I ask.

"A Havahart," David says dryly, then chuckles.

I hold up the bank deposit slip. It says the squirrel drowned. "Aaaaah! I was teaching it how to swim," David says. "That's the way I killed it. I put it in the fishpond, and it didn't swim." "Teaching it how to swim" is a taxidermic euphemism for drowning, which results in less darning than bullet holes. At certain times of the year, squirrels are classified as pests and can be legally "liquidated" (Bruce's word; David says "killed") on your own property. That's what David did.

Psychologically, the first cut—scoring the belly with a razor blade—is the worst, and I feel like a medical student making her first incision. Bruce guides me to the middle of the chest bone, but my untrained hand is unsteady, and I'm terrified that I will cut too deeply and rupture an internal organ. The razor blade is dull. We exchange it for a sharp one as a violin concerto on the radio builds to a crescendo.

After I score the chest, David hands me a rosewood scalpel that he made for Bruce on the occasion of the tiger he skinned for Great Adventure amusement park. It's engraved TO DBS FROM DAD, 1974. (Bruce's first name is actually David.) "There you go, Petunia," he says.

With the scalpel, I cut through the scored skin, then work my way to the outer edges of the body, loosening the pelt, which I peel off the animal's delicate rib cage. The ribs are as tiny as a leaf's veins; they protect the internal organs, now fully exposed. "You want to go to the outside of that pink meat," Bruce instructs. My latex gloves are wet and covered with tiny hairs; hardly any of them are gray, because a gray squirrel's hair is mostly bands of black and white. Slippage—when hair comes off in clumps—is a taxidermic nightmare. The few strands on my gloves do not constitute slippage. "Very good on this side. Gee whiz, look at that! You can go down on the right. I don't see any holes," says Bruce.

The squirrel is now lying on its side, both knees skinned and exposed, its sack of organs a tiny water balloon. "I'm really proud of my knees," I say, surprising myself. Then I turn the squirrel over to skin its back, feeling the scalpel run against the ridges of the spine. I skin the body, then the legs down to the delicate ankles. Soon the entire skin easily lifts off the back. I reach an impasse: disarticulating the hind legs by cutting the ball joint out of the hip socket. "Use the scissors, but don't cut the skin. Are you able to feel that joint? It's right there. Now cut down here. Use your finger like a pencil," says Bruce.

Mum-Mum I am not. I puncture the lower intestines (I can't tell one organ from another), and something resembling soupy baked beans spills out. "Oooooh! Something just fell out of the body!" I shriek in horror. I'm beside myself, repulsed and disheartened. I put down the scalpel and look to Bruce for help. He deftly sutures up the gash in seconds. "Just like *ER!*" he says.

"I can't stand it! I don't want to look at *thaaaat!*" David mocks. His taunting eggs me on, makes me want to finish the job and not wimp out.

Somehow, I manage to sever the ear skin from the ear canal and then loosen the nose and the lips. "Stay close to the skull. You can trim the meat off later," David coaches. It's impossible to discern skin from cartilage from skull. "Stay close to that bone. Stay right by the skull. Come over toward me a little. Not your *body*—your *knife!*" says Bruce.

"That's where your thumbnail would come in handy," says David. "You don't wear gloves when you prepare a steak!"

The single bulb dangling from the ceiling is not sufficient for this intricate work. Before I disconnect the eyelids from the eye orbit in the skull, we measure the milky eyes: ten millimeters. Then Bruce turns an eyelid inside out and demonstrates how one severs such delicate tissue. Now I have to "turn" the other one. I can't! "C'mon! It's your initiation!" David wails.

"Feel it!" coaches Bruce.

The eye is still connected to the skull by a film that must be cut through. If I puncture the eye, the aqueous humor will squirt out. For a visual person, nothing is more revolting than slicing an eye, and the opening sequence of Luis Buñuel's 1929 film *Un chien andalou* floods my memory like a nightmare. So does high school biology, when I nearly fainted while dissecting a sheep's eye. This requires more stamina than both of those things combined.

"Don't worry about puncturing the eye! The *eyelids* are what you've got to worry about," says David.

My forearms are covered with blood. Somehow, I manage to cut the membrane between the eyelid and the eye. Nothing squirts out. David pours me a cup of instant coffee with powdered Coffee-mate. The Coffee-mate resembles borax and arsenic, but I no longer have qualms about drinking and eating in the workshop.

"You're doing fine. You'd be out of here if you were having trouble," Bruce says.

"That's why we didn't get you a vomit bag," David says with a laugh. "I figured if we didn't have a vomit bag, you wouldn't vomit."

Finally, I detach the last foreleg from the body. The skinned squirrel rests in a heap on the table. Bruce says I can tidy up and go home right after David and I prepare a "sketch sheet" to use as reference: an outline of the extracted carcass (posed) that we will use to determine the form of the artificial body.

My cell phone rings. It's my mother, preparing Thanksgiving dinner. Can I pick up a large roasting pan and string beans? Of course, right after I sketch my flayed squirrel onto a piece of nonglossy paper.

David hands me a reference file filled with nature photographs of squirrels to inspire a pose. But the pose I have in mind comes directly from my personal observations in New York City: a squirrel racing across a wire, its body elongated, its eyes intently focused on something beyond the viewer. David takes the carcass, elongates it, and traces its outline to show its anatomy, its proportions, and the articulation of what's underneath the skin. The sketch sheet emphasizes its hips and shoulders—pivot points where the anatomy comes together. It will be my sole reference when I return next month to make the artificial body.

As I wash up and look for my purse, Bruce tightens the tail in a vice and yanks out the long bone with pliers in one swift movement—something you can do only if you've been skinning squirrels your entire life. "That's impressive," I say, and it truly is. Bruce is elated and buoyant. David finishes the sketch, we both sign it, and Bruce says, "This is the first ten percent of the taxidermy process of doing a squirrel."

Over the course of the next six months, the window display of Schwendeman's Taxidermy Studio changes from turkeys and skeletons to groundhogs to a big domestic rabbit for Easter. The workshop also contains new batches of snakes, wading birds, and deer heads. Each time I arrive, the worktable is already set with that day's tools, the thawing pelt, the sketch sheet, and the hairless frozen body in plastic wrap, for reference.

Of all the procedures, fleshing is the most tedious, the most repellent, and it smells. Bruce compares the process to removing the meat from a walnut shell without breaking the shell's paper-thin partitions. I spend an entire day nipping and extracting tiny bits of meat with scissors and a small knife, paring down the neck, the ear tubes, the lips, the tiny toes (with a toe probe), even the split tail, until my eyes blur and my hand aches. Then I surrender the pelt to Bruce, who has to redo my crude eyelids and the underside of the face. He also has to sew up the holes I made when I got sloppy and pierced the skin. Finally, the skin is ready to be tanned. For this, Bruce uses an antique glass salimeter (passed down from Schwendeman to Schwendeman, as if it were the family Bible) to measure the sodium content of his new pickle. Then order number 6499 — "Squirrel on a Wire" — takes a long, salty bath.

On one visit, we make the artificial form. When I step inside the workshop, Bruce, who has decided that we should work in tandem, is grooming a squirrel of his own. His squirrel is not ordinary; it is rare and exotic: an albino he's been saving for a special occasion. Today he's going to set its pink eyes (glass bulbs the color of calamine lotion). Bruce's own eyes happen to be burned-out from too much squinting at whiskers, eye rings, and tiny toes. He could use reading glasses but prefers a blue metal magnifying visor (circa 1960) typically worn by jewelers or watchmakers. He looks through the visor's square lenses to set the pink eyes. Then he pauses and hands me four wires to sharpen on an electric file until the points can easily impale skin. These wires will be used to make the limbs. For the rest of the day, we work side by side, mentor and apprentice. The master, David, stops by periodically to repair a hornets' nest, to report his bird sightings, and mostly to hassle Bruce — and me.

I wind the wire limbs with excelsior, using a motion that feels like spooling a kite string. I wind and I wind until the limbs look leglike—that is, the thigh is not where the foot should be and the foreleg is not as fat as the hind leg. (I have to redo them more than once.) To make the tail, Bruce shows me how to wind another wire with cotton thread until it matches the extracted tailbone (in front of us for reference). We do the same for the body. I like winding. It puts me in a Zen-like state: it keeps my eyes from staring with macabre curiosity at the fleshing beam (used to skin big animals), the steaming cauldron of deer-skull plates, and all the other oddities that evoke a medieval apothecary. Soon I imagine myself as an apprentice to the spinning docent at Colonial Williamsburg. It's not so far-fetched. The soft-bodied technique is, in fact, 250 years old, although this shop is a holdout, not a tourist attraction.

On another visit, David walks into the workshop at nine A.M. with three foam squirrel heads he cast that morning. They are still warm from curing. We choose the best one, carve eye orbits into it, and coat the sockets with smooth clay. Bruce goes over to his junk drawer and digs around for the perfect glass eyes. When he hands me antique black bulbs from Germany, I feel great. He'd never waste them on a rogue. I'm finally working with confidence, when David tells me to insert the artificial body into the treated skin. It does not fit. It is too fat; it has a potbelly. "Stretch it!" David yells. Like I'm zipping up super-tight pants or cramming a child's foot into a stiff ice skate, I squish and compress the body, then stretch the skin with all my might, trying to make it fit. David helps me. We stretch. We pull. Somehow we get the body inside the skin.

David sings, "Oh, the ham bone's connected to the thigh-bone . . ."

Meanwhile, Bruce, done with the albino, is now grooming a different squirrel, this one for Yale's Peabody Museum of Natural History. I glance at the Yale squirrel (plump, confident, can tackle any artificial tree), then at my scrawny New Jersey rodent. Its hams look undernourished; its femur lacks authority; its tarsus is skeletal; the back of its skull is concave. Bruce hands me an old tobacco tin filled with tow and tells me to plump wherever the squirrel needs muscle and fat. "These are my favorite tweezers. Don't bend them!" he booms. With chopsticks dexterity, I take small puffs of tow and pad the "bones" under the skin. The squirrel needs considerable plumping, it turns out. I plump and I plump. Lost in thought, still plumping, I'm jolted alert by David's voice: "Don't lump it up!" Watching me from his rocker, which is held together with duct tape, he shakes his head and raises his eyebrows. "Okay, Petunia. Do you have a needle and thread?"

I spend several hours sewing it up. (Stitching paw pads is a very strange sensation. Imagine stabbing a needle through a thin eraser.) Then I move on to the finishing work, the part where a taxidermist can play God or Mother Nature by deciding whether his or her replica will look pensive, content, or vicious. Regretfully, I forgot to study the preskinned squirrel's face, so I have no choice but to approximate. I trim off the excess mouth skin, then tuck the loose flaps into the crooked mouth slot (tight as military sheets, I'm afraid). A slight frown, perhaps, but the wonder of taxidermy is the zillions of magic tricks it offers, enabling you to alter nature. A sprightly tail and eager, wide eyes should compensate, I hope, for the grimace. I slide the eyelids up and down on the glass eyes, making the squirrel look drunk, then guilty, then panic-stricken. I surgically enhance the eyebrows with papier-mâché paste to give them definition and make the face cuter. The legs are a bit lopsided, and the shoulder padding has slipped down inside the arm as if it were a furry sleeve, but my fingers are too cramped to open the thing back up and resew it. So I shine up the eyes with cotton dipped in gasoline, then stick long pins into the face to immobilize the skin while it dries.

On my last visit to Schwendeman's Taxidermy Studio, I coat the paw pads, lips, and nose with a secret Schwendeman's beeswax concoction, then sculpt and paint them. Finally, I dot the corners of the eyes with shellac until they glisten with the dew of heaven, and the squirrel springs to life. "It looks great," David says. I smile with pride.

Before I go home, Bruce wires the squirrel to a dowel so that I can transport it back to Brooklyn. Once it's affixed to the rod, I can picture how amazing it will look inside the display case I've designed for it. The squirrel will be racing across a black wire above the doorway of a seedy basement apartment that is lit by a bare yellow bulb. I've named the case *Gray Squirrel, Yellow Dawn*.

10

GRAY SQUIRREL, YELLOW DAWN

IN 2005, EMILY MAYER was competing in the World Taxidermy Championships for the first time. When she arrived at the Crowne Plaza in Springfield, Illinois, a bellhop looked at her and said, "So you're a rock star?"

"No! A rat star!" she snapped, and walked inside.

I followed her through the lobby (buffalo heads on baggage carts; deer heads on escalators) to room 407. We were sharing a room for the next five days, and we were both uneasy about the competition. She set her stainless steel rat case on one of the beds, grabbed a beer from the minibar, and rigged up a work area near the window. Then she unhinged the case and extracted four extraordinarily succulent *Rattus norvegicus* specimens with translucent feet. "Bloody hell!" she shouted. A fluorescent light bulb for one of her displays had broken in transit. "Oh, bugger!"

A minute later, Paul Rhymer showed up with my squirrel. He had driven it from his house in Maryland so I wouldn't have to take it through airport security. Rhymer's Smithsonian ID serves as something akin to diplomatic immunity in the eyes of U.S. Fish and Wildlife Service agents. When Mayer had landed at

JFK International Airport two days before, customs officers had seized her rat case, and she'd had to spend an entire day filling out paperwork to get it back. Mayer's "USFWS Form 3-177: Declaration for Importation or Exportation of Fish and Wildlife" listed eleven items:

FOUR Rattus norvegicus (brown rat)
ONE Oryctolagus cuniculus (European rabbit fetus)
THREE Mustela nivalis (weasel)
ONE Micromys minutus (harvest mouse)
ONE Canis familiaris (domestic dog)
ONE Melopsittacus undulatus (Budgerigar parakeet)

I introduced Rhymer to Mayer. He glanced at her BITCH .COM T-shirt and said, "I want to make a T-shirt that says IT'S JUST TAXIDERMY!"

She nodded. "I want to make one that says I DO IT WITH DEAD ANIMALS."

He sat on one of the beds watching as I removed the squirrel from its cardboard travel box. The squirrel looked great, I thought; its fragile ears and tail had arrived intact, if a tad mangy. It was impressive for a first mount. Rhymer was silent.

The last time I'd seen him was at the Behring hall ribbon cutting, when I was admiring the orangutan he had painstakingly de-pickled. Now he was examining my juvenile *Sciurus carolinensis*. He rubbed his chin thoughtfully. His eyes roved from whisker pad to paw pad and back again. He was clearly puzzled by something, but he uttered not a word. Then, finally, he sprang up off of the bed and yelled, which is uncharacteristic of him.

"Wax!" he hollered.

Wax? He bent down, inspecting the squirrel more closely. His eyes lingered on its waxy brown lips. (They were a bit bumpy, I guessed. I'd never noticed that before.) He scrutinized its tiny paws with their sharp brown claws. He shook his head dourly. Then he grinned from ear to ear. He said nothing except, once again, "Wax."

Then: "That's old, old, old, old! The only taxidermist at the Smithsonian who used wax we called a waxidermist." Suddenly I understood what was going on. The Schwendemans had let me enter the most elite taxidermy event in the universe with a history lesson! The squirrel was perfect—for 1938. But it was not 1938. Suddenly, I remembered the day Bruce had sent me home with an old pamphlet published by *Modern Taxidermist* called "The Squirrel Mounting Book" by Leon Pray. Its brittle pages flaked when I turned them—which I didn't do much. Now I wished I had. Now I understood, and it was not funny. I was about to compete with a Model T.

Yes, the old methods may exist these days only at places such as Schwendeman's Taxidermy Studio (where Mum-Mum's beeswax is in fresh supply and antique salimeters measure the salt content in Pup-Pup's secret recipe for pickle), but here, at the WTC, where judges inspect anatomy with an obsessiveness that verges on oblivion (as one photographer aptly put it), beeswax paws and lips would be embarrassingly arcane.

Rhymer hadn't finished his lobster in time for the competition, so he coached me on how to modernize the antique squirrel in twelve hours. "You can sculpt out these lips, and since they're wax, you can heat them up on this light bulb," he said, pointing to the lamp on the nightstand that separated my bed from Mayer's. "You can take a toothbrush and fluff it up. Buy a sculpting tool at the trade show—a deer-lip tucking tool will cost around five to fifteen dollars. Then dig out the lips. Go to Jo-Ann Fabrics and buy dark umber craft paint. Scrape and rebuild the paw pads with epoxy."

No other competitor had a third-generation Smithsonian

taxidermist in his or her hotel room acting as coach. I was exceptionally lucky, if deflated.

I defended my squirrel, though. Had I been drowned by an old, unsentimental taxidermist, I can't say I'd look this good. Its imperfections gave it character: its rust-stained bib and brown incisors showed that it had cracked its own nuts (a pampered zoo captive it was not); its thin whiskers evoked Clark Gable's elegant mustache; even the wax anatomy was noble in this sea of store-bought plastic. Okay, so you couldn't look up its nostrils to see its brain (its nostrils were stuffed with papier-mâché paste — the mark of a beginner), yet I'd made everything — except for the glass eyes and, of course, the "derm" — by hand. My squirrel had personality; it was humble and wiry, a fighter who'd survived in the shadow of the New Jersey Turnpike. It had, if just barely, the vital spark of life.

No matter. Rhymer would not buy my excuses. Taxidermy, like basic mathematics, is empirical; you can't compete with a fantasy creature. Again and again, the taxidermists I'd met had told me: taxidermists are restricted to duplicate what nature has already created. (If only Rhymer had accompanied Charles Darwin on the voyage of the HMS *Beagle*, I thought, the world would not still be arguing about natural selection.)

Rhymer shook his head, his mind clicking. He grabbed a notebook by the phone and sketched squirrel feet so that I'd have reference when I rebuilt the paw pads. His eyes followed the long seam that ran ventrally from the squirrel's sternum to its anus, as if the crude stitches were primitive surgery. "You can minimize the seams by fifty percent by pulling out the hairs from under the thread with a sewing needle. Then take a toothbrush or a wire brush and back-brush it to make the fur look softer," he said, quickly adding, "Even city squirrels are fluffy."

Then he turned toward Mayer, who was in a DO NOT DIS-

TURB zone, feverishly working, and said, "Look at how fluffy her rats are. Squirrels are glorified rats with fluffy tails!"

As he was leaving, he said, "The angle on your back leg is harsh. Wrinkled skin needs to be tucked in, and make the wax feet less lumpy." The door clicked shut. Mayer looked up and snorted, "It looks like a football!"

In the morning, Mayer tossed me tweezers and said, "They'll work better for extracting the soft fine hairs out of the seam — *which is dry and brittle.*" I refluffed the squirrel and set it in its display case. The judging started at five P.M.; I had only a few hours to preen. "Boy, is it warm, but I dare not open the window because of dust," Mayer said, breaking an intense stretch of silence. She looked like a mime. She wore white muslin gloves so she wouldn't smudge her Plexiglas display case. She held it up to the window, her huge brown eyes scanning for fingerprints. That night the case would enshrine one of her three competition pieces, *The Dogs Bollocks.*

Mayer considers a title change. The Americans might not understand; they might find it distasteful. You see, in England, the expression "the dog's bollocks" is slang for "the best ever" (whereas "absolute bollocks" means "absolute rubbish"). For Mayer, however, it also literally means canine testicles. The testicles in question once belonged to a neighbor's terrier named Gus. Gus overstepped his bounds one day, as dogs tend to do, and Mayer noticed. It was a bad day for Gus. "He raped my bitches, so I had him castrated," she said coolly. Now Gus's testes floated in a small vial of vodka. A rat so alert it was terrifying mischievously rolled the testes down a laboratory shelf, dismantling a scientist's experiment. Mayer, who loves and identifies with rats and finds them intelligent, had captured more than just rat anatomy; she had captured the very spirit of the species — its playfully defiant soul. Mayer's lab rat sought revenge!

When she'd first showed me the piece in Norfolk, she'd called it a Damien Hirst knockoff and said that she'd apologized to him for it at a party. Hirst had said, "That's not a knockoff; that's a compliment!"

I carried *Gray Squirrel, Yellow Dawn* down in the elevator and through the grooming area. Had it been 1880 and this was the first Society of American Taxidermists competition, the squirrel would have been displayed among creatures lovingly preserved by pioneers who innovated a distinctly American style of taxidermy. Today their descendants were converging in a hotel ballroom. I stepped inside, holding my squirrel. The officials manning the doors read the label and exclaimed, "That girl's from Brooklyn!" One of the guys, Dave, was from Louisiana; he had on a CRAWFISH TIME T-shirt. He and an official named Carl carried the squirrel to the far back corner, directly behind an island of deer heads. They set it on a long table marked NOVICES.

Dave said, "How many pieces do you see like that squirrel? None. How many squirrels do you see like that? Every day!" This buoyed my confidence, making me feel less the waxidermist—until Carl pointed to the crowd that had gathered in the middle of the ballroom. They were excited about something, but I couldn't see what. Looming high in the air above their heads, however, was the most stupendous, most glorious set of antlers imaginable. "Look at the Irish stag over there," Carl said. "That's a pretty unique deal there. Obviously, it's extinct. He used three different skins to make it, and he actually got the pattern off of ancient cave paintings. Those antlers are like nine feet across!"

It was the biggest, most powerful stag in the ballroom, and people were drawn to it like a doe to a lek. Ken Walker had arrived the day before; now he was in Re-Creations, touching up his rack, which had got scuffed up in the cargo trailer during the thirty-hour drive from Alberta. "Customs went great," he boasted. "I'm sure it was that Smithsonian stamp in my passport!"

Walker no longer resembled Grizzly Adams. He had shaved and cut his hair. He worked the crowd. "I took a huge chance," he told his fans. "It's a gorgeous animal. Moose are impressive, but they're ugly. This is beautiful. You can see the light through the septum! I'm happy. You can give me a pink ribbon, a purple ribbon . . . ," he said, beaming. "Hopefully on Saturday, I'll be able to sing. They have a karaoke machine and everything." His eyes radiated the excitement of pulling off the impossible. Walker had wrestled with prehistory and won.

Now he had to beat the score sheet. It should be easy, considering he was the only competitor in Re-Creations. Everyone else had dropped out. "No one wanted to lose to a Canadian's fake animal," he said with a shrug.

I congratulated Colette and said it must be a relief to be here. She shook her head and said, "Show me the money!" Then Ken sprinted downstairs to the trade fair to raid the Russian-made lion eyes before they were sold-out.

Downstairs, in the café, Mayer's assistants, Dave Spaul and Carl Church, were drinking cans of Red Bull. They've worked with Mayer for years: they've gone to Hirst openings with her, seen her spend an entire week painstakingly mixing colors for cow hooves, and watched her collapse from exhaustion on the kitchen floor. They know that this type of devotion is absurd, that no matter how hard a taxidermist tries, he or she can never bring the animal back to life, yet they admire her persistence. Still, they wondered how the Americans would view her rats. "At our shows, we accept her work as different and outrageous because she's known for that, but out here it could be viewed differently. She's never been judged before by people who know so much about anatomy and techniques," said Spaul.

Church added, "It could offend people. It's like the testicle thing. I must have seen a dozen white-tailed deer eating corn on the cob. There's nothing wrong with that, but you'd never see a white-tailed deer in a gallery. But you would see Emily's work in an art gallery in London and see it next to a Damien Hirst, and it wouldn't look out of place."

At two P.M., Mayer, with a final fluff with a paintbrush, surrendered her rats to the show officials who carried them inside for judging. I headed over to Novices through flocks of vibrant birds and deer galore: whole deer; truncated deer; deer transformed into planters; deer hollowed out into fountains with running water; deer trapped in barbed wire. One deer display was extraordinarily weird: two deer heads stuck to a frozen pole by only their outstretched tongues. The title rivaled that of a Damien Hirst sculpture: *As in Nature, One Hand Helps to Feed the Other, Just Like in Life We Can Always Use the Help of Another.*

Novices was filled with mounts from as far away as Australia (a kangaroo head) and as nearby as Waynesburg, Ohio (a turkey), and Belding, Michigan (a yellow perch). I scanned the rival mallard hen, the bufflehead, and the gray fox. A trio of pintails named *Rites of Spring* sat near the panfish dubbed *Last Day of School.* In the middle of the table, a Milltown gray squirrel raced across a wire.

People stopped by to comment. John Schmidt, the master sculptor who makes manikins for Van Dyke's supply company, said, "Ain't no country squirrel. Usually you see cornstalks and that kind of stuff instead of wires. You didn't use a form — that makes you a sculptor."

Markku Natri from Finland said, "It looks like a cat."

Then Roger Martin, the guy who had donated 250 specimens for the Behring hall, said, "You're one of the smartest competitors I've ever seen. All you can see is the light bulb. It's like looking straight into the sun. Everything is in plain view, but you can't see it. Great strategy!"

Finally, Mayer approached. She glared at my squirrel and snarled, "It looked like a football. But now it looks like a baseball. It's better than that trumpeter swan in murky water that looks like a coffin."

At the WTC, it is customary for the judges to critique all the mounts to help competitors improve as taxidermists. My judge, Jessica Stevens, a pretty blonde from Alabama in a leopard-print cardigan, gave my squirrel an 85, a second-place ribbon, but ticked my score sheet with numerous violations. She glanced at the squirrel, took a deep breath, and led off with the positive: "I know it's an urban squirrel. You used your imagination." She smiled again. Then she continued: "Anywhere you have shrinkage, I want you to rebuild it." She pointed to the ears and hind feet. "You've got to retexturize and even it out. You want it to be plump-looking." I nodded, though I happen to find svelte squirrels attractive. "If it was falling off and stunk, I would not say that," she said with empathy.

She shined her penlight onto the right hind leg. She examined its narrow face, directing the light onto its eyes. "Its eyes are not in alignment." She grabbed a photograph of a squirrel. "*This* is what we're trying to achieve. See how soft he looks? Around the mouth is where you had the most problems. Make the mouth slot as small as possible. Tuck it from the outer corners in toward the center—that applies to deer or bobcats or whatever. Tuck in your nose . . ." The nose. I was in trouble. The poor thing would have suffocated if it had been alive, which it was not, a fact that offered some comfort as Stevens pointed out more faults with my anthropomorphic double. "You've got to put pins or something in the nostrils. If you're going to be a squirrel taxidermist, you've got to start looking at squirrels." I lowered my head and nodded.

"It's going to be hard to get this personal reference unless you're at a zoo and can get some good photos. The basics are still there. This animal is harder than any large animal because of the details—the tiny feet, the tail. I would never be a squirrel taxidermist. I have to for my clients, but they're not my love. Your love may be squirrels, because you're not going to come upon a bobcat in the city." Again she was right.

She flashed an incandescent smile and continued. This was humbling, but I took it seriously. "You're dealing with such delicate features. You're dealing with a tail that has a bone, and if the bone doesn't come out intact, you can't get the fluff or the flow. If you tear a squirrel tail up, you're not going to duplicate its expression. You've got to learn to blow it out with a hair dryer. I don't want it blown out like a porcupine, but it should be soft like you see in nature. It's hard to duplicate what God made. They are like people. They are not all the same."

She paused, working up her nerve. She was about to ask me to feel the squirrel's genitals. I grimaced. I arched a skeptical eyebrow. I stared right into her eyes. She stared right back. Neither of us was smiling. Then, reluctantly, I reached in and felt around. I did not feel sex organs. What I felt was a thready knot. My squirrel was, anatomically speaking, a Barbie doll, as my editor later explained. Grinning, Stevens said, "We have to deal with genitals—whatever—especially with males. If it's just squished up there . . ." She paused, blushing. "It's hard to critique a life-size bear for a male [taxidermist], but you have to do it. And they have to deal with it."

Then she summed up: "I'm looking forward to you enjoying this—not just for your book. You might develop this into a hobby. You might become a competitive taxidermist. It's opened up a whole world to you that you never knew existed. This is an art, and now you appreciate that. You may have thought taxidermy was just stuffing an animal—mounting an animal—we hate that term. But it's an art. We don't want to be thought of as Norman Bates. We are artists, and we have a great respect for God's creatures."

That was the official critique. Now Jack Fishwick was walking toward Novices. He had just judged hundreds of birds, yet he had fuel for one last squirrel. "The light bulb's the wrong color! This should be the red-light district," he said disarmingly, before he went for the jugular. "Squirrels on wires aren't this shape. I don't think you fully understand what you are doing. The hips are two big lumps, and they stand out. The ears need to go in more. You should have taken two squirrels and skinned one to study its anatomy. You're blind! A lot of American taxidermists hunt turkey, and the closest they get is thirty yards before they die. I think it's very good for a first attempt . . . but you have been hanging around taxidermists for the past two years—perhaps the best taxidermists in the world. You have an advantage! You are not starting at rock bottom. You have tons and tons of info you could have studied."

"I could spend thirty years studying Picasso, and when I'm done, I'm not going to be Picasso," I said.

"Taxidermy is not art. It's a highly skilled craft," he said.

"You mean I could be as good as Emily?"

"Yes—if you're dedicated enough. Anybody could be the best in the world. But not anybody has the dedication."

"What about the Carl Akeleys of the world?" I ventured.

"He wouldn't stand up to the work that's done today. Our best is better than he was. Mankind always improves."

Only in hindsight do I realize that he was right: my squirrel missed the mark because I didn't love it enough. I didn't have the reverential love for the species that consumes all great taxidermists, both in Carl Akeley's time and now.

In the end, Mayer took fourth place in Small Mammals. Her rats had tied for first place with a fawn and a cougar and its cub, but the judges considered erosion molding unconventional and gave her fourth place. They also docked the rats because their eyes were asymmetrical. After the show, Mayer said, "Animal faces are never symmetrical." She held a mirror up to half of her own face and said, "See how strange I'd look if my face were symmetrical. No one's face is symmetrical!" The big winner that day was the fawn, which took Best of Show.

That night, Fishwick was having dinner with a group of European taxidermists in the hotel restaurant. One of them was Peter Sunesen from Denmark. Sunesen's shop, Naturværkstedet, is as meticulous as a dentist's office. He is among the best bird taxidermists in the world, and Mayer has hired him for Hirst commissions. He's won the Danish, European, and Scandinavian taxidermy shows and has taken the WTC twice. He loves to do taxidermy, and he loves to talk about it. "I'm an Aries; I can talk forever," he said. I didn't doubt that. The best taxidermists talk like they preserve, each word a preenable feather. But my mind had gone into anatomical overdrive, and so I said, isn't it a bit odd to compare an Irish elk to lab rats, for example, to determine Best of Show? "It's a world show, and it is a *show*," he said. "We'll never know who's the better composer, Lennon and McCartney or Mozart. They all did brilliant music, and so it's a matter of taste, of preference. Some of the things in this show are impressive one time, but it hasn't got the lasting effects upon you. To improve too much is to get away from music.

"I love to watch birds, to hunt them, and eat them; everything about them. But it's the *live* birds that interest me — the excitement of getting it right. Can this curlew fool the birder? That's the standard I try to obtain."

He paused and added, "It's the same intimate sense that you have for your spouse. Someone who knows you intimately will know you have gained weight or that you are tired, but the judge who doesn't know that species won't know that. When I walk into that room, I see versions of nature that are distorted and wrong, and then every so often I see the real thing . . . but it's *rare*. It's the jizz that will tell them apart: the nervous action . . . The jizz is made up of everything."

Later that night, the BYOB wind-down party was being held in one of the Crowne Plaza's large banquet rooms. Unlike the previous night's awards ceremony, with its teenage "Liza Minnelli" in a sequined gown belting out "All That Jazz" and its tuxedo-clad taxidermists reciting the Lord's Prayer, this was just a party. People were seated at round tables, chatting, drinking, having fun. It was as dark as a nightclub, and it felt like one, too.

In the front of the room was a big stage with a microphone and a karaoke machine. People had already signed up to sing their favorite songs. One of the first to perform was Jerry Jackson, the blond taxidermist from Michigan, who had competed in Novices with a deer head and a raccoon. Jackson and his wife went up onstage and sang a duet, "Summer Lovin'" from *Grease*. Jackson is normally humble and introverted. Onstage, however, he let loose. He and his wife harmonized, filling the room with teenage romance. They finished. Everyone clapped. Then they sang "Falling in Love with You."

Soon the dance floor was a swaying mass of crooning taxidermists. Mayer, Fishwick, "Vinnie the Butcher," and Team Sweden were all twirling and twisting. I looked around for Ken Walker.

I didn't see him, but everyone knew he was going to sing. At some point, someone belted out "We Are Family," prompting more and more people to get up on the dance floor. By the time Roger Martin played the harmonica, the room was packed.

I sat in the back, nursing a drink. Eventually, Ken showed up at my table. He was talking nonstop, happy with his blue ribbon—already over the sting of his hulking stag losing Best of Show to a Bambi-like fawn. "How are you going to end your book?" he asked. I shrugged and said, "It's still going on." He leaned in and mentioned something about those old mounts that the Smithsonian had destroyed. He shook his head but didn't dwell on it. Not here. Not tonight at the World Show. The MC was calling him up onto the stage: . . . "Three time World Champion and world champion singer is going to sing . . ."

Ken ran up and grabbed the mike. He nodded, scanning the crowd, revving up. He's done this a million times at clubs all over Alberta. His hunter's hands clutched the mike. He tapped a steady beat with his trapper's feet. He was wearing a khaki hunting shirt, not the requisite black suit. He had no props: no guitar, no black sunglasses. But it didn't matter. He had the jizz.

The first five notes were electrifying: *doo doo doo doo doo*. It was one of the most famous rock songs ever—the only song that outsold the Beatles when it was released in 1964 (two years after Ken was born). Everyone hummed the guitar riff before he sang a word; they knew this song by heart. He tapped the beat, his head nodding.

"Pretty woman walking down the street . . . Pretty woman, the kind I like to meet . . .

"You're not the truth . . . No one could look as good as you . . .

"Mercy."

His voice was rich and smooth and had the incredible Orbison range: the range Bob Dylan said made you want to drive a car off of a cliff; the voice of a professional criminal; the voice that could jar a corpse.

"Cause I need you . . . I'll treat you right . . . Come with me baby . . . Be mine tonight . . ."

"Pretty woman stop awhile . . . pretty woman talk awhile . . . pretty woman yeah, yeah, yeah . . ."

More and more people joined the dance floor. Everyone was swaying and singing. I watched from the back, taking notes. The falsetto was spot-on, the growl beyond masterful. If you close your eyes, his parents said to me, you can't tell the difference.

So I closed my eyes. My heart wanted to dance. My heart wanted to throw this notebook off a cliff. I squeezed onto the dance floor, swaying and stomping with everyone else. For a moment, I forgot I was in Springfield. I forgot who was onstage. Something Ken once said flashed in my mind: "I idolized Roy Orbison. Always have. And that's why I was able to get as close as I did."

Now Ken sang, "But, wait . . . what do I seeeeeee . . ." He held the word in suspension for several seconds. It hung in the air like the shrill cry of an exotic bird. And then it struck me: Ken had brought Roy Orbison back to life.

SOURCES

··········

Behind many a stuffed animal lurks a
thrilling story of travel and adventure.

—WILLIAM HORNADAY, 1896

•

The history of taxidermy, natural history, habitat dioramas, and museums is central to Karen Wonders's amazingly comprehensive study
"Habitat Dioramas: Illusions of Wilderness in Museums of Natural
History" (Ph.D. diss., Uppsala University, 1993); Stephen Christopher
Quinn's *Windows on Nature: The Great Habitat Dioramas of the American Museum of Natural History* (Abrams, in association with the American Museum of Natural History, 2006), which also contains beautiful
photographs; and Stephen T. Asma's *Stuffed Animals and Pickled Heads:
The Culture and Evolution of Natural History Museums* (Oxford University Press, 2001). Asma explains with considerable delight why people
have always been drawn to the macabre and the strange, and nothing is
quite as macabre and strange as a museum of natural history.

An immensely fascinating book about the natural history mania
that swept the United Kingdom from 1820 to 1870 is Lynn Barber's *The
Heyday of Natural History* (Doubleday, 1980). This profoundly affecting
book about natural history in the pre- and post-Darwin eras provided
a rich context essential to my understanding of the world in which the
taxidermists I wrote about lived and worked. For an understanding of
how the trade was practiced in the nineteenth century, I relied on pop-

ular turn-of-the-century taxidermy manuals and on Christopher Frost's self-published *A History of British Taxidermy* (1987), which describes the era from 1820 to 1910, when Britain was the center of the taxidermic universe, having taken over the role from France and not yet relinquished it to the United States. Pat Morris's splendid article "An Historical Review of Bird Taxidermy in Britain" (*Archives of Natural History*, 1993) chronicles taxidermy's early development. *An Annotated Bibliography on Preparation, Taxidermy, and Collection Management of Vertebrates with Emphasis on Birds* by Stephen P. Rogers, Mary Ann Schmidt, and Thomas Gütebier (Carnegie Museum of Natural History, 1989), called the "blue book" for short, is a trove of facts and sources.

For information about specific bird species, I used the *Sibley Guide to Birds* by David Allen Sibley (Knopf, 2000). For mammalian taxonomy and phylogeny, I relied on the Princeton Field Guides book *Mammals of North America* by Roland W. Kays and Don E. Wilson (Princeton University Press, 2002) and numerous Web sites, including the National Museum of Natural History's Mammal Species of the World Database, www.nmnhgoph.si.edu/msw. Also see the International Union for Conservation of Nature and Natural Resources Red List of Threatened Animals, www.iucnredlist.org.

Taxidermy is an obscure topic for which no central archive or comprehensive book exists. If it weren't for the taxidermists themselves —who love to preserve things—countless old manuals, scrapbooks, memoirs, and catalogs would have perished. Thankfully, several taxidermists and taxidermy collectors generously lent me sources from their impressive personal libraries. Additionally, I spent weeks at the AMNH archives and the Explorers Club library in Manhattan.

1. SCHWENDEMAN'S TAXIDERMY STUDIO

The idea for this book grew out of an article I wrote for the *New York Times,* "When a Polar Bear Needs a Pedicure," which ran on March 26, 2002. For that piece, the AMNH's exceptionally knowledgeable senior project manager, Stephen C. Quinn ("Mr. Diorama"), gave me a private tour of every diorama and display in the museum bearing the mark of David Schwendeman.

Anyone who has had the distinct pleasure of hanging around Schwendeman's Taxidermy Studio for fifteen years (or fifty years) will get to meet every living Schwendeman, every Milltown neighbor and friend, every fellow birder and curiosity seeker who loves to poke around in such anachronistic shops of wonders. In addition to many enjoyable talks with David and Bruce Schwendeman and their extended family and friends, Rose Wadsworth (the AMNH's former exhibition coordinator for living invertebrates) wrote me two anecdote-filled letters and sent me an assortment of photographs, memos, relevant book chapters, and news clips. Further sources include the following articles: "Memories and Lessons from a House of Nature," *Home News,* March 23, 1986; "Taxidermy—All in the Family," *New York Times,* October 23, 1977; and the AMNH's employee newsletter, *Grapevine* (May/June 1983 and January/February 1987).

William Hornaday's quote is from his popular manual *Taxidermy and Zoological Collecting* (Charles Scribner's Sons, 1891; I used the 1916 edition). This book was used as the basis of Elwood's popular correspondence course, established in 1904 and undertaken by several living taxidermists quoted in this book.

Information on Ker & Downey is from *Ker & Downey Safaris: The Inside Story* by Jan Hemsing (Sealpoint Publicity, 1989).

It is still possible to see Misty at the Beebe Ranch in Chincoteague, Virginia. In July 2010, Roy Rogers's horse Trigger was sold at auction for $266,500 to RFD-TV, a family values network based in Omaha, Nebraska. The network also bought Roy's German Shepherd Bullet for $35,000.

Charles Darwin's foray into taxidermy is discussed in Stephen Asma's *Stuffed Animals and Pickled Heads.*

A *New York Times* article on rebuilding Deyrolle ran on November 15, 2008.

My source on contemporary antifur campaigns was Andrew Bolton's *Wild: Fashion Untamed* (Metropolitan Museum of Art and Yale University Press, 2004).

The *New York Times* obituary for Douglas Herrick ran on January 19, 2003.

The Third Annual Report of the Society of American Taxidermists (Gibson Brothers, 1884) contains a bibliography of taxidermy, in which the obscure methods used in the 1700s are described. Additional methods can be found in Amandine Péquignot's "The History of Taxidermy: Clues for Preservation (*Collections: A Journal for Museum Archives Professionals,* February 2006) and *An Annotated Bibliography on Preparation, Taxidermy, and Collection Management of Vertebrates with Emphasis on Birds* by Stephen P. Rogers, Mary Ann Schmidt, and Thomas Gütebier, which does a great job of defining the role of the museum taxidermist.

I found Peale's correspondence with Washington in the Harvard Museum of Comparative Zoology guide *About the Exhibits* (1964, 1985).

The story of Bécoeur is expertly told by L. C. Rookmaaker, P. Morris, I. E. Glenn, and P. J. Mundy in "The Ornithological Cabinet of Jean-Baptiste Bécoeur and the Secret of Arsenical Soap" (*Archives of Natural History,* 2006).

William Hornaday's quote about jealous, narrow-minded taxidermists ran in *Science* on July 24, 1880.

John James Audubon's effort to animate bird skins with wires is from *Audubon and His Journals,* vol. 2 (Dover Publications, 1986).

Pat Morris's article on arsenic exposure and the life spans of Victorian taxidermists, "Stuffing for Longevity," was published in *New Scientist* in August 1982.

Stephen Quinn's *Windows on Nature* has wonderful mini-biographies of the AMNH'S diorama artists; this is where I read about James Perry Wilson and the first renovation of the Hall of Ocean Life. The rest is from David and Bruce Schwendeman and AMNH press releases.

Facts about the Biology of Birds renovation came from AMNH's employee newsletter, *Grapevine* (May/June 1983).

2. THE CHAMPIONS

Retired Milwaukee Public Museum taxidermist Floyd Easterman generously shared documents from his personal archive with me, includ-

ing the SAT annual reports of 1881, 1882, and 1884 and William Hornaday's personal scrapbook of newspaper clippings. Mary Anne Andrei's
fastidiously researched article "Breathing Life into Stuffed Animals:
The Society of American Taxidermists, 1880–1885" (*Collections: A Journal for Museum Archives Professionals,* November 2004) was extremely illuminating, as was an interview I had with her by phone.

America's approach to taxidermy is described in Karen Wonders's
Habitat Dioramas. This is where I learned about the tradition of American sportsmen such as Theodore Roosevelt and the Boone and Crockett Club.

For panda information and information on Hsing-Hsing, see "China's Panda Ambassadors," http://news.bbc.co.uk/2/hi/asia-pacific/
4508873.stm; "Animal Info—Information on Endangered Mammals,"
http://animalinfo.org/; and the National Zoo's Web site, http://
nationalzoo.si.edu/Animals/GiantPandas/default.cfm.

No one can describe *A Fight in the Tree-Tops* with more animation
and wit than its creator, William Hornaday. I found his lively words in
his memoir *A Wild-Animal Round-up: Stories and Pictures from the Passing
Show* (Charles Scribner's Sons, 1925) and in Andrei's article "Breathing
Life into Stuffed Animals." Wonders's *Habitat Dioramas,* from which I
got Hornaday's quote "I love nature . . ." from *Two Years in the Jungle*
(1885), provided the context in which I could view *Tree-Tops* in its era.

William Hornaday's account of Ward's Natural Science Establishment, "The King of Museum-Builders" (*Commercial Travelers Home
Magazine,* February 1896), is incredibly vivid. Likewise, *Natural History*'s March–April 1927 issue has articles by famous Ward's grads such
as Frederic A. Lucas and William Wheeler, who lovingly describe the
place. The Harvard Museum of Comparative Zoology guide *About the
Exhibits* (1964, 1985) also has a section on Professor Henry Ward and
his magnificent quarry.

3. THE MAN WHO HUNTED FOR SCIENCE

Sources on Carl Akeley, his African expeditions, and his taxidermy
process come from many places, including primarily the AMNH ar-

chives (his personal papers, journal, telegrams, correspondence, press bulletins, and records, as well as those of his widow, Mary Jobe Akeley) and to a lesser extent the Explorers Club library in Manhattan. I also relied on the following works: Akeley's memoir *In Brightest Africa* (Doubleday, 1920; I used the 1923 edition); *Carl Akeley's Africa*, an account of the Akeley-Eastman-Pomeroy Expedition by Mary Jobe Akeley (Blue Ribbon Books, 1929; I used the 1932 edition); *The Wilderness Lives Again* by Mary Jobe Akeley (Dodd, Mead, 1940), which describes his step-by-step preservation process. Roy Chapman Andrews's essay "Akeley of Africa" (*True,* June 1952) provided thoughtful insight into the character of this complex man, as did Robert Rockwell's memoir *My Way of Becoming a Hunter* (Norton, 1855). Stephen Quinn's *Windows on Nature* contains images from the AMNH's archives and behind-the-scenes information on the making of African Hall. The May 1914 issue of the *American Museum Journal* (14, no. 5) is about Akeley, as are the essays "The Autobiography of a Taxidermist" (*Natural History,* March–April 1927) and "Carl Akeley's Enduring Dream" by George R. Price (*Reader's Digest,* September 1959). The March–April 1927 issue of *Natural History* is devoted entirely to Akeley's legacy and contains glowing commemorative essays by his dearest friends and colleagues: Kermit Roosevelt, Baron de Carter de Marchienne, F. Trubbee Davison, George Sheerwood, Frederic Lucas, William Wheeler, and Henry Fairfield Osborn.

Of all the Akeley books and articles, none is as passionately researched and rendered as *African Obsession: The Life and Legacy of Carl Akeley* by Penelope Bodry-Sanders (Batax Museum Publishing, 1998). I relied on this book for specific details about his early life and career, his time at Ward's, and his Congo expeditions.

I attended the June 2004 elephant radiography press conference at the museum, where I interviewed the conservation team while they shot images of the elephants. The *New York Times* ran a piece on the elephant project on June 4, 2004.

The Roosevelt-Smithsonian expedition of 1909 is described in Karen Wonders's "Habitat Dioramas."

The alleged elephant substitution is from Bodry-Sanders's *African Obsession.*

I found descriptions of Ward's Natural Science Establishment in the aforementioned memoirs and books; in Hornaday's profile of Ward, "The King of Museum-Builders"; in the Harvard Museum of Comparative Zoology guide *About the Exhibits* (1964, 1985); and in Robert Rockwell's memoir *My Way of Becoming a Hunter.*

"Zoological Collections in the Early British Museum—Documentation of the Collection" by Alwyne Wheeler (*Archives of Natural History,* 1996) summarizes the British Museum's collections, sources, and importance. The origins and contents of famous AMNH collections (those of Prince Maximilian of Wied, P. T. Barnum, and Roy Chapman Andrews) are from two old AMNH guidebooks (1953, 1972) and from the *New York Times* obituary of paleontologist James Hall (August 9, 1894).

The Thomas Barbour expedition is from the Harvard Museum of Comparative Zoology guide *About the Exhibits* (1964, 1985).

Peale's information is drawn from many sources, chiefly Charles Coleman Sellers's *Mr. Peale's Museum* (Norton, 1980) and from Lynn Barber's *The Heyday of Natural History.*

The account of Roy Chapman Andrews's expedition is from *Science Explorer: Roy Chapman Andrews* by Jules Archer (Simon & Schuster, 1968).

Charles Waterton's quote is from the 1889 edition of his expedition memoir *Wanderings in South America* (Macmillan).

Taxidermists originally portrayed the dodo as looking like it had swallowed a Gouda cheese and the goblin shark as having a shovel-like protuberance on its forehead. The fat dodo theory was debunked in Andrew C. Kitchener's study "On the External Appearance of the Dodo, *Raphus cucullatus*" (*Archives of Natural History,* 1993). An anatomically accurate rendering of the goblin shark can be seen in *Sharks and Rays of Australia* by P. R. Last and J. D. Stevens (Fisheries Research and Development, 1994). A goblin shark with a shovel-like protuberance is depicted in *The World Encyclopedia of Fishes* by Alwyne Wheeler (Mac-Donald, 1985).

Additional information on Akeley's first expedition to the Congo to collect gorillas is primarily from his article "Gorillas—Real and Mythical" (*Natural History*, September–October 1923). I also used documents from the AMNH archives, including Mary Jobe Akeley's personal correspondence and an essay by Professor Henry Fairfield Osborn.

The *New Yorker* published a delightful review of African Hall called "Africa Brought to Town" on May 2, 1936. David Schwendeman's vivid memories brought the ribbon cutting alive.

Frederic A. Lucas's quote about what to call the modern taxidermist is from *Natural History*, March–April 1927.

4. HOW THE ORANGUTAN GOT ITS SKIN

In addition to many thoughtful conversations with John Matthews, Paul Rhymer, and Ken Walker, I interviewed National Museum of Natural History collections manager Linda K. Gordon, curator in charge James G. Mead, and conservator Catharine Hawks, as well as conservation scientist Amandine Péquignot, Centre de recherches sur la conservation collections at the Muséum national d'Histoire naturelle in Paris, and Frank Greenwell, Smithsonian taxidermist from 1957 to 1999. The Smithsonian's mammal hall press conference, where museum scientists and administrators spoke and then led reporters on guided tours of the new hall, took place in November 2003. I was on Associate Director for Public Programs Robert Sullivan's tour. The Smithsonian's Office of Public Affairs provided statistics and facts about the old West Wing and the new Kenneth E. Behring Family Hall of Mammals, as did the November 2003 issue of *Smithsonian*.

British Natural History Museum fish curator Oliver Crimmen ("We're just a bunch of state-funded Tony Perkinses") took me on two fascinating behind-the-scenes tours of the museum. At Wandsworth, the museum's gigantic off-site storage facility, we came upon a donkey that looked as if it had laughed so hard it burst its seams, and we began to talk about why people humanize mammals. Crimmen said, "It will be a sad day when I stop anthropomorphizing." Only now do I realize how deeply his words influenced how I approached this book.

The *New York Times* reported Lawrence M. Small's resignation in

"Report Faults Oversight by Smithsonian Regents" on June 19, 2007. "History for Sale" (*Washington Post,* January 20, 2002) chronicles Small's efforts to privatize the Smithsonian through big-time donors; I relied on this for figures and context, including the protest memo signed by curators at the National Museum of American History and also for information about Kenneth H. Behring. The Archaeological Institute of America ran an online feature on Small and Behring called "Crisis at the Smithsonian," www.archaeology.org/online/features/smithsonian/behring.html, September 19, 2002.

For accounts of how Behring tried to import the trophy remains of the argali sheep, see "Controversy Surrounds Rare Sheep in Canada" (CBC Radio Transcripts, http://archives.foodsafetynetwork.ca/animalnet/2001/8-2001/an-08-19-01-01.txt, August 17, 2001). The Humane Society's online feature is called "Trophy Hunting," www.hsus.org/wildlife/hunting_old/trophy_hunting/, n.d. "How to Bag Your Own Endangered Species" by Linda Gottwald ran in *USA Today* on February 3, 2000. Also see the Safari Club International's Online Record Book, www.scirecordbook.org/login/index.cfm.

A *New York Times* feature titled "Friends Matter for Reclusive Creature of African Forest" (October 12, 2004) describes how scientists based in the Congo continue to study the okapi.

William Hornaday's quote is from the 1916 edition of *Taxidermy and Zoological Collecting.*

Though separated by ninety-three years, Ken Walker's nine-month appointment at the Smithsonian echoed that of his hero, Robert Rockwell, who worked there for nine months in 1910. I drew information about Rockwell's time at the Smithsonian from his autobiography *My Way of Becoming a Hunter.*

Of all the brief accounts of James Smithson's bequest, my favorite is in Lynn Barber's *The Heyday of Natural History.* For a history of the Smithsonian Institution, see http://siarchives.si.edu/history/main_generalhistory.html.

After the mammal hall opening, several newspapers and news services reviewed it, including the *Washington Post, Winston-Salem Journal,*

Albany (N.Y.) Times-Union, Atlanta Journal-Constitution, Dallas Morning News, Austin American-Statesman, Philadelphia Inquirer, Baltimore Sun, Chicago Tribune, Scripps Howard News Service, and Associated Press. Of them, the *Architectural Record*'s piece (November 1, 2004) was especially helpful in describing the high-tech wizardry designers used to create the hall's special effects and sound-and-light shows. Paul Rhymer's personal account appears in *Taxidermy Today* (August 2004). The Smithsonian's Office of Public Affairs' press materials provided further details about the massive renovation of the West Wing and its prior usage.

Sally Love's take on dioramas ran in the *Baltimore Sun* on November 28, 2003.

I read about the Fenykovi elephant's anus (and the giraffe's clay privates, mentioned earlier in the chapter) in the *Baltimore Sun* (November 28, 2003).

I learned about how the Natural History Museum evacuated specimens during World War II in William T. Stearn's book *The Natural History Museum at South Kensington* (Heinemann, 1981).

5. THE CHAIRBITCH

This chapter was drawn primarily from interviews with Emily Mayer and her family, friends, and colleagues. The *Times* of London's "Stuff Art: This Is a Life and Death Thing" (August 16, 2000) and Steve Baker's *The Postmodern Animal* (Reaktion Books, 2000) provided further insight into Mayer's career. For Mayer's take on her own artwork, I relied on her artist's statements in the catalogs for two of her solo shows, "Out of Context" (Campden Gallery, Gloucestershire, England, 2007) and "Material Evidence" (Triskel Arts Centre, Cork, Ireland, 1995). Mayer's master's thesis, "Representing Animality: The Nature of the Representation of Animals in Contemporary Taxidermy and Contemporary Sculpture" (Norwich School of Art and Design, 1990), demonstrates the deeply complex relationship Mayer has with animals, in art and in life.

I read about Damien Hirst in his books *I Want to Spend the Rest of My Life Everywhere, with Everyone, One to One, Always, Forever, Now* (Booth-Clibborn, 1997; I used the 2005 edition) and *On the Way to Work,* a series of interviews with Hirst by the British writer Gordon Burn (Universe, 2002; I used the 2007 edition).

Erosion molding is described in *A Guide to Model Making and Taxidermy* by Leo J. Cappel (A. H. and A. W. Reed, 1973).

Emily Mayer and John Loker let me keep their copy of *Dipped in Vitriol* by Nicholas Parsons (Pan Books, 1981).

Pets, Usual and Unusual by Maxwell Knight was originally published by Routledge and Kegan Paul, 1951. I used the 1962 edition.

Irmelin Mayer and I stayed up very late one night talking about Emily's childhood and flipping through family scrapbooks. The next day, she generously let me photocopy all the articles about Emily. The titles alone bear mentioning: "Girl Taxidermist Loves Job"; "OK, Where Does a Taxidermist Pick Up a Dead Camel?"; "Emily Can Ferret Out a Bargain!"; "She Keeps Bodies: Unusual Job for Emily, 19"; "Tinker, Tailor, Taxidermist"; "Chipping In with the Fish"; "Illustrious Corpses"; "Get Stuffed! If You'll Pardon the Expression"; "The Stuff That Dreams Are Made Of"; "Dead Clever; Change of Course as Emily Tackles Sculpture"; "Life After Death."

Emily and Irmelin Mayer graciously provided me with sources on Lotte Pritzel. These include *Lotte Pritzel: Puppen des Lasters des Grauens und der Ekstase* (Puppentheatermuseum, 1987); *Hans Bellmer,* a biography of the controversial surrealist by Peter Webb (Quartet Books, 1985); "'They've Got Souls of White Cotton, the Little Darlings!': Lotte Pritzel and Her Wax Figurines," an unpublished scholarly work by Barbara Borek; and "Fragments," Irmelin Mayer's unpublished autobiographical work about growing up in Nazi-era Berlin.

The quote comparing a Hirst show to Jack the Ripper perpetrating a crime is from Richard Shone's essay "Some Went Mad, Some Ran Away" in the catalog for the show (Serpentine Gallery, London, 1994).

For a deeper understanding of how England and America differed in their approaches to natural history and specimen collecting, see Joyce Chaplin's article "Nature and Nation: Natural History in Context," in *Stuffing Birds, Pressing Plants, Shaping Knowledge: Natural History in North America, 1730–1860,* edited by Sue Ann Prince (American Philosophical Society, 2003).

I read about how Lionel Walter Rothschild liked to outbid the British Museum in *The Heyday of Natural History* by Lynn Barber. "My Museum: The Walter Rothschild Zoological Museum, Tring" by Tring's bird skins preparator Katrina Cook appeared in the 2006 issue of *Taxidermist;* it describes the history of the museum and what it contains today. The anecdote about how the baron was blackmailed into selling off his peerless bird collection is from *Dinosaurs in the Attic* by Douglas J. Preston (St. Martin's Press, 1986).

For information about the Powell-Cotton Museum, see "Quex House and the Powell-Cotton Museum" by Richard Crowhurst, www.timetravel-britain.com/articles/museums/quex.shtml, 2006. Also see the Powell-Cotton Museum Web site, www.quexmuseum.org.

Charles Waterton may have been exasperating, but he was never boring. This made writing about him painful, because I had to omit how he used to crawl under a table and bark like a dog, along with just about everything he ever said or wrote. The surviving Waterton quotes and quirks are chiefly drawn from his somewhat reliable expedition memoir *Wanderings in South America.* I used the 1889 edition, which includes an endearing biography of the squire (complete with drawings of Walton Hall's pigpens, breeding tower, and lofty trees) by the Reverend J. G. Wood, as well as an explanatory essay on his taxidermy methods. I found his quote about possessing "Promethean boldness" and his use of Horace's "By laboring to be brief you become obscure" in an essay by Dr. J. B. Holder in the SAT's 1884 annual report; they are also in *Wanderings.*

For the account of the *Nondescript,* I used *Wanderings.* Author Errol Fuller e-mailed his own very endearing description, and Lynn Barber describes this "taxidermic frolic" in *The Heyday of Natural History.*

The Watertonian terms "pseudo-classical phraseology" and "complimentary nomenclature" are from the biography by Wood in *Wan-*

derings. "You must possess Promethean boldness . . ." and "A hideous spectacle of death in ragged plumage" are from *Wanderings*.

Montagu Browne calls Waterton an "eccentric genius" and "pioneer" and also describes his methods for making peacock faces and scraping out ape feet in his two manuals: *Practical Taxidermy: Manual of Instruction to the Amateur in Collecting, Preserving, and Setting Up Natural History Specimens of All Kinds*, 2nd ed. (L. Upcott Gill, 1884), and *Artistic and Scientific Taxidermy and Modelling* (Adam and Charles Black, 1896).

"Chairbitch is OK too" is from "View from the Chair," Emily Mayer's inaugural letter as chair to the guild journal, *Taxidermist* (2002).

Kim McDonald's article "E-bay—You Are Being Watched! Internet Auctions and the Natural History Specimen" ran in *Taxidermist* in 2006. The Get Stuffed scandal has been widely publicized in the United Kingdom. The *Independent* ran a story on it at the time on February 2, 2000, and the *Guardian* covered it retrospectively on August 8, 2008. The *Birmingham Evening Mail* reported that the Metropolitan Police Wildlife Crime Unit seized more than twenty thousand endangered species in 2000.

The history of the Guild of Taxidermists is from Emily Mayer's graduate thesis, "Representing Animality," and Christopher Frost's *A History of British Taxidermy*.

Information about Rowland Ward and his illustrious wildlife studio primarily came from Pat Morris's self-published monograph *Rowland Ward: Taxidermist to the World* (2003), which also has amazing photos. Front and Wonders ("Habitat Dioramas") also cover Ward.

"The Antiquity of the Duchess of Richmond's Parrot," Pat Morris's account of how he x-rayed the duchess's stuffed African grey parrot, appeared in *Museums Journal* 81, no. 3 (1981). I went to Westminster Abbey to see the parrot in 2003.

6. MR. POTTER'S MUSEUM OF CURIOSITIES

Daphne du Maurier was inspired to write *Jamaica Inn* after an ill-fated outing on Bodmin Moor. The story goes like this: One day she was staying at the Jamaica Inn and went out riding in the moor with a friend.

A storm broke, and they were forced to seek shelter in an abandoned cottage. Eventually, their horses led the way through the treacherous moor back to the inn. For further information about du Maurier and her relationship to Cornwall, see www.dumaurier.org, which has a bibliography and numerous related links.

The infamous Jamaica Inn—its smugglers, ghosts, murderers, and barren moor—is described with suitable gore and gothic relish in the resort's souvenir guide, *Jamaica Inn and Museum.*

I read about Peale's, Scudder's, and Drake's museums in the SAT annual reports and also in Charles Coleman Sellers's *Mr. Peale's Museum.* I also visited the American Philosophical Society in Philadelphia, site of the original museum.

I read about the Victorian mania for natural history and the state of science museums in the pre- and post-Darwin era in Lynn Barber's *The Heyday of Natural History.* This, combined with the general history of taxidermy, helped me create the context in which Walter Potter lived, worked, and built his stupendous collection.

Bruce Schwendeman and Emma Hawkins generously supplied me with materials from their personal archives, including early catalogs of Mr. Potter's Museum of Curiosities before it moved to Cornwall. I relied on these to write about Potter's life—what drove him and how he approached taxidermy—and also to trace the evolution of his museum from 1861 to 1986, when John and Wendy Watts bought it. For the museum's post-1986 history, I relied chiefly on the Bonhams press release, interviews, and newspaper articles.

Pat Morris's splendid article "An Historical Review of Bird Taxidermy in Britain" describes the bird displays at the Great Exhibition of 1851, including John Hancock's gyrfalcons and the original usage of the word "jizz." *A History of British Taxidermy* by Christopher Frost chronicles taxidermy's rise and fall. It also describes the era's leading taxidermists, such as Hancock and Herrmann Ploucquet and how they practiced their trade during taxidermy's most faddish epoch. Montagu Browne's *Practical Taxidermy* describes how the Great Exhibition of 1851 led to the rise of artistic taxidermy in Britain.

Charles Waterton's quotes are from his book *Wanderings in South America*.

Calke Abbey is a 1622 country house filled with glass cases containing fascinating collections acquired by several generations of the Harpur-Crewe family. Sir Vauncey Harpur-Crewe's late-nineteenth-century natural history cases—including domed birds, butterflies, and eggs; Egyptian curiosities; a crocodile skull; deer heads; and fossils—are still on display in period rooms that have been restored by the National Trust, which has owned the property since 1985. I toured Calke Abbey with the exceptionally knowledgeable Pat Morris. For those unable to visit, the National Trust's guidebook (1989) provides an excellent virtual tour.

For information about El Negro, see "Gaborone Journal; Africa Rejoices as a Wandering Soul Finds Rest" by Rachel L. Swarns, http://www.nytimes.com/2000/10/06/world/gaborone-journal-africa-rejoices-as-a-wandering-soul-finds-rest.html?sec=&spon=&pagewanted=all. This article appeared in the *New York Times* on October 6, 2000.

I discovered the wonderful word "anthropomorphophobic" in *The Postmodern Animal* by Steve Baker.

Details about Errol Fuller appeared in *New Scientist*, May 2004; the *Vancouver Sun*, May 15, 2004; the *Guardian*, November 13, 1999; the *Observer*, April 10, 1994; and the *Spectator*, November 8, 2003.

Richard Taylor's campaign to save the museum was reported in the *Guardian* on September 8, 2003. Damien Hirst's efforts to buy Potter's appeared in the *Financial Times* on September 24, 2003, and in Cornwall's local daily, the *Western Morning News*, on September 24, 2003, which also reported that Bonhams said it had no record of Hirst's offer. His letter in the *Guardian*, titled "Mr. Potter, Stuffed Rats and Me," ran on September 23, 2003; see www.guardian.co.uk/artanddesign/2003/sep/23/heritage.

Ye Olde Curiosity Shop, on the waterfront below the Pike Place Market in Seattle, has human mummies.

For information about the post-auction legal dispute, see "Strange Case of Damien Hirst and the Stuffed Squirrel Sale," *Times* (London),

December 6, 2007, http://entertainment.timesonline.co.uk/tol/arts_
and_entertainment/visual_arts/article3007089.ece. When I asked Bonhams whether the legal dispute had been resolved, the auction house
had no comment.

7. IN-A-GADDA-DA-VIDA

Facts about Damien Hirst and his artworks, including his quotes, are
primarily from *On the Way to Work* by Damien Hirst and Gordon Burn;
Damien Hirst, the exhibition catalog for his show at the Museo Arche-
ologico Nazionale in Naples, Italy, in 2004; *I Want to Spend the Rest of
My Life Everywhere, with Everyone, One to One, Always, Forever, Now;* and
Carol Vogel's critiques in the *New York Times.*

I read about "In-A-Gadda-Da-Vida" in Martin Gayford's article
"Would You Adam and Eve It?" in the *Telegraph Magazine* (February 28,
2004). The *New York Times* ran a piece on the replacement tiger shark
on October 1, 2006. The newspaper and magazine reviews of "In-A-
Gadda-Da-Vida" were all published in February and March of 2004.

I read about Francis Bacon in *Francis Bacon* (Centre Georges Pom-
pidou, 1996) and in Steve Baker's *The Postmodern Animal.* Hirst describes how he feels about Bacon in *On the Way to Work.*

The *New York Times* published an article that describes crucified
cows on October 1, 2006; Damien Hirst describes the similar concept
in *On the Way to Work:* "I want to do a cow hacked open like that with
its arms open. I'm going to do three, sixteen foot. A whole crucifixion.
Can't resist it. Sixteen-foot tanks. Massive. With all cows skinned and
peeled apart . . . Fantastic."

8. KEN AND THE IRISH ELK

The basis for Edmonton's "inferiority complex" is from a discussion I
had with my friend Tim Tokarsky, an Edmontonian who studied geo-
physics. I was also incredibly lucky to find myself seated next to Leah
Dolgoy, another spirited Edmontonian, on the flight to Alberta.

In addition to Ken Walker's encyclopedic knowledge, my primary source for information about *Megaloceros giganteus*—phylogenetic, historic, and cultural—was the Irish elk chapter in *Extinct* by Anton Gill and Alex West (Macmillan, 2003). I also used the following articles, essays, and academic papers: "A Lesson from the Old Masters" by Stephen Jay Gould (*Natural History*, August 1996); "The Phylogenetic Position of the 'Giant Deer' *Megaloceros giganteus*" by A. M. Lister, C. J. Edwards, D.A.W. Nock, M. Bunce, I. A. van Pijlen, D. G. Bradley, M. G. Thomas, and I. Barnes (*Nature*, December 2005); "Why Antlers Branched Out" by Valerius Geist (*Natural History*, April 1994); "Irish Elk Survived After Ice Age Ended" by Sid Perkins (*Science News*, November 6, 2004); "DNA Pegs Irish Elk's Nearest Relatives" by Sid Perkins (*Science News*, October 1, 2005); "Giants Survived Human Onslaught" by Ross MacPhee (*New Scientist*, November 13, 2004); "Survival of the Irish Elk into the Holocene" by Silvia Gonzales, Andrew Kitchener, and Adrian M. Lister (*Nature*, June 15, 2000); "The Case of the Irish Elk" (www.ucmp.berkeley.edu/mammal/artio/irishelk.html, n.d.); "Extinct Giant Deer Survived Ice Age, Study Says" by James Owen (*National Geographic News*, October 6, 2004); "Extinct Giant Deer's Descendant Found in U.K." (www.ucl.ac.uk/media/library/giantdeer, September 4, 2005). I found "The Giant Irish Deer—A Victim of the Ice Age" by Frank Mitchell on the Irish Peatland Conservation Council Web site, www.ipcc.ie/infoirishelk.html; it originally appeared in the *Shell Guide to Reading the Irish Landscape* (Town House & Country House, 1986).

Seamus Heaney, the great Irish poet, was deeply moved by Ireland's peat bogs and mined them for inspiration. I read about this in "The Great Irish Elk: Seamus Heaney's Personal Helicon" by William Pratt (*World Literature Today*, Spring 1996). In it, Pratt says, "Heaney had described his own creative process as if it had lain for a while in the earth beside the Great Irish elk: 'I have always listened for poems, they come sometimes like bodies come out of a bog, almost complete, seeming to have been laid down a long time ago, surfacing with a torch of mystery.'"

I read about the Chauvet cave in *Dawn of Art: The Chauvet Cave,* the *Oldest Known Paintings in the World* by Jean Clottes. "Grotte Chauvet Archeologically Dated" by Dr. Christian Zuchner of the Institute of Prehistory, University of Erlangen-Nuremberg, appeared in *TRACCE* (February 2000). This incredible iconographic study compares seven megaloceros paintings and motifs from different periods and caves in France.

British anatomist Richard Owen's questions about the skeletal and muscular structure of the Irish elk are from Gould's essay "A Lesson from the Old Masters."

The alarming rate of extinction is sadly easy to document. The United Nations figure is from "Global Diversity Outlook 2," a paper prepared by the Convention on Biological Diversity (2006). The *New York Times* article "A Rising Number of Birds at Risk" ran on December 1, 2007. The frightening statistics about China's dwindling mammal species and an account of its last two Yangtze giant soft-shell turtles both come from a particularly affecting article in the *New York Times* by Jim Yardley called "Then There Were Two: Turtles' Fate Shows Threat to China's Species," which ran on December 5, 2007. On June 12, 2007, the *New York Times* reported that the last two white rhinos in Zambia had been shot by poachers.

9. I STUFF A SQUIRREL

All flawed squirrel anatomy described in this chapter is my fault alone and in no way reflects the squirrel output at Schwendeman's Taxidermy Studio. David and Bruce did their best to turn a stuffer into a taxidermist; the rest was my undoing.

William Hornaday's quote about "stuffed monstrosities" is from his essay "Common Faults in the Mounting of Quadrupeds," which appeared in the SAT's 1884 annual report. This report also contains the information about the 1883 SAT convention and the exhibit "A Taxidermist's Sanctum."

Taxidermy manuals are fascinating to look at and to read. I mention four of them in this chapter: *The Breakthrough Mammal Taxi-*

dermy Manual by Brent Houskeeper (B. Publications, 1990); Montagu Browne's *Practical Taxidermy* (1878); Oliver Davie's *Methods in the Art of Taxidermy* (1894); and William Hornaday's *Taxidermy and Zoological Collecting* (1891; I used the 1916 edition).

10. GRAY SQUIRREL, YELLOW DAWN

Leon Pray was an American taxidermist who wrote one of the most popular taxidermy manuals in the United States. In 1972, his *Taxidermy* was in its twenty-sixth edition. Bruce Schwendeman's exceptionally rare first-edition copy of Pray's "The Squirrel Mounting Book," a pamphlet published by *Modern Taxidermist* in 1938, sat on my desk for years, unopened.

I read about Roy Orbison on several Web sites, including *Billboard* online, Wikipedia, and RoyOrbison.com.

ACKNOWLEDGMENTS

WITHOUT THE PEOPLE who shared their lives with me, this book would not exist. My heartfelt thanks go to David and Bruce Schwendeman, Ken Walker, and Emily Mayer and their families. These gifted artists welcomed me into their homes and studios, fed me, lent me books and articles, and answered my questions until I finally understood. I will miss hanging around their workshops.

My thanks to all the taxidermists, collectors, scientists, curators, conservators, antiques dealers, artists, and enthusiasts for their unstinting contributions to this book. Taxidermists David Astley, Larry Blomquist, Carl Church, Jack Fishwick, Frank Greenwell, Jerry Jackson, Joe Kish, Dave Luke, Roger Martin, John Matthews, Paul Rhymer, Dave Spaul, Jan van Hoesen, and countless others helped me gain an understanding of their art form. Jessica Stevens was the kindest judge an amateur squirrel mounter could hope for.

My research was made easier by the assistance of the staff of the American Museum of Natural History library. I am grateful to thank Floyd Easterman for providing me with copies of the SAT annual reports and William Hornaday's personal scrapbook. Karen Wonders traded me a copy of "Habitat Dioramas" for a copy of *Still Life;* my book could not have existed without her scholarship. Conservator Catharine Hawks referred me to important sources and leads. Emma Hawkins faxed me two old Potter's catalogs. Conservation scientist Amandine Péquignot was a big help in the eleventh hour.

Fish curator Oliver Crimmen took me on two fascinating tours of the Natural History Museum storeroom and gave me useful articles; Pat Morris and Mary Burgis served as superb guides in England; and Steve Quinn led me around the AMNH dioramas and reviewed my Akeley chapter for accuracy. And Stephanie Adler-Yuan tackled the daunting task of fact checking the entire book.

A writer couldn't ask for a smarter agent, friend, and editor than Tina Bennett. Tina believed in this project through its growing pains and through what turned out to be many changes in the publishing world. Only Tina saw the potential of taxidermy before it was fashionable. Her exact words were, "Who knew there was so much life in taxidermy?"

I am indebted to David Corcoran of the *New York Times* for assigning the germinal article and *Studio 360* for producing my radio segment on the Schwendemans.

Andrea Schulz and Eamon Dolan, book editors extraordinaire, vastly improved the book on every level, from armature to hiding the seams and imperfections. I thank them for their encouragement, insight, and wit, as well as for challenging me to do what I thought was impossible: write with authority *and* be myself. Christopher Moisan's jacket design is as beautiful as it is arresting. Thanks also to Svetlana Katz, Rick Tetzeli, Lindsey Smith, Barbara Jatkola, and everyone at Houghton Mifflin Harcourt.

Of all the people who now know more about taxidermy than they ever thought possible, I'd like to thank my very supportive parents, Marcia and Paul Milgrom, and the other Milgroms:

Steve, Robin, Arthur, and Jake. My friends, whose moral support was boundless, deserve a week at the spa on me: Frieda Alutin, Erma Estwick, Camille Korschun-Bastillo, Lorraine McCune, Nathalie Schueller, Lisa Waltuch, and Ulalume Zavala. And, of course, I'd especially like to thank Eric, Sabine, and Greta for their incredible patience and for believing that all families take vacations to see Jeremy Bentham and talk about squirrels at the dinner table.